WHAT OUR REA[illegible]

Keepers of the Dream is inde[illegible] and dresses it up for the 21st c[illegible] metamorphosing mothers, corrupt catacombs, living art, sweetness and madness, hope and loss...all through the eyes and hearts of seekers and dreamers on the quest to truth and belonging. Celeste Adams's story swirls you along an inner journey of discovery and the spiraling breath of the ancient goddess energy embraces the reader as delightfully as it does the intriguing characters in *Keepers of the Dream*.

—Pamela Jaye Smith
Founder of Mythworks

This magical and heartwarming tale celebrates the sacred trinity of mother, daughter, and earth spirit as it embraces the kinship between goddess spirituality and ecology. It is a highly original and entertaining myth for the new millennium that takes a stand for the living earth, and challenges old myths that threaten our planet. I highly recommend this delightful story that has otherworldly tones of magical realism, and the power and beauty of a legend.

—Sheila Laffey, Ph.D.
Environmental Film Producer

Keepers of the Dream is a visionary tale of mythological proportions; an invitation into the inner sanctum of the earth feminine and the unified field of her creative consciousness. This book is both revelatory and deeply transformative, it is a torch flame of truth. Celeste Adams paints word pictures that are exquisitely captivating. Spirit chills poured through me on the first and second readings...

—Donna Strong
Author, Healing Facilitator

Celeste Allegrea Adams weaves a magickal web of myth and mystery, of spirituality and sensuality. Her mastery of imagery satisfies the senses on all levels...the physical, mental/emotional, and celestial. She invites the reader to a three-fold journey down the river of inspiration and dreams—not only to other physical locations, but also to a deeper part of oneself, awakening the sacred archetypes within every woman to rise to their full potential, encouraging the goddess in every one of us to dance beyond the veils between the worlds.

Mahira Naraperi
Temple Dancer and Wiccan

The modern world—perched on the threshold of a new millennium—had never experienced the likes of the self-proclaimed Creatrix, Eartha Mae. Nor were they ready for the whiskey-swigging archaeologist Betina Sharp or the sixteen-year-old waif, Evangeline. What this curious trio has in common with each other is an inexplicable whisper of voices in the wind, a chorus heard by many disenchanted souls yet heeded by none...until now. What they discover on their journey is a revelation older than time...and more potent than the contents of Pandora's box.

—Christina Hamlett
Author of *The Spellbox*

KEEPERS OF THE DREAM:

A Myth for a New Age

Celeste Allegrea Adams

CREATRIX STUDIO

We can all be keepers of the dream by holding a vision of possibility in our hearts

LIBRARY OF CONGRESS CATALOGING-IN-PUBLICATION DATA

Adams, Celeste Allegrea.
Keepers of the dream : a myth for a new age / Celeste Allegrea Adams. – 1st ed.
p. cm
"We can all be keepers of the dream by holding a vision of possibility in our hearts."
LCCN 2001118540
ISBN 0-9721943-0-4

1. Goddess religion—Fiction. 2. Spirituality—Fiction. 3. New Age movement—Fiction. I. Title.

PS3601.D355K44 2002 813'.6
QBI33-650

For Information, contact:

Creatrix Studio
PO Box 3775
Santa Monica, CA 90408-3775 USA
Email: CreatrixStudio@aol.com

Visit our Website: www.CreatrixStudio.com

Cover Image: Jean Marie Mayer
Cover Design: Alex Djolakian
Typesetting: Gus Dawson and Alex Djolakian

Printed in the United States of America

"If you bring forth what is within you,
what you bring forth will save you.
If you do not bring forth what is within you,
what you do not bring forth will destroy you...
For whoever has not known himself has known nothing,
but whoever has known himself
has simultaneously achieved knowledge
about the depth of all things."

— The Gospel of St. Thomas

To my mother, Pearl Adams,
who celebrates creative expression above all else.
To my father, Edwin Adams,
who finds supreme happiness in nature
and who has the soul of a mystic.
To my sweet and beloved sister, Julie,
and to my visionary soul-sister, Yuki.

To the spirit of the fire that fills me with eternal passion,
to the holy wind that whispers in my ear and tells me things I long to know,
to the ocean that soothes me with the calming rhythm of its waves,
to the rivers that take me to distant lands,
to the desert that gives me stillness to find the truth of my desires,
to the forest where I breathe in the fullness of life,
to the cave that takes me deep into the mysteries.

To the leopard that runs with me,
and the butterflies that flutter in and out of my thoughts
and who celebrate all things beautiful.
To the nomads I have met in my travels,
who shared their bowls of couscous, and warmed my heart
and invited me on their journey.
To the whirling galaxies that sweep me away into their ecstatic symphony.
To those who have known my highest self
and who believe in my deepest desires.

To the mystics, visionaries, and rebels
with whom I've celebrated profound moments in my life,
and to the wanderers and spiritual warriors that I've met on my life's journey.
To those who dedicate their lives to creating beauty in the world through their art
and to those whose art is their prayer.
To the lost children who roam the streets . . . call out, believe, always believe.
To all those with whom I've shared sacred moments of my life,
I dedicate this story to you.
I am grateful.

CONTENTS

PART ONE

CHAPTER ONE

A STRANGE WIND

Betina had reached a time of dissatisfaction. The smallest thing made her irritable. She was drinking too much, eating too little, arguing at the slightest provocation, not sleeping enough, and blowing things out of proportion. She wasn't happy with the paper she planned to deliver at the Archaeological Congress in Athens. It seemed uninspired, though perfectly acceptable—but it was never her ambition to be perfectly acceptable. She even dreaded the predictable papers she would most certainly hear. She always knew the conclusions after just a few introductory sentences and she had lost all patience for hearing things she already knew. In her own work, she was tired of offering reasonable and comforting answers that obliterated greater truths and deeper mysteries. She feared that she had forgotten her pursuit of wisdom and replaced it with a neurotic assemblage of inconsequential details.

Betina scheduled a few weeks of travel before the conference so that she could revisit some of her favorite archaeological sites in Malta and Turkey and take photographs for upcoming lectures. During those weeks, she met with a remarkable group of people. It began with a trip to Malta and Gozo, where she had gone several times in the past. Betina visited several well-known megalithic temples including Santa Verna, Ggantija, Tal Qadi, Ta Hagrat, Ghar Dalam, and Hypogeum which all bore witness to a civilization that thrived thousands of years before Christ. She spent a couple of days at Tarxien, exploring three separate temples. Each ruin had been carefully studied and written about by numerous historians and archaeologists. But it was another site, unknown to researchers past and present that captured her attention. It was an old woman's private cave that remained foremost in her mind. Its energy was vibrant and alive and had a strange magnetism that drew a small group of women into its depths.

It was by chance that Betina learned about the cave.

She had been having coffee every morning in a cafe near her hotel in Valetta, that was owned by an old and frail Maltese woman who wore a dark wool shawl over a long black dress. Her fine white hair was wrapped in a tight bun, and when she smiled her eyes sparkled with a glow that revealed a resplendent spirit.

Her husky grandson looked like he was in his late thirties, close to Betina's age. He brought her *pastizzi,* a boat-shaped delicacy of ricotta cheese and egg. As Betina picked up a fork to take a bite, she wondered why he watched her so intently. Was he sensing something of her character, or of her destiny? Was he thinking that she looked pale and tired, undernourished and overworked? Did he find it strange that she was traveling alone, or was he wondering where she came from and why she was visiting his village?

He asked her name and she said it was Betina Sharp. He repeated it several times and invited her to their home for a late lunch the following day. The old woman stood by the kitchen holding a mushroom, larger than both her hands, and eagerly waited for her response. Betina planned to spend the day doing research at the main library on the island, but something about this invitation intrigued her and she agreed to visit them. When the grandson nodded to his grandmother, she clasped her hands together and pressed them tightly to her heart.

Betina rode in a taxi that passed over rolling hills covered with dry grasses and shrubs. The taxi paused while a flock of sheep scurried across the road, then continued on its way. Betina delighted in the cavalcade of smells. The perfumed fragrance of honeysuckle, spearmint, and sage blended with the tangy odor of cow manure. They finally stopped at an old rustic house made of stone that had a few goats in the front yard. The old woman met her at the gate wearing an embroidered apron over the same black dress she wore the previous day. She clapped her bony hands together, then held them to her cheeks. Her broad grin revealed gold crowns on several teeth, which glistened like sparkling jewels. She brushed aside Betina's shoulder-length hair to gaze into her eyes, as if she was looking into her soul; then wrapped her arm around Betina's slender waist and led her through a small door to the dining room. Her grandson held out his arms and gave Betina a warm hug, then offered her a chair at the table.

The old woman immediately went into the kitchen, bringing out a savory rabbit stew cooked in wine and herbs, topped with mushrooms, laid out on a terracotta platter. She sat down and tore off a crusty piece of rosemary bread, fresh out of the oven, then dipped it in virgin olive oil and topped it with anchovies. She handed it to Betina, motioning for her to eat it. When Betina smiled in appreciation, the old woman clapped her hands a second time. She sighed with satisfaction as Betina enjoyed the wine that came from the vineyard behind the house.

After the meal, the old woman insisted on taking Betina to a cave, which had an entrance obscured by jagged rocks and shrubs, where a few sheep grazed. It was the same green mound that she passed in the taxi, but it hadn't occurred to her that beneath it were ancient chambers. To get to the cave, they stepped over rocks that crossed a stream of pristine water. The old woman believed that the stream created a perfect medium, a fifth element for the world of spirit, to move through. The grandson held aside branches of a thorny shrub, and they slipped through a narrow entrance, supported on either side by limestone slabs, which formed a triangular archway in the earth. Betina was the first person, outside of the old woman's family and close family-friends, to enter into this underworld. Since the old woman had no granddaughters of her own, she wanted Betina to know about this special place.

They stood in the subterranean temple, looking at the earthen red walls, illuminated by the old woman's torch. The bright flame cast elongated shadows of their bodies on the stone creating an eerie, otherworldly atmosphere. Betina ran her hands over the walls and felt a spiral pattern cut into the rocks. As her fingers moved along the circular path, her senses heightened, and she thought she heard the sound of distant music.

"*Saxa loguntur*," the old woman whispered with great seriousness.

Betina understood her words of Latin, 'the stones speak.' She breathed in the pungent air and absorbed the beauty and power of the sacred place. They walked toward three old women, sitting in a circle in the shadows, softly singing a song whose words she could not understand. The cave was dark and damp; the sound of the stream rushing over rocks echoed throughout the underground chamber. Betina wondered how the women could stand to sit in there, day in and day out.

The grandson translated the old woman's Maltese. "My grandmother say that her mother take her to this place when she was baby. Her grandmother came here and the ancestors came before that. Each day she sit in this spot. Her friends sit too. There's a presence...something that comforts...something that heals. She asks if you can please to tell what it is."

Betina had hoped the old woman would have answers for her, not more questions. But as she sat with them, she began to understand something of what they experienced. She felt a strange spiraling wind, like a cool hand reaching out for her, carrying with it the beautiful scent of perfumed gardens. The old woman often felt the touch of this same wind and said that it brought a calming energy. It healed the women of arthritis, lumbago, nervousness, and sleeplessness, and it even put an end to hot flashes for a few women who had entered menopause.

After sitting with them for several hours, absorbing the energy of this power vortex, Betina took a taxi to a shop near the hotel where she stayed and bought a bottle of wine from a local vineyard. She walked down a narrow winding street made of cobblestones, passing a cafe where old men drank afternoon tea while playing backgammon. Farther up the street, a plump old woman sat on a stoop, resting her swollen feet on a stool, while mending a shirt. Another woman chatted with a friend and gently fanned an infant that suckled at her breast. At the corner, an old woman in a wheelchair and a young boy in shorts and a cap, sat by an opened door, peeling potatoes. The comforting scent of bread baking in their oven wafted out through the streets.

Betina was warmed by the scents and images of old-world domesticity but was glad to rest and reflect on the day's events, in the privacy of her hotel room. She sat by the window enjoying a glass of Maltese wine and listened to the strained high-pitched voice of a singer in a neighboring bar: "*Rabbi i-kuragg taqtax qalbek.*" She knew the meaning of the song. "Have courage, don't lose heart." Humming along, she jotted notes in her journal about the cave, then folded her clothes in preparation for a flight to Turkey.

Betina took a bus from Istanbul to the ancient city of Ephesus. It was once the center of a cult dedicated to Artemis, Mistress of Wild Things, known to the Romans as Diana. The ruin was at a midway point on Turkey's West Coast, overlooking the Mediterranean Sea, south of the Dardanelles. One of the Seven Wonders of the World, Ephesus was also said to have been the last domicile of the Virgin Mary.

The statue of Artemis didn't move her on an emotional level, though every detail was intriguing for its symbolism. Artemis's head was crowned with a twin tiara made of triple towers, all kinds of creatures adorned her form, and she had numerous breasts covering her torso. As Betina studied the statue, she became aware of a guard who leaned against a stone wall, twirling a string of prayer beads around his index fingers, while staring at her. He was a small man with a slender build, neatly dressed in a carefully pressed tan uniform. Eventually he approached her; he told her a curious story in fluent English. He said that being in the presence of the statue had saved him from suicide after he lost his wife to a long illness. He spoke in a matter-of-fact manner about the times when milk sprayed out of the multi-breasted statue.

Betina listened politely but didn't know what to make of the things he told her. She was eager to be on her way. Wandering into a cave not far from the statue of Artemis, she soon realized that it was the same one that she had explored on her first visit at nineteen—when she promised herself that she would become an archaeologist. She knew then that she wanted to be surrounded by this world of mystery and myth. Shortly after making that vow, a Turkish man, in his mid-twenties, entered the cave and approached her. He looked like a university student, with fashionable black-framed eyeglasses and a pinstriped shirt. Grabbing her by the arm, he pulled her toward him, to kiss her on the lips. She tried to push him away, but he twisted her wrist and attempted to rip open her dress. A vicious struggle ensued until finally she broke away and ran out of the cave. Consumed with fury and struggling to catch her breath, she hid amongst a bus load of tourists that had just arrived.

Now, almost twenty years later, the anguish of that moment was replaced by a strange calm that radiated from a gathering of animals near the cave entrance, where the violent incident had taken place. A donkey, two chickens, and a goat sat peacefully together—the image reminded her of the peaceful cohabitation of animals depicted in paintings of the Garden of Eden.

Reflecting on the dreaminess in the eyes of the animals, her thoughts were soon interrupted by approaching footsteps. The guard that she had spoken to earlier suddenly appeared at the cave entrance and sensed the agitation she felt by his presence. She wondered about his intentions and was somewhat relieved when he explained that he was just checking on her safety. He pointed to the goat and said that she followed him there that morning. He didn't have the heart to make her go home and figured that the goat sensed the healing energy that radiated from the cave. He noticed that the cataracts in the goat's eyes had begun to dissolve, and that she could move around without bumping into things.

He believed the animals were hearing things that people couldn't hear and sensing things that most humans could not perceive. The guard explained that once he had arrived at dawn to find a boar, a deer, a wildcat, two wolves, and a couple of local dogs gathered in a circle. Even his cat joined this strange communion of animals. It soon became his job to disperse the animals because it was feared that they would attack one of the tourists. Despite his efforts, the animals hid out in the mountains and late at night they would congregate at the cave entrance. The guard looked into Betina's eyes and told her that the animals were harbingers.

Finally he left her alone with the gathering of animals. She tried to understand how her first experience in this cave, as a teenager, related to this moment. It seemed that the man who attacked her was also a harbinger, telling her that in order to get at the significance of ancient archaeological treasures, she would have to withstand many trials and tests. The attempted rape was the first of the tests she would endure to have access to the mysteries. Perhaps the animals were also harbingers, as the guard suggested, in that they had a sense of the miraculous events that were to come.

Betina mused over the strange occurrences all evening. After dinner she spoke to two young men, tourists from England, who were on their way to India to see a woman from a small Indian village who was revered as the Mother. They told her about unusual activities they had witnessed at a church in Bosnia. Their story sounded intriguing and since she still had a couple of days before the conference started, she decided to take a detour to this small town.

Betina boarded a bus from Ephesus to Istanbul and then another one from Istanbul to Belgrade. She arrived just in time to catch yet another bus headed to Mostar. Sitting in the seat directly across from hers was a moist-eyed grandmother whose tears seemed ready to roll down her round and wizened face. After tightening a gray scarf over her head, she slowly took a loaf of bread out of an old basket. She broke off a morsel of the stale bread then fed it to her teenage grandson, who had no hands. As the bus passed bombed out mosques and churches covered in graffiti, Betina thought about all the destruction that had taken place in the name of religion and ethnic cleansing—she assumed the young boy was a casualty of war as well.

When Betina got off the bus, several Italian tourists got on wearing rosaries and t-shirts with the words 'pray, pray, pray' above a silk-screened image of the Virgin entitled Our Lady of Medjugorje. As a taxi driver put her luggage into the trunk of his car, he tried to convince her that she should visit Medjugorje, since the church she wanted to see was just a shell of its former self. Nevertheless, she was determined to stay on course and insisted that he take her there. They drove past burned-out houses and traveled across roads that had large potholes and even craters. She realized that the country was still devastated from the war and didn't have the economic means to make repairs. These detours slowed them down and they did not reach the church until the late afternoon.

The taxi driver dropped her off, shrugging his shoulders and shaking his head as he drove off. Dismayed to find that boards fenced in the church, preventing her from getting a good view of it, she wandered around the building several times hoping to find an entrance. Finally noticing that one of the boards was loose, she pushed it aside and crawled through the small opening. Walking over the rubble, surveying the ruins, she tried to imagine the role this church had played in the village throughout the centuries. She wondered how many weddings had taken place there, how many Christmas and Easter masses, how many christenings. As her fingers traced a spiral design on a collapsed wall, she thought about the kinds of rituals that might have been performed there, before the church was built. Perhaps it had once been a sacred grove or a place that inspired healing.

Passing under an archway toward the partial remains of an altar, Betina stopped in front of a fragmented fresco. She assumed that it was a depiction of the Madonna or perhaps a black Madonna. Only her eyes and dark-skinned hands remained, and the outline of a head with stars in her hair. She found herself praying, asking for meaning, for direction, and for the diminishment of her continual state of dissatisfaction. She was surprised at the depth of her longing and seriousness of her intention as tears flowed from her eyes.

Although the church was in ruins and seemed abandoned, there were dozens of new votive candles honoring the fragmented image in the fresco. Lighting a few of the candles, she smiled appreciatively as the small flames shone through the blue glass candleholders, bringing the altar to life. She realized that hours had passed since she arrived at the church and although it had become dark, she had not even checked into a hotel. Focused on the candles, she did not want to leave this sacred place.

She must have been in a deep meditative state for a couple of hours when she heard a clicking sound, slowly building in intensity. Opening her eyes, she saw a young man, whose name was Samir, tapping his foot. Moments later a girl behind him, who later introduced herself as Vesna, made a loud whooshing sound with her mouth. Surveying the ruins, she noticed more than a dozen teenagers moving in a synchronized dance. Several of them grabbed sticks and banged on the collapsed walls, while others rushed up the crumbling stone steps that led to a bell tower. Standing at different levels on the steps, stomping their feet and tapping their chests, they created body-percussion sounds.

Zoran, the youngest boy in the group, bungee jumped from the bell tower, diving headfirst into the courtyard. His long black trench coat fanned out around him like a parachute and his hair grazed the pavement, but the ropes that were tied to his feet prevented him from crashing into the cement. He quickly untied the ropes and joined in the pandemonium, making jerky movements as though an electrical current was moving through his body.

They cheered when a bolt of lightening exploded in the black sky, and danced even harder when a sudden downpour of rain turned the earth to mud. But just as suddenly as the rain started—it stopped. The rainmakers became silent and took a moment to catch their breath. Vesna tore off her wet clothes and laid them out on stones by a fire that someone had managed to make in the only dry corner of the church ruin. Several others did the same. In no time the energy started to build, with naked bodies covered in mud, slam dancing into each other. Eventually they all collapsed, one on top of another, like a mass of helpless sea creatures washed ashore, with writhing arms and legs strewn everywhere, gasping for air. Slowly, a new rhythmic configuration began to pulsate within this twitching pile of sea life. This ever-quickening beat wove its way over the walls of the bombed-out churchyard, drifting under the doors, through the broken windows, and into the dreams of the sleeping town folk.

After Vesna dressed, she approached Betina, looked her over, and sat down next to her. Betina was surprised that her style of dress had similarities to the Gothic styles she had seen in Boston, London, and Berlin. Although she had once witnessed a young Gothic group performing a ceremony in a cemetery in Saint Petersburg, she never expected to find a similar group in such a remote region of Bosnia. Vesna wore worn-out army boots and a black lace dress that was shredded under the arms and around the hemline. Her black fishnet stockings were torn in several places and held together by safety pins. She wore black lipstick with heavy eyeliner, had dark raccoon eyes, and ears pierced in a dozen places with small medallions of saints and emblems from every religion. Her shoulder-length, raven-black hair had a dead flower tied onto a small braid and was streaked with red. Betina wondered if she wore a crucifix, a crescent moon and star, an ankh, a peace sign, and a pentacle around her neck as a decoration or because it was her way of embracing all traditions. It occurred to her that this Gothic-styled attire set them apart from their Christian and Muslim families and unified them as a tribe.

Vesna spoke in broken English saying that she was drawn to this old church, because it was a place of dreaming. Sometimes her friends would dance until sunrise, since it was the only place they could sleep without having nightmares of surprise attacks and bombings. "We'll all be dead soon…we long for death…we prepare for it. We celebrate what we cannot stop. Maybe we are already the living dead. This is how we want to die…dancing." She explained that she also danced so that she could dissolve into the rhythm of the music and forget that she was the child of a man who raped a fourteen-year-old girl at gunpoint and impregnated her. Her teenage mother abandoned Vesna by the side of the road when she was two; after she was found she was taken to an orphanage. At twelve, she ran away from the orphanage and moved in with this wild and angry tribe that had become her family. Now she was pregnant and determined to love the child that was growing in her womb, even though she had never been loved.

Samir, the oldest of the group, had a ring in his nose and another in his lip, and wore a tattered antique military trench coat. He spoke of the loss of the beautiful home that his parents and grandparents and even his great-grandparents had lived in. The bombs destroyed the precious instruments that his family played every Sunday after dinner while his mother sang. His father's enormous book collection, including volumes of first editions, had been destroyed. His mother had lost the photographs and 8mm films she took of the family on holidays and outings. The only thing remaining in the bombed-out ruins of their home was silverware passed down from his great-grandmother, to his grandmother, and then to his mother. When the family resettled in another town, Samir did not stay with them but joined this band of dancers and musicians. He connected to this tribal family because he was filled with confusion brought on by the war and could no longer find comfort in the love extended to him by his wonderful parents. He spoke of chronic nightmares and the only moments of peace he found were amidst these ruins.

Zoran said that jumping from the bell tower every night relaxed him since he had a nervous disorder. His hands trembled, his eye twitched, and a severe case of eczema made him look like an old man in a young boy's body. Betina suspected that he wrapped the large trench coat around him to hide in it and to keep people from seeing his twitching and trembling. When Zoran lifted his shirt, Betina noticed scars that were probably caused by shrapnel. He pulled out a small white bunny that he kept close to his chest, and held it to his cheek, breathing in the exquisite sweetness of this timid creature. He stroked the soft fur with his fingers, and watched protectively as he let Betina hold his pet for a few minutes.

Betina sat with these children through the night and listened to each one's story. Zoran leaned against her, shivering from the cold, and told her that they often saw the face in the fresco come alive. Vesna said the eyes moved, and chipped pieces of the face filled in so that they would see the full portrait of a warm, gentlewoman. Samir explained that it was the older image that came alive, the image that was under the newer one of the lady. The woman in the older image was buxom and rounded, with full rosy cheeks and cherry lips. Zoran nodded, adding that she often held her hands out as she whispered encouraging words. They said this happened when a strange wind blew through the ruins, followed by a mist that calmed their fears and soothed their spirits. They loved this place that had been their home since they discovered it six months before.

Although a number of journalists visited the church ruins when a rumor circulated that the children were seeing a Marian apparition, interest quickly faded when official validation by the Vatican was not received for this sighting. They said that the visions that were described did not appear to be related to visitations traditionally associated with the Virgin Mary. Over the past two thousand years, Mary had appeared in sacred places around the world, in a globe of pure white light, wearing a long dress, with her head covered. Her feet were usually surrounded by mist and she sometimes held her son in her arms.

The newer Madonna that covered the emerging older image of the rounded mother caused embarrassment to the Christians. Although journalists reported that the fires had turned the Virgin's skin black, Betina wondered if a black Madonna or Magdalene had been superimposed over the rounded Mother in a continuation of goddess worship, made to look Christian. Betina thought of the stories of the painting of the Black Madonna in Czestochowa, Poland

and the apparition seen by Juan Diego in the 1500's in Guadalupe, where he was instructed to build a church. There was also the fourteen-year-old girl who lived in the Pyrenees, named Bernadette, who experienced eighteen visitations from Mary, over a six-month period, never knowing who the lady was until the last apparition. In 1862 the apparition was considered authentic and Lourdes became a center of healing and miracles. Although the list of visitations over the past century was enormous, the apparition seen by this band of children was regarded with suspicion. She was like that icon of prehistoric art—the Venus of Willendorf—come to life. But since she looked nothing like the virgin, stories began to circulate that the place was possessed by the devil.

Betina realized that under the peaceful gaze of the woman in the fresco, a miracle had indeed taken place at this church ruin in the way that these Muslim, Roman Catholic, and Serbian Orthodox children secretly came together. They did not hate one another, and some of them showed the promise of finding pathways to heal their burden of despair. They were children of mothers who died in rape camps and of fathers who had committed crimes of rape; children of fathers who had been tortured or who tortured; children whose parents had prayed in the historic Aladza Mosque or in Roman Catholic churches. These were children who had lost everything, including a need to identify with any religion or ethnic group. They were simply too weary to fight their parent's religious wars.

When Betina arrived in Athens, she was preoccupied with the curious stories she had heard on her travels. She needed a few hours to sort through her experiences, beginning with the strange energies in the cave in Malta and in Ephesus, and with the children at the church in Bosnia. But there was no time for reflection: the agenda for the Archaeological Congress was packed with lectures and panels. Betina felt some remorse when she told the chairman of the symposium that she would not be delivering her paper that week. Mostly she felt relief since there was so much on her mind.

The morning presentation examined the destruction of numerous historical sites in Iraq and other neighboring countries, and the potential significance of a number of artifacts found in a secret chamber, revealed after a bomb opened up a tunnel underneath the ziggurat in Ur. The archaeologist alluded to the discovery of a collection of 'Gold Tablets' and inferred that the significance was to be as important or more important than the Dead Sea Scrolls. This was followed by a report of the ongoing efforts of a multi-cultural team of archaeologists to reconstruct artifacts that had been damaged in the National Museum in Baghdad in 2003, after American forces entered the city. There was also an intriguing report of the successful use of infrared aerial photography in locating lost cities in the jungles of Peru.

After a tea break, Betina listened with interest to Peter Fagan's paper, perhaps the most controversial of all those given at the congress. She knew it would be shredded, and labeled pseudo-science or cult archaeology. Peter was the youngest speaker, still in his twenties, and spoke with enthusiasm and vitality as his long blond ponytail bobbed in the air with every gesture of his expressive hands. He had a bounce in his steps as he moved around the lectern discussing tonal resonance in the pyramids in both Egypt and Mesoamerica. He believed that the design of the pyramids had many functions, including the amplification of sound, which was of great importance during rituals that took place in these temples. A full-scale attack was launched against him when he finished, but he laughingly brushed it off, complaining that his critics were too closed-minded to consider the obvious.

Peter and Betina left the congress midway through a final presentation and went to a lively Greek restaurant popular among the locals, whose exterior imitated the facade of the Greek Parthenon. They ordered fish dishes—octopus with sauce and baked shrimp with feta—and a bottle of ouzo. Several Greek men were clapping while a young man slowly danced the zeibekiko. When the clapping died down, Peter asked, "Why didn't you deliver your paper? You were listed in the program as a presenter."

"I had nothing new to say," Betina replied as she lifted a hyacinth out of a vase and smelled it. "I'm bored with the paper I wrote. I don't want to impose it on anyone. Not one sentence reflects my original purpose for going into archaeology. I started to write another paper about some curious events I recently witnessed, but my thoughts are scattered. I have no clear interpretation for the things people have told me and what I've seen with my own eyes. I plan to turn it into a proposal for further research."

Peter had no difficulty understanding her feelings. He told her he had been spending all his time at Palenque. He experienced an extraordinary high one afternoon as he climbed the steps of this ancient pyramid in Mexico and then descended into its depths. He said he heard the voice of the earth, resonating, reverberating against the walls, and speaking a forgotten language. That was how he stumbled upon his theory of tonal resonance.

He took her hands in his and kissed them, and asked her to go to Palenque with him and experience it on mushrooms. As he stroked her palm and forearm, she braced herself so that she would not succumb to his charm. She noticed her reflection in a wineglass. She had become so thin; there were dark circles under her eyes from a resistance to sleep. She hadn't bothered to put on any make-up in weeks or perhaps months.

"I dream of being with you again," he said as he brushed aside a golden lock of curly hair, fine as a child's, that fell across his eye. "It's like..."

She put her fingers on his lips so that he could not continue.

When she removed them, he quickly inserted one last comment.

"I love the struggles you've chosen for yourself in life."

She laughed hesitantly and then stopped, rethinking his comment. "Chosen?" If there was a second that she had considered his invitation, it now was lost. It made her remember how often she could not appreciate the way he looked at things. She avoided his intense eye contact, feeling herself weakening to his power as he ran his hand down her upper arm. Even though he had girlfriends in several cities around the world, there was an occasional moment when she found him convincing in his devotion, but in any regard, she always found him enjoyable.

"Earth speaks. I want you to hear its song," he said as he took out an embroidered Guatemalan pouch from his pocket. He showed Betina his private stash of Psilocybe mushrooms that he said grew abundantly in Chiapas, Mexico.

She was tempted, but declined his invitation and told him she planned to fly to Amsterdam the following day, to visit a cousin she hadn't seen in many years, and then she had to get back to Cambridge. He sighed and withdrew the mushrooms.

"It's a pity to experience this bliss all alone," he said as he put the bag back in his pocket.

It was a pity, she thought to herself, but she was on a mission, and the mission was to discover what her mission might be.

It was impossible to stay seated any longer. Four men, with arms wrapped around each other, danced around them and one of them grabbed Betina by the hand. She reached for Peter's hand and he followed after her. Soon, more than a dozen people circled the dance stage, smashing plates whenever the spirit moved them.

"I could really get into this," Betina whispered to Peter, as she threw a plate against the wall. He nodded and threw another two, then stomped on some fragments that landed near his feet. After a few more dances, Betina's feet started to hurt. "I've been walking for weeks…the spirit's willing, but the body's weak."

They sat down at their table and Peter took off her Greek sandals and began massaging her feet. The waiter brought them another round of ouzo and *bougatsa*, Peter's favorite desert.

"Well, since I can't persuade you to join me in Mexico…I'd like to recommend that you visit a man I met in the Yucatan. His name is Wolfgang Hertzog and he lives in Amsterdam. He's a reclusive chap, who has an extraordinary private collection of antiquities. Apparently he smuggled things out of many different countries and hid them in his mansion." He wrote down his friend's address on a napkin and insisted that she visit him.

They parted shortly after that. She felt a pang of remorse at turning down Peter's invitation, as she recalled their escapades at the Archaeological Congress several years earlier. After sitting through tedious readings of papers that went from early morning to late afternoon, they would spend the evenings in trendy clubs in Paris. Peter always seemed to know the club owners, and they never had trouble getting in. They were always escorted past sleek models with angular faces, and actresses with alluring red lips, dressed from head to toe in tight black leather. Many of the women knew him and blew him kisses.

She remembered how he whispered in her ear, "After more than a few drinks, it's possible to forget their vapidness."

After dancing all night and more than a few drinks, she would find him beside her in her hotel bed. His hair was longer then, well below his shoulders. Running her fingers through this golden mane, she indulged in its softness and flowery fragrance. She remembered how he rolled over when she stroked the silky skin on his back and how he slowly open his eyes, with the sweetest smile on his face. She thought that Psyche must have felt this same intoxication when she discovered the secret beauty of Cupid.

CHAPTER TWO

THE MUTE BOOK

Betina's cousin, Faye, had to visit her mother-in-law in the hospital the morning Betina arrived in Amsterdam. With a few hours to kill, Betina went shopping in antique stores. She found a remarkable velvet cloak, which drew her attention, because of the intricate antique embroidery around the hemline and sleeves. Putting it on, she sensed that this beautiful cloak had a distinguished past and had been worn by some extraordinary people. She knew she had to have it. When she reached into her purse for her wallet, she accidentally pulled out the address of the antiquities collector that Peter had given her. She was about to throw it out, but changed her mind. She paid for the cloak, put it on, and decided to visit Peter's friend.

It was a violently windy day. Heavy gray clouds loomed over the city blocking light, hope and comfort. She passed shadows of solitary figures wearing hats and scarves, shielding themselves with large umbrellas as they hurried for refuge from the pouring rain.

Wolfgang Hertzog's mansion was surrounded by a wrought-iron fence and protected by a pack of vicious dogs that charged to the gates at her approach, flashing their hungry fangs at her. She rang the buzzer, announced herself, and to her surprise, the gates opened without any further inquiries as to who she was or what her purpose might be.

A housekeeper stood at the door. Her black hair, streaked with gray, was in a tight bun, and her white blouse and plain black skirt were perfectly pressed. She examined Betina with disdain and Betina immediately became self-conscious, realizing that she must've been a terrible sight. Her hair was wet and disheveled from the rain, her umbrella had blown inside out, and beads of rainwater streamed down her raincoat forming a puddle at her feet. As Betina wiped her face with a handkerchief, the housekeeper told her that Wolfgang would not be receiving any visitors because he was sleeping. She suggested that Betina come back the following day and quickly closed the door in her face, before she had a chance to utter a word. Betina lingered at the door for a moment, stunned by her gruffness. She decided to forget about meeting the antiquities collector.

Betina spent the late afternoon with Faye, who had restored works of art for various museums over the past fifteen years, and was now working in the Rijksmuseum. They looked at seventeenth-century Dutch paintings by Frans Hals, Jan Steen, Jan Vermeer, and Rembrandt, as well as the fifteenth-century masters from the northern low-countries. They studied a nativity scene of Christ in a manger surrounded by angels. Betina thought of the way Peter recited Milton's *On the Morning of Christ's Nativity*, a few years earlier, when they spent Christmas together in Edinburgh after the close of an archaeological conference. Peter was a walking anthology of European and American poetry. He reminded her of how Milton had incorporated the theme of the music of the spheres in his writings; in this particular poem, the angels sang out when Christ was born, with music that had never been heard before, setting earth in perfect balance. He said that finding that perfect harmony was the thing that was needed to set our magnificent planet back on its course.

While her cousin made a phone call to check on the status of her mother-in-law, Betina browsed through the museum shop and selected a poster of Vermeer's painting of a woman baking bread. She stood on line to buy stamps so that she could mail the picture to Jane, an old friend from her student days at Harvard. Betina's cousin returned, just as she paid the postmaster for the postage.

Faye had a look of relief on her face: her mother-in-law was recovering. Strolling past paintings in the permanent collection, Faye described the conservation work she had done for the museum. "In Italy, I helped restore a painting by a lesser-known Renaissance painter, Dosso Dossi. The x-ray that they took of the painting showed that the artist had originally drawn in a figure of a knight. Later, he covered it up and painted in a dog. This led to the popular interpretation that a good witch was trying to free the knight from a spell that put him into a dog's body."

"When the painter 'repents'...pentimento...isn't it?" Betina asked.

She nodded. "It's exciting to access original concepts and intentions. The earlier images under the newer ones reveal so much about the thought process of the artist. Sometimes paintings are painted over by a second artist. Occasionally, the original image is more significant and I have to remove the top layer of paint."

As Betina listened to her cousin, she began to think of the fresco in the church where Vesna, Samir, and Zoran spoke of seeing an emerging image of a large woman under certain atmospheric conditions. She wondered what year the Madonna was superimposed over the earlier image.

Faye broke her train of thought when she pointed to two paintings, worth millions of dollars, that were gifts from Wolfgang Hertzog's private collection. Betina was amused by the coincidence of seeing his name on the gold placard beneath the painting. She wondered how Peter had developed a relationship with this extremely wealthy, but intensely private man, but quickly reminded herself that he had a fluid nature that always led him to extraordinary people and situations. She wondered if seeing Hertzog's name on the placard was somehow a sign that she should try once more to see him.

Though the rains continued the next day, she did not let that stop her from returning to Wolfgang's mansion. She passed through the gates, only to be informed by the housekeeper that he could not be disturbed. She was told in that same disinterested tone to try back the following day. Again, the housekeeper closed the door in Betina's face before she could say a word. Returning a third time, Betina was told that Wolfgang was still too ill to see visitors.

Recognizing that the housekeeper's stern rebuffs caused her curiosity to build rather than subside, Betina visited the mansion a fourth time. This time she was admitted into Wolfgang's foyer and passed under an enormous crystal chandelier. The housekeeper solemnly escorted her up a winding flight of marble stairs to his bedroom. Betina looked at an emaciated figure lying in bed, attended by a young nurse, who offered her a seat beside him. Wolfgang motioned to the housekeeper to come to him. Drawing her ear to his lips, he whispered to her, in a feeble voice. A moment later she left the room and return with a package. He took the package from her and ran his fingertips over the heavy brown paper wrapping, as if he could sense the energy of the mysterious object.

A layer of shiny transparent skin, thin as filo leaves used in Greek pastries, was tightly stretched across long thin bones in his hand. The blue veins stood out like major highways on a map—the thicker ones were like the system of rivers that were the main arteries in Europe. Looking out the only window in the room not fully covered by a heavy curtain, Betina saw the Ijsselmeer River, which flows into the Rhine. She imagined Wolfgang as a young man sailing down this river, and on rivers all around the world. She could see him on the Indus, the Yangtze, the Congo and the Amazon. She could see him on the Nile, stopping in Cairo, haggling with an Egyptian merchant over the price of an illegally confiscated scroll from the Tombs of the Kings. She saw him wandering through the markets in Alexandria, where ancient thought and wisdom converged in this city built upon the delta triangle. She could see him in his youth, searching for prehistoric vessels and figurines, and exploring old shops in Baghdad. If he were well, he would probably have been the first to collect artifacts from the National Museum in Baghdad, after the lootings in 2003.

In a faint but dignified voice he said, "I was expecting you. This is yours, Ms. Sharp."

Betina was startled that he knew her name, but realized that the housekeeper must have told him. After all, she had tried to visit him on three other occasions.

"It's a pity that so many other manuscripts by this visionary thinker were destroyed. This is all I have."

She asked him where the book was from and what language it was written in, but no answer was forthcoming. Instead, he turned his head away and motioned to the housekeeper to usher her out of the room. She told Betina that he could not be disturbed any longer, his health was too delicate. While the nurse adjusted the flow on an intravenous bottle, the housekeeper saw Betina to the front door and shut it in her face before she had a chance to say another word.

As she rode in a taxi back to her cousin's house, she listened to the steady click of the windshield wipers, clearing away the mild flow of raindrops. After arriving at her cousin's house, she went straight to her bedroom, and carefully unwrapped the package. She studied the finely crafted leather cover of the book and was nearly breathless as she turned to the first page. Surprised that it merely contained a faint sketch, she turned to the next page, and then the next. Her heart sank when she found that none of the pages of the manuscript were complete. The pages had lines on them, where images and writing would be, but had not been filled in.

The next day, as the rain stopped and light from the sun broke through the dark clouds, she approached Wolfgang's home, hoping for information regarding the manuscript. This time the guard dogs did not charge at her; but remained at a distance and whined. Betina knocked at the door for a long time until the housekeeper opened it. Her face was puffy, her eyes were red as though she'd been crying for hours, and her hair was coming out of its bun, long strands falling down her back. She realized how deeply the housekeeper must've cared for Wolfgang as she told her, in a broken voice, that he had passed away during the night.

The housekeeper invited her in. They sat in front of an empty fireplace. The heavy wine-colored velvet curtains were drawn, shutting out all but a few shafts of sunlight that shone through the moth holes, illuminating dust particles in the air. The only life remaining in the house was the ticking of an antique grandfather clock. The chimes were mournful, discordant, and several hours off their mark. It even seemed that the bells sounded for the last time, in this place where time stood still. Betina was pleased when the housekeeper piled logs in the fireplace and started a fire to warm the place.

Tears flowed from the housekeeper's eyes as she said, "I understand nothing about the meaning of life. How can we be here one day and gone the next? Why be here at all? For what? It's for naught. It's meaningless."

On the plane to Boston, Betina noticed that the sadness she had been carrying since her final visit to Wolfgang's home, was dissolving. Instead, she felt a slight buoyancy in her spirit and moments of lightness in her being. She reflected on the series of events that had transpired as the plane ascended higher into the sky.

Betina glanced at a young Dutch couple in the seat next to hers, looking sweetly into each other's eyes; their dreaminess did not goad her into her usual cynicism. They had each other, but she had the manuscript. Wanting to look at it again and hold it in her hands, she reached into the overhead rack and took out her briefcase. The manuscript was still there, wrapped in her soft velvet cloak. Even though it was an unfinished book, or rather a book that had hardly even been started, Betina sensed that it still had great importance. Drawing it close to her heart, she noticed that it radiated an unusual kind of energy. Rubbing her eyes, she saw a fireworks display with sparkles of illumination. As she drifted off to sleep she dreamed of talking to her old boyfriend, Andrew.

When her dream suddenly shifted, she found herself wandering through a tunnel. That same mysterious wind, which she felt in the cave in Malta and in the bombed-out Bosnian church, came whirling through the tunnel, carrying with it an earthen scent of the underground world. A dim light guided her down the entire length of the tunnel where she heard an old woman's gentle and melodic voice. She could not identify the voice, but somehow it seemed familiar.

"You've finally come," the old woman said. "There is so much to tell. Now is the time to begin."

Betina moved through the tunnel, seeing patches of vaporous colors--ochre red, lavender, celestial blue, and forest green. The sound of chanting was coming from a great distance. She struggled to identify some of the words, but could not even determine the language. Again she heard the old woman's soft voice:

"I will tell you many things—of my life, of my time, of the truths that I have known. I know you long to understand these things."

Betina wondered why this old woman presumed to know what she longed for. Intrigued, she waited for the voice to continue, but that was all the old woman said. Before she could tell if there was a human form that accompanied the voice, she found herself back on the plane, next to the same Dutch couple—now sleeping in each other's arms. Betina wondered if it was sleep deprivation that brought on this vision. It was as if her mind tuned into another station, picked up a different frequency, and transported her out of her dream into another world.

The plane pierced billowy clouds. Beneath them was the vast ocean, so like her mind. At times there were moments of stillness in which she could see all things clearly, and could find peace in the purposefulness of her endeavors. At other times, periods of chaos destroyed any sense of order and direction, pointing to the absurdity of her efforts.

Betina recalled the voices of Vesna, Samir, and Zoran, and in the swell of the deep waters their voices merged with those of lost children living on a new-world delta. She heard their songs and felt their despair. These voices were from children who would one day enter into her rapidly transforming life.

CHAPTER THREE

SCENT OF ROSES

On Bourbon Street in the French Quarter of New Orleans, Evangeline, a sixteen-year-old runaway, sang an impassioned rendition of "Motherless Child." Though this song brought tears to her eyes, she loved to sing it since it always attracted an appreciative audience. She imagined it moved so many people because they shared that same heartache for a mother's love that would endure over time and circumstance—the kind of love that was as eternal as the stars in the night sky, and as vast as the mighty oceans and endless deserts. Businessmen, store owners, delivery boys, and tourists alike would stand around her, enraptured by the depth of feeling she emoted in her song. For that one moment, they were bonded in their deepest longings.

She had a natural elegance about her, seeming like a lost princess, wandering through life in search of the magical path that would take her back to her royal origins. Like the goddess Persephone, captured on canvas by the Pre-Raphaelite painter Dante Gabriel Rossetti, she had sweet red lips, a slender nose and ivory skin. Adorning her neck were gold chains, lockets and fake pearls. She often wore rings on her fingers and earrings with semi-precious stones. She was delicate and regal, with fine brown hair cascading down her back. The lavender velvet cloak that she liked to wear over her slightly tattered, antique satin dress set her apart from other women who passed her by on the street, dressed in current fashions. It was as though the world she grew up in had not shaped her—she belonged to another time and another place.

Her eyes were extraordinary: lavender, with a dark ring around the iris and a few dark specks near the pupil. They held a mystery and intrigue that captured the attention of everyone who met her. Whenever anyone thought of Evangeline, it was her eyes that came to mind, and always they stirred up wonder about who she might be.

After abandoning her father, Evangeline lived with four other runaways. Salome, her best friend, ran her knuckles over a washboard, and as she played, time ceased to exist. The rhythms and melody sent Salome soaring through exotic lands where she retrieved forgotten memories, returning only when the music stopped. She had a soft, exotic beauty; her perfect caramel-colored skin shone in the sunlight and her long, curly black hair smelled of the deep green forest. She was tall and slender and when she walked, little bells on her ankle bracelet would sing out along with the chiming of gold medallions of Yoruban gods that she wore around her neck. Salome—who was angelic music solidified into matter—often longed for emancipation from the restraints of human form.

Salome's boyfriend, Christian, played the guitar. He was seventeen, just a year older than Salome and Evangeline, and wore an old spiked jacket, cut at the shoulders. He was the only one in the group from out of state. Despite his parents' pleas, he had no intention of returning to their upscale Colorado home. He felt none of the love they claimed to have for him, and nothing they had to offer could match the happiness he felt in Salome's company. She helped him understand something of who he could be. When he met her at a drug rehabilitation program, it was love at first sight. He often wrote songs to honor her and never wanted to be separated from her.

Evangeline, Salome, and Christian first met Tex while he was digging in a dumpster for food, behind a popular Cajun restaurant. He claimed he had no name, so Christian called him Tex for his insistence on wearing cowboy boots wherever he went. At eleven, he was under 4′ 5″. The boots added two inches to his height and to his confidence. He even had the name Tex tattooed on his shoulder, over a tiny drawing of his boots. He had white Irish skin that turned rosy just moments after being in the sun. Usually, it was streaked with dirt from the streets, and he had to be reminded to wash his face before it turned completely black.

Raider was thirteen when Tex discovered him digging for food in the dumpster that Tex had claimed as his own. After an argument and fistfight over dumpster rights, the two boys became friends. Tex introduced him to the others as the one who had been raiding his dumpster, and soon the boy's name became Raider. Since he was the last to join the group, he never felt secure about his position, but stayed with them because he couldn't find a better place for himself. Everyone had someone, he thought. Evangeline had the dream of her mother, Salome and Christian had each other, Tex had Evangeline, but Raider believed he had no one. He had no memories he could treasure, no hope for the future, no faith in the present and he couldn't shake the feeling of being an intruder wherever he went.

Tex and Raider sat on the sidewalk, banging makeshift drums, trying to lose themselves in the rhythms. They weren't drawn to Evangeline's slow songs, since they didn't like the emotions it stirred in them, so they pushed the rhythm. Like the tribe of abandoned children living in the Bosnian church ruin, Tex and Raider wanted to vent their rage, not access their sadness. They were ready to launch into a song of their own that they'd been practicing together for a couple of weeks, but first Christian wanted to take a collection, since "Motherless Child" always brought in the biggest tips. They never forgot the faces of the people who gave them money, nor did they forget those who listened to them play and walked away. It took so little for them to survive, but it took everything they had to gather the little bit they needed.

Salome stopped playing her washboard, distracted by a man in the distance who was searching the streets and storefronts. He was gaunt and intense with a gray complexion and turkey neck, long wiry locks and a scraggly salt-and-pepper beard. She grabbed Evangeline's arm and shook it, pointing in the direction of the man.

Malcolm suddenly caught sight of Evangeline, his daughter, and screamed out to her, "You can't hide from me forever!"

Evangeline pushed her way through the crowd and ran down the street to get away from him, but he chased after her. She increased her pace and saw that he was getting farther behind. Finally, he stopped and grasped his chest with both hands, trying to catch his breath. Evangeline disappeared around a corner.

Walking along the shore of the Mississippi, she looked over her shoulder to make sure that Malcolm was not still following. When she felt certain that he would not find her, she whispered in the wind, "Do you think of me, the way I think of you? Do you search for me? Oh Mother, if I could talk to you, I might have a chance in this world. I imagine that you are wise, that you are kind, that you are everything I need." She heard Salome calling out to her, then saw her running up the path along the river's edge. Finally she caught up to Evangeline.

Evangeline, happy to see her, said, "You know most of my secret places." They walked in silence until they reached the little cottage where Evangeline lived as a child. They sat on the stoop in front of the modest wooden house that had a dilapidated picket fence running around it, with a swinging door that was always halfway open. They watched a woman read a bedtime story to two children in a second floor window. "Malcolm never thinks of looking for me here, but this is where I often come when I need to find a moment of peace." Evangeline whispered, "He told me that my mother abandoned me, but I never believed him. My dream is always the same. I hear her singing to me. She rocks me to sleep. I know she never left me." Evangeline hummed a few bars of the song; she closed her eyes and rocked back and forth, recalling the embrace of her mother's arms.

Now Evangeline lived with Salome, Christian, Tex, and Raider in an historic house that had been abandoned for years in an area commonly called the slave quarters. It was on a side street in the French Quarter, where there were few pedestrians, and little chance that their secret hideout would be discovered. Since the windows had been boarded up and there was no electricity, Evangeline worked by candlelight, cutting up potatoes and onions and frying them on a gas-powered griddle.

Christian sat at the kitchen table and finished counting the day's take from their street performances. He hoped they all might all be able to go out for some Cajun delicacies, but realized they only had enough for beans and potatoes. Christian complained that it was always the same old grub: fried potatoes, mashed potatoes, bean soup and refried beans.

Later that evening, Evangeline lay on a mattress with her eyes focused on a candle burning on a wood crate, that served as a night table. Seeing the answers to her prayers in the heart of the flame, she was momentarily comforted by a feeling that her dream of finding her mother would manifest. She didn't know how or when it would happen, but she felt certain that things would not always be as they were. Her thoughts were interrupted by Tex, who was sitting in a corner of the room, smoking a water pipe:

"I'm lifting right off the ground. I'm almost floating."

Evangeline was about to respond, but was distracted by Salome and Christian who were in an adjoining room. Christian had set aside his guitar and was making love to Salome—the floorboards creaked with every move they made.

"Cool it," Tex said, as he threw a pillow at Christian. "You go at it every night!"

Christian shouted back, "You'll get yours. Quit whining."

Evangeline whispered, "Come here. I can't sleep either." After making a space for him on the mattress, Tex got up and lay down beside her. Evangeline watched as Raider covered his head with a blanket. "You can join us too, Raider. You don't always have to keep to yourself."

Raider said nothing. Evangeline felt the usual sense of frustration at not being able to reach him. He was always withdrawn, always suspicious, always ready to defend himself at the slightest provocation. Evangeline often wondered what terrible things had happened to him that had severed his desire to communicate. She often felt guilty showering her affections on Tex, whose resistance usually broke down after a tender gesture and a few comforting words.

Tex was wearing pajama bottoms and no shirt. Evangeline held him close and touched the scars on his chest with her fingertips. "It makes me sick to think that someone hurt you like this."

Tex turned away from her, "The ol' man."

"The ol' man…You mean your father did this? You never told me that before."

"Why should I?" Tex rolled his eyes.

"It would be good for you to tell someone."

"The only thing that would be good is if it never happened. Talkin' don't change nothin'! It's a waste of time."

Evangeline ran her fingers through his hair and stroked his forehead. "What happened? I want to know."

Tex sighed and sat up, putting his cheek on his fist. "Nothing happened, 'cept that the ol' man came home and found me drinking his whiskey. Guess he wanted it for himself, 'cause he was furious. He said he'd been a failure as a father 'cause he hadn't taught me nothin'. This time he was really gonna teach me. He slashed me with his knife." Tex stopped talking and stared at the wall.

"Then what?" Evangeline nudged.

Tex continued reluctantly, "Then my sister came home and saw me bleeding everywhere. She called the cops and they took him away. Then an ambulance came for me. I got out of the hospital after two weeks."

"What happened to your father?"

"He's in prison," Tex said in a voice devoid of feeling.

Evangeline kissed his scars and asked, "Have you heard from him?"

"I wrote him a letter, but he never wrote back." Tex slammed his hand on the wall. "What's this to you, anyway!" He said angrily. "I'm so unhappy. Maybe I want to die." He took a tattered picture out of a crate in a corner of the room. After studying it for a few minutes, he showed it to Evangeline. It was his father sitting in an old tractor with a toothpick in his mouth, and bruises on his face. "Once, I thought he knew it all. I wanted to be like him. Now I know he's the last person I wanna be like." Tex watched Evangeline as she looked at the photo, then he touched the collection of medallions that Evangeline wore on several silver chains around her neck. "I guess you must need lots of protection."

Evangeline laughed. She lifted one of the chains over her head and put it around Tex's neck. He smiled when he saw that it had a silver heart on it.

"There's a whole world of people out there that want to love you. Your father just wasn't one of them." Reaching for a tube of salve, she rubbed the soothing gel onto his back.

"I wish I hadn't been born," said Tex.

"Why dream of dying when you can dream of having the life that you want?"

"I'm tired of your bright ideas. You always say the same stuff 'n it means nothin' to me. I'd rather die than dream somethin' that ain't never gonna happen," said Tex.

"Well, why don't you just get some sleep for now," said Evangeline. As Tex closed his eyes, she thought about how she had waged a private war to break through the wall Tex had created. She had been chiseling away at that hard mass of despair for so many months, but had barely made a dent. Where her own faith came from remained a mystery to her, but it was solid in her like an inner orb of light that shone out of her lavender eyes, setting them on fire.

She let her hair loose and it curled down her back to her waist, so soft, so full, so lush. Holding on to a strand of it and wrapping it around his hand, Tex brushed his cheek against the exquisite softness, before drifting off to sleep.

An hour before dawn, Evangeline sat on the balcony, wearing her silk kimono. She whispered, "I see you in the first rays of the morning sun. I feel your presence in the scent of a rose." Evangeline moved toward an altar she had made for her mother, which had a small collection of crystals, shells and dried flowers. She lit a stick of incense, then added a few feathers to the collection.

She thought of the years when she had lived at home with Eartha Mae and Malcolm. She remembered sitting in a corner of the living room, when she was five, mesmerized by the tranquil movement of boats on the Mississippi and the steady rhythm of waves. Her father broke this spell of enchantment, when he began pacing back and forth across the room. He started grilling Evangeline about the whereabouts of Eartha Mae. She remembered feeling confused and stressed by his endless questions. Now she wondered if perhaps her mother had been off with other men. As Malcolm's irritation grew, she wrapped her mother's fringed shawl around her shoulders for comfort, smelling the lingering scent of rose perfume that her mother always wore. Malcolm lifted her up, tore the shawl from her hands, and carried her off to his truck. They drove through the night toward his underground shelter, which he had built on a small piece of land in the bayou. As they drove, he told her over and over that he had made a terrible mistake in marrying Eartha Mae. He hadn't seen her for what she was. He also told her that he would make sure she didn't follow in her footsteps.

On their first night in the underground shelter, he told her he had experienced a revelation. It had come in a flash, like the vision that transformed St. Paul. He heard a voice telling him to let go of any hesitation and gather the black sheep that had gone astray—he was destined to become their leader.

Evangeline watched him in the candlelight of the shelter as he dug his fingers into his own flesh and scratched his stomach and thighs so that his skin bled profusely. He took a metal rod from a shelf and flagellated himself with it. Sitting for hours on end in a corner, in the darkness, he beat his head and back, till blood oozed out of the wounds. The blood became crusty around his eyes and his hair became knotted like a Rastafarian. Eventually, he completely forgot about her.

Day after day she watched helplessly as he sank deeper into insanity. She began to believe that this man couldn't be her father and started calling out to her mother. As Evangeline's difficulties deepened, Eartha Mae dominated her thoughts; her powers became superhuman.

Although the shelter was built using a high-quality prefabricated design, considered to be the best model available in the country, it did not hold up to its ten-year warrantee of being waterproof. Water still seeped in during heavy rains. When that happened, all kinds of creatures slithered into their hideout. Evangeline endured centipedes and snakes and even a baby alligator. As the water level rose inch by inch, Evangeline watched as styrofoam cups became sailboats and a doll's head became a buoy. It wasn't until the rats came that Malcolm finally awoke from his stupor. That was her first experience with Malcolm in the shelter, and each sojourn that followed was more traumatic than the previous one.

Those childhood memories dissolved, as an ephemeral trail of sparkling light guided her out into the courtyard, toward a neglected garden behind their house, where all vegetation had died. But tonight, the garden came to life as she entered through the decaying stone archway. Vines of ivy shot up around the entrance, and spikes lifted of their own accord, out of the paws of a stone lion. When the lion was free from its entrapment, the blood began to course through his veins, and he stretched his back and roared. The marble angels on the water fountains turned in Evangeline's direction and spread their wings, as they stood up on their toes to guide her through. The leaves of a willow tree softly stroked her shoulders and back, like dozens of tiny fingers. A lush pink rose blossomed before her and whispered, "Dance with us tonight." Evangeline closed her eyes and heard a rhythm and a melody in the soft voices of the flowers, in the rustle of wind through the trees, in every breath she took. She became supple like the willow branches and leapt through the air and around the perimeter of the garden until she became breathless. Entranced by the magic of this place, she lay down on an ancient stone bench in the midst of the perfumed garden. She let go of thoughts of the harsh realities of life and sank into a deep state of dreaming.

She played with the first rays of sunlight on her hand. Opening her silk robe, she shut her eyes and lay back as the soft morning light kissed her flesh. Dozens of butterflies glided into the secret garden and swirled around her naked body. The flutter of their luminous golden wings tickled her and she laughed with pleasure when she received a hundred butterfly kisses. Arching her back, she opened every orifice to receive the sublime gifts of the enchanted garden and the mysteries of the dawn. She whispered to herself, "I am not who people think I am. I am not the person Malcolm thinks I am. I am not the person I appear to be when I stand on the street corner. In this garden I remember who I am. I am the daughter of the one who is magnificent. Hear my voice and come to me. Carry my voice, oh great wind. Take it to my mother so that she might know of my longings."

Evangeline called out, with a depth of intention and solidness of faith that caused her soft voice to rise up to meet the majestic and compassionate North Wind. It carried her words past a flock of swallows, through the gray smoke of industrial plants, over pasture-lands where cows grazed, and above fields of corn and barley. Finally her voice reached Lake Itasca, the source of the Mississippi, where her mother and two companions were camping.

CHAPTER FOUR

THE CALLING

It was an unlikely trio, yet they stayed together for several years, zigzagging across the country in search of Evangeline. As time passed, Eartha Mae's hope of finding her lost daughter turned to despair. The old truck that they had been traveling in had broken down for good; they left it by an abandoned railroad station. The prospect of having to continue their journey on foot was too much for Eartha Mae. She was slowing down. Lacking further ideas for new directions to explore, she withdrew to a cave, where she slept much of the time, cutoff from the world like a bear hibernating in winter. Her two companions, Virgil and Oakie, waited for her to awaken. At first they were patient, but slowly they became frustrated, wondering if she would ever arise from her slumber.

A twelve-year-old, sandy-haired boy found them camping in a wooded area that bordered Lake Itasca. He had been collecting leaves from different trees for a school project when he discovered them. He came back several days in a row and watched them from a distance. He told no one that there were three squatters living in a cave, not far from his family's home. When the small boy, Petie, realized that they were hungry and had no means to buy food, he worried that they would die of hunger. Sometimes he woke up in the middle of the night, wondering how he might help them.

At first he bought food for the squatters with the money he kept locked in a little bank above his bed. He even sold his bicycle to his friend to buy more groceries, but they were a hungry group and soon went through all the food he provided until there was nothing left. Sneaking large quantities of food out of his mother's pantry, he gave them cans of soup and beans, canned tuna, and boxes of cereal. He made them oatmeal when his parents weren't around and brought it to them in a pot in the morning. He brought them blankets from his bed, and an old mattress and cot that had been stored in the attic. He took pride in taking care of the three of them and saw it as his personal responsibility, telling no one about their secret relationship.

Eartha Mae was grateful for all the gifts he gave her. She told him he was the sweetest child she had ever met, aside from her daughter, who had that same generous spirit. Petie liked sitting close to her and enjoyed hearing about her adventures around the country. The more he fed her, the more stories she would share. He had never seen anyone quite as large as her, nor had he seen anyone eat so much. Soon he was preparing meals every day—packing them in a picnic basket, and carrying it to the cave in the evenings.

But as time passed, Eartha Mae became even more overwhelmed with despair. She had no idea which way to turn on her search for Evangeline, nor did Oakie or Virgil have inspired ideas of their own. She dragged a mattress to a corner of the cave and slept for days. When Petie brought them food, she devoured it in seconds then went back to sleep. Since her only source of comfort came from food, she grew larger each day. Virgil and Oakie understood the sorrow that she felt over her daughter, but it had been ten years since their separation and they wondered how much longer she would mourn. Whenever they suggested that she let go of the idea of finding her, Eartha Mae had a fit. She threw her shoes at them, swatted them with her sweater, and chased them down the road casting rocks at them. She yelled at them to stay away from her until they could offer an intelligent strategy. She even threatened to cut them out of her life if they continued to tell her to give up her quest to find Evangeline. For weeks she stomped around and grumbled about how insensitive they were—they had never lost a child.

Virgil and Oakie didn't want to leave her and finally had to accept that there was no point in telling her to forget. She wanted solutions from them, but every suggestion they offered seemed pointless. Helping her maintain her faith, they soon realized, was the best way they could help her. She would find Evangeline. They promised her that.

When Jane, the young boy's mother, began to notice the strange disappearance of food and various household items, she became puzzled and began questioning her son. Petie was not very good at lying and after several attempts to disguise the truth, he finally told her about the vagrants.

"I felt sorry for them. They had nothing to eat. Whenever I brought them food, they were so grateful. Oakie, the funny one, would jump up and down...he ate the cereal right out of the box with his hands. He always asked me how he could send away for the prizes. I gave him our address. Is that okay?"

Jane didn't look pleased, but her reaction was no surprise to Petie.

"The other one, Virgil, was always off by himself. Always thinking about things, I guess. The lady's as big as a bear. She used to tell stories, but then she became sad...now she sleeps. Maybe she's sick, I don't know."

His description of the trio intrigued Jane since she had an outgoing nature and a curiosity about people that surfaced when her husband was out of town. She listened to Petie's accounts with great interest, but did not mention their presence on their land to her husband, Phillip, fearing that he would have the police escort them away for trespassing.

When Phillip was away on business in Hong Kong, she asked Petie to invite them to dinner. Virgil and Oakie had a hard time waking Eartha Mae from her sleep, but they sparked her interest when they told her that she had been invited to dinner. When they promised that there would be plenty of food and pastries, she slowly got up and dressed. Unaware of the weight she had put on, she was surprised to see that even her favorite dress no longer fit her body. The seams ripped apart when she tried to slip into it, so she had to drape a shawl around her waist to cover up the tear.

Jane spent the day cooking—it had been a long time since she had cooked a dinner for anyone besides her family, and she wanted this to be a special occasion for all of them. Petie was pleased by her efforts. He spent the day with her, helping to make a pie and designing cookies with smiling faces. She enjoyed spending her time this way, though a part of her still ached for the academic world she had once shared with Betina; the world she left when she quit her Harvard doctoral program and married Phillip.

Jane and Petie greeted Eartha Mae, Oakie, and Virgil when they arrived at the front door. The house was not as remarkable as some of the other homes Jane had lived in, but it was pleasant enough, and she had done everything to make it warm and inviting. Her husband was an architect who had a reputation for bringing nature into the structures he designed. He had designed all their homes, including their adobe home in Arizona, which had gently rounded earthen-walls and an indoor waterfall. Their New England home had an earth-covered roof that supported a wild garden. After several years of perfecting that house, they sold it and moved to this home in Lake Itasca, which had large picture windows that let in plenty of morning and afternoon sunlight. The living-room window overlooked the lake and the front yard extended to the shoreline.

Virgil and Oakie were dazzled by the splendor of the place. They sat in the living room, which was elegant and spacious. Jane had an instinctual understanding of how to create harmony and comfort, by using earth-tone colors on the walls. Eartha Mae made herself comfortable in a large leather armchair that faced the fireplace. She looked up at the mantle above the fireplace that had family photographs and a beautiful collection of a dozen Hopi Kachina dolls, all of them bearing messages from the spirit world. Virgil and Oakie sat on a couch covered in a fabric that had an American Indian geometric pattern. Vibrant flowers flourished in large terracotta vases that lined the picture windows.

Jane brought out a tray of hors d'oeuvres and set it on a coffee table. Without a second thought, Eartha Mae put the tray in her lap and devoured the stuffed mushrooms and cheese puffs. When there was nothing left on the tray and no other food in sight, she settled back in her chair and looked into the fire. In a wistful voice she said, "Every night, I sang to my daughter in front of our fireplace. She smiled and laughed, 'tll she drifted off to sleep. Nothing has ever been sweeter."

Throughout the dinner and late into the evening, Eartha Mae spoke in a dreamy voice about her last days with Evangeline. Her mind became a loop of repeating memories. There was the time when Evangeline was three and gave her an exquisite bouquet of wild flowers that she picked along the Mississippi. There was the special way that Evangeline took care of her pet rabbit. There was the unforgettable picture she made when she was six: Eartha Mae as a tree, with birds, squirrels, and raccoons on her branches; bears and foxes on her shoulders; and a smiling six-year-old Evangeline in her belly. She had roots that went deep into the ground—she was earth herself. Eartha Mae loved this picture and hung it over the fireplace. She studied it for weeks after Malcolm ran off with Evangeline, and wondered about the meaning it had for her daughter. She was so engrossed with personal thoughts of this painting, that she could not hear any of Jane's questions.

"Was there a missing person's investigation? Have you considered grief therapy so that you can begin to move…on?" She paused, realizing that Eartha Mae might resent her comment. "How long has it been?"

"It's like it happened yesterday for her," Oakie whispered helplessly.

"It's been ten years, but there's been no healing," said Virgil, holding back his frustration.

Jane recognized the depth of Eartha Mae's depression and inability to let go but her attempts to communicate with Eartha Mae were unsuccessful. Jane realized that it wasn't her place to judge Eartha Mae's feelings, since she might feel the same way if someone ran off with Petie. She watched with amazement as Eartha Mae silently ate the entire pie that she baked for all of them. Even after Jane cleared away the plates, Eartha Mae remained at the table, mumbling to herself, picking crumbs off the tablecloth and licking them off her fingertips.

While Petie showed Oakie his favorite intergalactic computer games, Jane joined Virgil in the library. She found him flipping through books of poetry that had been required reading in her undergraduate college classes.

"How did you meet Eartha Mae?" she asked.

"It was five years ago, in San Francisco." Virgil recalled the after-hours bar where they met, which he frequented nearly every night for six months. He knew he was going downhill, numbing himself with alcohol, desperately trying to block any feeling or thought. One evening, Eartha Mae sat next to him and they fell into a conversation. She had just arrived in town by bus and passed out photos of her lost daughter to the customers in the bar. Virgil studied the picture of Evangeline and remembered thinking that the six-year-old child looked like an angel, with curly locks of hair flowing down her back, and clear shining eyes. She wore a white-lace dress and the sun illuminated her from behind, creating a gold aura around her.

Virgil knew how it felt to be lost. He had never had a sense of belonging. There was no place that seemed like home and no ethnic group that he felt like he could call his own since he had a Japanese mother, and a father who was American Indian. He was a man who had lost everything, and with each loss he withdrew deeper into himself. When Eartha Mae took hold of his hand that night in bed, and commented on his beauty, he found a rush of buried sexual feelings return to him.

They rode back to his hotel on his motorcycle. Laying in bed, Eartha Mae held him in her arms and stroked his hair. He was amazed at the effortless connection that developed, but at the same time he was afraid of the dependency he might begin to feel. Slowly the stone in his throat began to dissolve and Virgil told her something of his life. His father had drifted off when he was a boy. His mother worked long hours to provide for him, so he was alone even as a child. When he dropped out of school, he took to hanging out at local bars and then became a drifter like his father. At fifteen, he hitchhiked to Mexico's Baja California and camped out in an abandoned trailer on the harsh desert land, away from both natives and tourists. He found shelter in abandoned Spanish missions, and inside unusual rock formations and caves with petroglyphs. Later, he lived in a thatch hut on the coast and watched the migration of gray whales.

After nine months he became restless. He hitched to Tijuana, where he spent his days drinking and panhandling. For a time, he worked as a carpenter, but soon found himself drifting out of that life and heading for the Sierra Madres. He thought that by getting away from people and living alone he would learn the truth of things.

His hair became long and unkempt and he grew a bushy beard. He believed that separating himself from people was the smartest thing he had ever done. Venturing deeper and deeper into the mountains, he swore to himself that he would never return to civilization, but would preserve what he called, 'the purity of his spirit.'

Virgil made no plans for his survival and soon found himself without the willpower to forage for roots or berries, or to trap the smallest game to satisfy his hunger. His hope for enlightenment turned to despair and he began to sense that he was in a critical situation. Secluded in a hut made of branches and resting on a mattress made of leaves, he wondered if all along he had a death wish and had set himself up to die of starvation in the middle of nowhere.

Discovering that he was near death, a farmer drove him to a village shaman, who performed a healing ceremony on him. After a long recovery, he returned to San Francisco hoping to see his mother, whom he hadn't seen since the age of fifteen, twelve-years earlier. When he found out that his mother had died, his depression deepened. Without resources to take care of himself, he held up the owner of a liquor store. That impulsive act resulted in a six-month prison sentence for robbery. After his release, he managed to find a job that enabled him to pay for a hotel room and buy a motorcycle—it was shortly after that he met Eartha Mae in the bar.

Virgil loved finding Eartha Mae's arms protectively entwined around him when he woke up in the morning. He loved sinking into the fullness of her body and touching her voluptuous soft flesh. With time, he began to blossom and experience a renewed sense of possibility. He began moving again, shedding the excess weight that he had put on from drinking. Eartha Mae was astonished at the person that was emerging.

Eventually he began to sense that she was drifting away from him, returning to recurring thoughts of her past and of her daughter. When he realized that he would not always be the center of her world, he began to let go of some of his expectations, and watched with sadness as she hardly noticed. Despite this, he knew he wanted to stay with her since he couldn't remember when he had ever experienced so much tenderness and understanding.

They traveled together on Virgil's motorcycle for a few years after that, passing out flyers describing Evangeline's disappearance, in cities and small towns all across the United States. It was in Lincoln, Nebraska, that Virgil's motorcycle broke down, and it was there that they met Oakie. He had been living with his Aunt Olive and had never been out of Lincoln, though he always dreamed of seeing something of the world. Virgil assumed that Eartha Mae invited him on their journey because he owned a small truck of his own: he never imagined that it might be because she enjoyed his company. In any case, that was how the three of them joined up in their wanderings.

But Virgil shared none of these thoughts with Jane, nor did he hear any of her other questions, so she left him alone in the library, disappointed by her inability to learn more about him.

After dinner, Eartha Mae, Oakie, and Virgil returned to their cave and Eartha Mae immediately fell asleep on her mattress. Who could say how long she lay there? Maybe it was just a week, but Virgil and Oakie began to think she had been there since the beginning of time. She often said that since she could not create the life she wanted, she preferred to sleep and to dream.

They all had dreams that night that carried them back in time, to a pristine world. Eartha Mae's dream took her to the primordial beginnings, where all life forms flowed from her. Virgil saw the land lush with ancient plants and prehistoric animals. In this cave of dreaming, he saw himself running with the bison, taking part in a stampede across the Great Plains, and drinking from a clear pool of water. Soaring above the land, through the billowy clouds that covered the mountain tops, Oakie had a bird's eye view of the rivers and turquoise lakes, and the forests with singing birds.

When Virgil awoke, he began scratching images from his animal dreams on the wall with a metal blade. Oakie covered his hands in berry dye and stamped handprints on another part of the wall. During the next few days, they managed to cover large sections of the cave walls and ceiling as they waited for Eartha Mae to awaken from her slumber.

Eventually there came a soft voice, echoing down through the chambers of the underground cavern, calling out, "Eartha Mae! Eartha Mae!" Virgil and Oakie looked at each other and then around the cave trying to locate the source of that mysterious voice.

When the voice called out a second time, Eartha Mae rubbed her eyes as she sat up in bed. "What voice is that?" she said with irritation. "Who wakes me from my dreamy dreams?"

Oakie was startled by Eartha Mae's words and jumped up, knocking against a pile of empty soup cans that came crashing down around him. Virgil shook his head in disdain, tired of Oakie's clumsiness and bungling.

The voice called out again and Eartha Mae asked, "What is that voice? Small as a robin, persistent as a cricket." She got up from the old mattress and put on a bathrobe then walked to the cave entrance, which overlooked Lake Itasca. She saw that the land was dry, the trees were dying, and the lake was covered with a thin layer of pea-green algae. Eartha Mae opened her arms toward heaven and cried, "My kingdom is a wasteland. The crops are withered. Disease is rampant. Despair rules the land. Where are the bison? Why don't I hear the trumpeting of the bull elk and the catamount?"

Oakie and Virgil followed her as she walked around the lakeshore and looked at the fish that lay gasping for life beside dozens of dying crabs. Even the geese were weak and several struggled to fly but could not lift off from the ground no matter how hard they flapped their wings.

The little voice called out again, "Eartha Mae! Eartha Mae!"

Eartha Mae looked around, "There it is again. A voice with so much sorrow. So much sadness."

"Maybe it's the wind in the trees," Oakie suggested.

Eartha Mae shook her head, "It comes with the wind, but it's not the wind. It comes from a great distance." She faced south and the gentle wind blew through her hair. "Yes, it comes from the south. It's a calling. It's the voice of our new direction. The river will take us there."

Eartha Mae walked a little farther and turned to Oakie and Virgil, "I believe that if you turn from your destiny, if you choose a weaker path, you will destroy yourself. You cannot resist a calling. If you do, you become stagnant, like a lake that is overgrown with algae. There's no movement. The light cannot penetrate its depths."

Virgil watched as she paced up and down and put her hand to her chin, then scratched her head. He suspected that she was hatching another one of her tiresome plans and was afraid to hear what it might be.

"You must build me a vessel to sail down this mighty river," said Eartha Mae.

Oakie frowned and said, "I can't build nothin'," then he perked up and added, "but I'm good at breaking things."

Eartha Mae glared at him, "There's a journey we must take. A long, long journey. We must go south!" she commanded.

"What do you mean by south?" Virgil asked. South to Antarctica? South to Brazil?"

Eartha Mae offered no further explanation, though she expected Virgil and Oakie to follow along without question.

It was one of those moments when Virgil wondered how much more he could take of her whims, but when he imagined living on his own, he knew that he was desperately attached to her. They had spent so many nights and days holding one another, stroking each other's face, becoming connoisseurs of the scents and tastes of each other's body. When he felt completely alone, her body became his island of calm in a turbulent world that cared little whether he lived or died. He knew he couldn't leave her and go out into a world where no one else would see the beauty in him, or appreciate the things he could do.

Later that day, Petie led Virgil and Oakie to the town dump, where they searched through mountains of trash. In addition to plenty of barrels and boards, they found an old couch, stuffed chairs and a chest for personal things. There was even an old generator that would provide electricity for the vessel that Eartha Mae wanted them to build. Virgil told Petie that he would make a mobile out of the old silverware, and that Eartha Mae would probably be able to use the rolls of colorful material to create a canopy that would shade them from the sun.

Virgil walked back to the camp at a fast pace, carrying an assortment of items, while Oakie and Petie lagged behind. They stopped when they noticed a kitten in a bird's nest and watched as several baby birds spread their wings and jumped from branch to branch. The kitten tried to imitate them but fell from the nest, into Oakie's hands. He held the kitten close to his chest, kissing it on top of its head, and whispered, "Don't worry, I'll take care of you. I'll never let anything happen to you." Then he hid the kitten under his jacket. He told Petie that he didn't want Virgil to see it, because he wanted to take it with him on their journey and he knew Virgil would try to stop him.

Over the next week, Virgil worked on building the houseboat from the boards and planks that he found in the garbage dump. When they ran out of boards, Eartha Mae told them to chop down a few trees to complete the deck. Although Petie worried that his mother would not approve of the loss of the trees, he decided not to discourage them, since it was the only thing holding up the completion of the houseboat. Petie chose the trees and made sure there were no nests in any of them. Still, he felt much sadness at the thought that they would be taken from the forest that he loved.

Virgil looked appealing to Eartha Mae as he worked in the warm sun, wearing only loose shorts. The muscles on his tall, lean body rippled and bulged as he swung an ax high above his head, and down into the trunk of an oak tree. He mumbled with annoyance as he chopped down the tree, "Windage, it's all we are. Eartha Mae has us shifting direction with every new wind that comes our way. First it's go west, then north, then east, now it's south." Virgil chopped down several more trees and eventually noticed that Oakie had not even made a dent in the trunk of a small tree.

Eartha Mae held a big heart-shaped box of candies and rested on an elegant eggplant-colored chaise longue, which Virgil had brought back from the dump. She lay on her side in a position that accentuated her large curvaceous hips, her broad circular thighs and bulging belly. She turned on her stomach and kicked her little feet in the air, swinging her tiny sequined shoes with pink-feathered pompoms, on the tips of her toes. Contentedly, she tossed bonbons in the air and caught them in her mouth. When she noticed that Virgil and Oakie were slowing down, she snapped her fingers and told them to stop dillydallying and to get the show on the road.

Oakie was frustrated by her commands and sat down on a log, refusing to do any more work. This made Eartha Mae even madder and she reached for a whip, made of long fuzzy-tailed grasses, and snapped it in the air. Oakie glanced at her for a moment, then his attention shifted to the blisters forming on his hand. Virgil shook his head and grumbled at the way Oakie seemed to get out of everything. Moments later, Eartha Mae fell asleep and the whip slipped from her fingers. The last bonbon fell to the ground and was quickly snatched up by a hungry goose.

Eventually the houseboat was finished. Eartha Mae looked on in satisfaction as Virgil and Oakie loaded boxes of supplies onto it. Virgil checked his wooden chest to see if he had forgotten anything. He took out a book that he had bought in a used bookstore in San Francisco. It was the *I Ching,* which he often consulted before setting out in new directions. He asked, "What will be the outcome of this journey?" Without taking the time to throw coins, he closed his eyes and opened the book to hexagram 15, which was 'Modesty.' He knew this hexagram by heart: it reminded him that the journey was more important than the outcome. He also packed a martial-arts manual and fingered his Tibetan beads, given to him as a gift by a man who led a poetry workshop in prison. He neatly folded his collection of colorful vests and sandals and loose cotton pants, then ran back to the cave for his drum and notebook.

Oakie packed his yellow boots and matching rubber raincoat, several favorite foldout books, and a private stash of peanut butter, maple syrup, jellybeans and animal crackers. He called out for his kitten, Boots, and found him crouched down in the tall grasses, not far from the houseboat. He watched as Boots made his way to the goose and sniffed its legs, but just before the goose had a chance to snap at Boots, Oakie picked him up. "You're a curious one. Hope that doesn't get you into trouble someday." Then he put a collar around Boots's neck, attached a leash, and took him on board the houseboat.

Virgil watched with a look of disbelief. "You can't take a cat down the river. Cats hate water...and I hate cats."

Oakie ignored him and held Boots tightly in his arms. Boots meowed and scratched and struggled to break free, as Oakie placed him in a makeshift cat house that stood next to his mattress.

Eartha Mae added a few finishing touches to the houseboat. From the rafters she hung the colorful Indian silk and chiffon fabrics that Virgil had found at the dump. She strung a dozen colorful Chinese lanterns from overhead beams and added an assortment of lime-green, cherry, and tangerine pillows for her eggplant-colored chaise lounge that they placed on a small platform in the center of the deck.

Jane came looking for Petie and found him standing on the shore, by the houseboat, just as it was about to pull out into the waters. She was impressed at the work they had put into making the vessel and was amused by the inventiveness of the hanging mobiles that Petie helped make.

Eartha Mae gave one last look at their Lake Itasca home, then took hold of Virgil's hand and climbed on board. "See the river flowing before us. It is so mighty and fast. Do not think of holding to the shore. The river will take us to our true destination. Push off!"

When Virgil pushed the houseboat out into the water, Eartha Mae flung her arms into the air and cried out joyfully, "Oh great river, calm our troubled spirits in your soothing arms. Comfort us in the day. Lull us to sleep at night. We put our faith in you to guide us through the darkness of these troubled times. Take me to my daughter. Take me to my long lost Evangeline." She paused for a moment then continued, "Great Wind, I ask you to bring me the voice of my daughter. Look kindly on us for we suffer so."

CHAPTER FIVE

MT. OLYMPUS

Betina walked through Harvard Square, past rows of coffee shops, street musicians, and vendors. She was feeling optimistic and could hear Humbert, the chairman of her department, say that her proposal was intriguing. He would most certainly tell her that she would receive the grant she requested for research into the remarkable phenomenon she had discovered in her recent trip. All her old enthusiasm was returning and she found herself walking at a brisk clip and breathing deeply as she hummed the song she heard from her hotel in Malta, "Have courage, don't lose heart."

She thought of the first paper she wrote for Humbert, when he was her undergraduate advisor. It described the movement in the sixties that brought together east and west and showed how the feminist and environmental movements were giving rise to the resurrection of modern-day goddess spirituality. Included in another paper she wrote, called "The Flower Child: Goddess of Innocence," was the psychedelic experiences of a dozen women who had taken LSD in the sixties. She recalled the interview she did with Estrella Estevez, a woman, who lived on the Commonwealth Commune. Estrella described transformative experiences of becoming one with the Goddess during a number of acid trips that she took while listening to the Moody Blues album, *In Search of the Lost Chord*. Estrella related it to the music known by our early ancestors that could tune a person to the fundamental vibration of the universe.

Betina recalled these papers with fondness, admiring their originality and playfulness—something that Humbert appreciated in his early years as instructor at the university. She felt a sense of longing for the work she had done as a freshman: it had magic and vitality, with new and aggressive perspectives on old subjects. In those days, she would risk everything to discover something new and to speak in an authentic voice. She wanted to get back to that style of writing to re-ignite her passion. Somehow she was able to convince Humbert of the relevance of these subjects to Eastern Mediterranean archaeology, though in his later years of teaching he would have insisted on a dry analysis of potsherds.

Betina tried to persuade herself that the funding committee, which Humbert now headed as Chairman of the Classics Department, would recognize the value of her new proposal. She ignored the tightness in her jaw, the twitch in her left eye, and tried to suppress any thoughts of uncertainty. Instead, she focused on spending nine months of uninterrupted time researching and writing her next book. But the truth was, her relationship with Humbert had become strained over the years. It started when she took to task one of his pet theories, in the first paper she published. Their relationship never recovered but became more difficult as the years went by. She sensed that her attack on his paper was a reflection of both her strength and weakness: it was self-sabotage but also a yearning for truth at any cost.

Just as Betina was about to open the door to the Classics Department, her purse opened and the contents spilled on the floor. She picked up scraps of papers, lipsticks and powder, pens and cigarettes. Reaching for some loose change, she pulled her lower back and stood still for a few moments while rubbing the aching muscles. Pausing in front of the door, she overheard Humbert talking about her to his colleagues.

"I'll never forget the time that Betina came after me like she was possessed. Hard to believe, that was almost twenty years ago. She told me she had read one of my books, and that she wanted to discuss it. She had an intensity about her. At first, I found her pleasant enough. But soon, I realized that she was unstable. After just a few meetings, she imagined that there was something serious between us. When she couldn't break my allegiance to Vivien, she fell into terrible rages. It was quite frightening. She couldn't accept that she was just a passing interest—not that she ever had my interest...she wouldn't leave me alone. I thought I'd have to call the police to get a restraining order."

Clark snorted, "And now, she wants a grant to develop these inane ideas."

Reynolds laughed sarcastically, "She's made more ridiculous claims in this proposal than most people do in a lifetime."

Humbert added, "She's abrasive, acidic..."

When Betina opened the door on Humbert, he stopped talking in mid-sentence with his mouth wide open. Clark and Reynolds turned toward her in astonishment, then looked away with embarrassment as she stood there glaring at them. "Is this how you pass your time, making up stories about me? You actually think you were the innocent victim of my uncontrollable desire? Only in your demented mind did that fantastical story happen."

"You were obsessed, my dear," Humbert smugly insisted.

She looked at him, dumbfounded, pausing to catch her breath. In a controlled voice she said, "I came here to find out if a decision had been made on my grant application."

Humbert avoided eye contact and began scraping and emptying the ash from his pipe. "We are not interested in…the emergence of the divine feminine…or the return of the great mother…or whatever else you are suggesting in this asinine proposal."

Betina was too stunned to respond and stared at him in shock.

Humbert smiled sardonically as he refilled his pipe with tobacco. "Perhaps I have not made myself clear. Let me try once more." With exaggerated pronunciation of each word he continued, "Your. Funding. Is. Denied. Period." Lighting a match, he breathed in on his pipe, making a loud gurgling sound as he sucked in again and again, smacking his lips on the mouthpiece. A few strands of tobacco fell into the hairs of his goatee, but he didn't care.

Betina hoped that the flame from his match might set his beard on fire. She waited a moment for her wish to manifest. When it didn't, she told Humbert she would turn in her resignation at the end of the semester. Her pride once again got the best of her, and she ignored any practical considerations or compromising positions. She thought he looked satanic as his eyebrows arched and the corners of his lips lifted into an amused grin. Then he blew a gray cloud of smoke in her face and turned to Reynolds and Clark who struggled to hold in fits of laughter.

Betina slammed the office door and made her way down the corridor with her head spinning from the shock of what had transpired. She realized that this was probably just one of dozens of stories he had manufactured as a front for his duplicitous lifestyle. She thought of all the stories she had heard about him. He had been seen riding a motorcycle dressed in leather and chains, cruising gay bars in Key West while his wife told everyone he was at a conference in Miami. Then there were stories about his wife's attempted suicides, her pleas of desperation and cries of loneliness that would sometimes spill out at their dinner parties after a few drinks, so that eventually there could be no more dinner parties. Betina thought of a half-dozen comebacks, but instead of saying any of them, she had just thrown away a lifetime of teaching. The rage that she felt a moment earlier toward Humbert turned back on herself.

She was not at all in the mood to give a lecture, but the students were waiting. She looked around the expectant class of graduate students and tried to gather enthusiasm when all she felt was despair. Betina began, "The prodigious power of the feminine is revealed in the earliest art works found throughout the Old World. She was worshipped as the guardian of childbirth, as a healer, as a source of wisdom. Her fertility powers are the most important of all her attributes. She provides the promise of a plentiful supply of food.

Notice the exaggerated fleshiness in her arms and thighs and in her rounded buttocks. Her very shape is reflected in the temples that were dedicated to her. There was a different world view then." As she looked into the confused and unfamiliar faces before her, it occurred to her that she was in the wrong classroom. She excused herself and made her way to a room on the floor above. She was too miserable to even consider how foolish she might have appeared to the students. The truth was, she didn't care.

She began again, "The Great Mother was revered worldwide and had many forms. One of her oldest manifestations was as Ishtar of Babylonia. To the Canaanites she was Astarte, to the Phoenicians she was Cybele. When warlike nomadic people from Asia and Northern Europe invaded the centers of Goddess culture, they established their Sky God in her place. The values of the Goddess were suppressed and the centers of her worship in southeastern Europe, the Near East, and India were destroyed.

"With the rise of the Sky God and of the all powerful monotheistic rule, patriarchy replaced...what some scholars term...matriarchical, matrifocal, matristic, or gynocentric societies. Since these terms are so loaded...I'll *simply* say...patriarchal systems replaced...egalitarian systems, and became the new world order. Everything that had been of value in the Goddess religion was now devalued. Man had dominion over the land, and the Great Mother became the Great Whore of Babylon. History was revised and women were written out of events in which they were the main characters. Women, more than any other group, bore the brunt of this revisionism. When the church disconnected from its ancient roots, denying the archetypal foundation that probably included Isis and Osiris, it created a virgin mother, a celibate and virgin son, and a patriarchy where women, sexuality, and partnership were repressed.

"Now, for the sake of balance, it's time to bring back the metaphor of the mother—or perhaps it is the case that the feminine principle is re-emerging regardless of our efforts." She took a moment to reflect on everything that she had said, then continued. "The truth is…this great mystery, this great creative force, doesn't have a gender. Creator, Creatress—Coin your own term, call it what you will—this isn't about gender." Several students had their hands in the air ready to challenge her, but Betina didn't have the energy to allow for a heated debate, and stepped over this landmine, for the time being, promising to address it at another time. "There are no words or images to describe this intelligence, or creative principle. All we have are metaphors, and, as mythologists have pointed out, when the metaphor for this mystery becomes the father, it creates a different field of influence in our thoughts and in society, than when it is the mother."

She paused again, suddenly overwhelmed at the realization that the course of her life had just changed directions and everything she worked for would now be lost. The pain of this was too much for her and she needed to catch her breath. She set up a slide projector and quickly inserted a stack of slides into the carousel. Then she took the only empty seat in the room, which was next to Lawrence, the only male in the class, and put the carousel of slides on automatic. She drew the shades closed and turned out the lights so that no one would see her as she struggled to gain her composure.

The slide show seemed to have accelerated into high gear or perhaps it was her distorted perception, but all she could see was a blur of images. It started with the Earth Mother of Willendorf, like an upside down tarot card waiting to be read, followed by the Earth Mother of Laussel, also upside down. There were images of the Goddess as life giver in a bas-relief from Çatalhöyük, two life-size heads of a bull cut into a plaster wall, and a reconstruction of a shrine at Çatalhöyük. There were slides of the Maltese Goddess that she had just taken on her recent trip; and an architectural plan of the Gantija Temple, which was backwards; followed by slides of the Snake

Goddess from the Palace of Crete. In a marble statue from Greece, Demeter held sheaves of wheat and had serpents around her eye like the Minoan Goddess.

She looked at the images that she had collected over the years with a growing sense of loss. There was a time when there was peace in her life, just as there had been in prehistory. But now she felt annihilated, like the dismembered goddesses in Sumer and Mexico. Her body scattered to all corners of the universe, as it had been for the dark goddess Tiamat, slain by Gilgamesh. She was broken in pieces, like the moon goddess Coyolxauhqui, killed by the war god Huitzilipotli.

She noticed that Lawrence grinned at her, longing for her attention, denying her the privacy she coveted in the dark corner of the classroom. She let the slides continue to flash without offering any explanation to the class as she tried to quiet her mind. In Titian's "Assumption of the Virgin," a bearded father God looked down on the Madonna. That was followed by the Byzantine Madonna of Czestochowa, and the Black Virgin of Notre Dame from France.

There was a painting of Salome made in 1886, by Edouard Toudouze, "Salome Triumphant," which Betina meant to contrast with a painting of Salome by the performance artist and activist Estrella Estevez. While Toudouze's contented Salome lay sprawled on a throne in her dancing clothes, with the head of John the Baptist by her side; Estrella's painting depicted an old but illumined Salome speaking to a group of spiritual seekers in a mountainous region in Northern Spain, far from her desert homeland. There were also images of Betty Crocker, Aunt Jemimah, and paintings by Judy Chicago. There were slides of Estrella in performance as the Earth Mother that Betina took when they were both students, but they were stuck together and she looked like Kali with six pairs of arms. As dozens of images touching on thousands of years of history flashed on the screen, she saw her own life flash before her as it is said to happen just before one dies.

Betina had much to say on these images, but now it was all she could do to collect her thoughts. Lawrence's smiles and glances suggested that the repetitive revolving slide show had gone on too long. She reluctantly turned it off, walked to the podium in the front of the room, cleared her throat, took a deep breath, drank a few sips of water, cleared her throat again, and continued her lecture to the few remaining students in her class. "Although the Mother Goddess passed into oblivion for thousands of years, her power is once again emerging in a new earth-centered spirituality. We are a civilization that chooses to survive: to do so we must organize around a new myth. We are at the tail end of the deconstruction of patriarchy. A new mythology emerges: an old one wanes."

She hurried out of the class, wanting only to return home so that she could shut herself off from the world and the deconstruction of her own life, but Lawrence was trotting after her. His clumsy pirouette over a foot-high link chain that protected the grass nearly caused him to trip. Calling out her name while gasping for his next breath, he waved his puffy hand in the air. Although she pretended not to see or hear him, he soon caught up to her just as she crossed the street.

Beads of sweat rolled down his forehead as he clasped her hands in his clammy palms and said, "The class was so inspiring. You're so amazing." He paused a moment to catch his breath, then continued, "I want to work for you, or with you."

Betina looked at him blankly and struggled to gather enough energy to answer. "I won't be teaching here after this semester. My work and my perspective has not been supported."

"How could that be? You're a pioneer in your field. An intrepid explorer!"

"How nice that you feel that way. If only you were on the grant committee."

He gave her an excruciatingly long bear hug that was so tight she could hardly breathe, then looked into her eyes and told her she was a Goddess.

What was it about Lawrence that always bothered her? On the one hand, he was more supportive of her work than anyone else, yet his support never pleased her because she believed he didn't understand her work—in fact, she suspected that he completely misunderstood it and had brought his own assumptions to it. Whenever he quoted her, it always seemed to be the reverse of what she said or implied.

He held her gaze too long. He held her hand too long. He resisted finding strength within himself. Instead he seemed to seek it in others. There was something unappealing to her, about the way he spoke of a *fairytale* goddess that seemed more like a combination of the good witch in the Wizard of Oz, with her magic wand, and the 1960's TV mothers that continued to influence cable viewers across the country. Her conflicted feelings toward him made her wonder about herself. Why couldn't she be more charitable? He made her consider how much her focus was on deciphering the archaeological meaning of the remains of the past, while his focus may have been centered on incorporating his vision of this great mother into his life.

Betina was always a researcher and explorer—never a believer. She had never put enough emphasis on the personal implications of her work, and she realized that this was what it was all about for Lawrence. Perhaps with all her battles to move up in her department, she knew more about the masculine world and less about the divine feminine. She wondered if Lawrence had a better understanding of it than she did. She was certain that the academic community she embraced all her adult life, had never allowed for the expression of the true feminine. Perhaps she had even taken on some of the misogyny that prevailed in the academic community—but that was something too disturbing for her to consider. At the same time, she knew it might be the key to unlocking some of her feelings. Maybe she was suffering from a kind of amnesia and had forgotten the true meaning of the feminine, just as the world around her had forgotten. She could not spin enough life into her artifacts, and her slides of artwork and ruins remained flat images: she was unable to weave a full-length story around them. It was as if one part of her brain could not connect with the other.

While walking home that afternoon, it struck her that the denial of her grant might have had something to do with her confusion and lack of regard for the very thing she was researching. Perhaps she had only taken a half step in proposing the subject. It troubled her to think that at the deepest level she might be as ambivalent as Humbert, Clark and Reynolds.

Although she had walked home from the university countless times, she lost her way and found herself in a shadowland, swimming past gray, faceless bodies, moving blindly through a murky underwater world, gasping for oxygen, deprived of sunlight. Drifting into slow motion in that water world, she passed old women moaning in doorways, and sleeping behind garbage cans. The conversations at a cafe that she floated past jangled her nerves. Everything was an assault: the piercing laughter, high-pitched voices, the deep drones, the rattling of china and silverware. It was all closing in on her, amplified and echoing in her head.

Her perception was skewed. Everything sickened her and had suddenly become meaningless. She could only see the insanity of her obsessions, including her neurotic drive and ambition to succeed in academia. She repeated in her mind that in one blow, her career had fallen apart, after twenty years of building. Destruction was effortless—creation so laborious. The mighty civilization of Atlantis swallowed overnight by a tidal wave; Pompeii buried in a flash under the ash of Vesuvius; Hiroshima gone in the blast of the first atomic bomb; thousands of Tibetan monasteries with priceless art destroyed overnight by the Chinese army; ancient Buddhas carved out of the mountains 1,500 years ago, blown to bits by the Taliban in Afghanistan. Her career at Harvard, over in a blink of an eye.

She found herself in the back row of a movie theater that was showing Bunuel's classic, *Exterminating Angel.* Without remembering how she got there, she felt as trapped and motionless as the characters in the movies. Although she was free of the entanglements of the ivy-towered world, she was still a prisoner caught under a spell with no will of her own. She didn't know how to fly out of the cage now that the door had opened.

Betina finally found her way back home, which was on a poorly lit Cambridge Street, where the wind was blowing newspapers around on the ground. When a section of the paper blew in her face, she was slapped with front-page images of old turbaned men pushing carts, and women in *burquas* with heavy bundles on their backs, fleeing military attacks in their villages. Suddenly, the difference between them seemed less pronounced. Grabbing the pages of the newspaper that covered her face like a veil, she crumpled them up in a ball and threw them on the ground. She passed a ragged old man, sitting on a stoop with his head drooping forward in his lap, mumbling to himself. She could see herself on an adjacent stoop too burdened to move, watching other people moving with purpose, commitment and direction through their day. Mourning the loss of the familiar world she was leaving, Betina wondered about the New World she would soon enter.

She was glad to be back in the comfort of her townhouse. Resting under a colorful wool afghan her mother had made, she nursed a glass of scotch, and listened to Bach's *The Passion of St. Matthew.* She looked at the pictures above her desk, taken at archaeological sites in Egypt. She was standing with several Egyptian assistants, next to the pillars at Hatshepsut's Temple. She couldn't lose this world.

Betina called her mother in a nursing home in Quebec City, where she had been residing for the past few years, with the vain hope that she might find a bit of comfort in talking to her. At first Frances recognized Betina's voice and they spoke about the weather and the unseasonable snowfall. She even asked Betina to move back to Quebec. But after a few minutes, Frances became confused and abruptly switched to speaking French, her first language.

"Pourquoi dérangez-vous mon sommeil? Retournez chez les vôtres. Cessez de m'harceler!" Frances paused. "Go back to your own people! Don't trouble me again or I'll call the cops and you can be sure they'll throw you in the slammer."

Slammer? Cops? Where was she getting these words? It was agonizing to see how rapidly Alzheimer's disease was setting in, taking over her once remarkable mind. Frances had graduate degrees in biology and philosophy and had been fluent in five languages, but now the languages blended together and everything she said had a surprising and unusual spin. It had only been six months since the diagnosis, yet in that short time Betina believed she had become a source of paranoia for Frances, rather than pleasure.

The conversation reminded Betina to live fully and not waste her time in despair since life was short and middle age would soon turn into old age. But that moment of illumination was quickly forgotten. Betina paced the living room, had another scotch, and called Andrew. She rambled on and on about how desperate things had become and how she needed to be with him. Soon she became annoyed at his inability to understand what she was saying. When she told him that he sounded as senile as her mother, he laughed and said that he was not Andrew, he was a Harvard law student. "It figures," she muttered to herself, "I'm as senile as my mother." Then she tried Andrew's number again. This time she reached him and managed to persuade him to come over.

Andrew was late, so she called his house a dozen times, only to get the same recording on his answering machine. When he finally arrived, he quickly kissed her on the cheek and sat down on her Egyptian camel-haired chair. She was nervous and compulsively lit a couple of cigarettes at the same time. "I'm so glad you're here. They attack my work with complete ignorance. They're making up stories about me. They have no conception of who I am or what I am about. They want to destroy me!"

Andrew shrugged his shoulders, "Maybe they're afraid of you."

"They call me reckless, outrageous, even acidic! They'll probably finance the Ararat project for the hundredth time. How many expeditions are they going to send to that mountain…and to find what, a few splinters of wood?"

"Oh Betina," Andrew sighed.

"Oh, I know…but they sat there, like the three brothers...Zeus, Poseidon, and Hades, on Mt. Olympus."

Andrew interrupted her, "And you, like Artemis. Independent of them."

She started pacing, "Thank you. Thank you very much, but you know I'm not independent of them. Humbert is right. I have alienated everyone. Do you think I'm acidic?"

She poured a glass of scotch for Andrew as she waited for his answer. He was always the proper Englishman, taking great care in choosing his words wisely. "Oh, never mind," she said. "Just drink! Of course I'm bitter and acidic. Andrew, why didn't it work between us? I thought of you all the time I was abroad." She filled her glass to the top with scotch and drank half of it before he responded.

Andrew chose his words carefully. "You were always possessed by your work."

"I couldn't trust anyone in those days. So many years have passed since then. Now that I'm ready to settle down with you, you've gone your separate way."

"You're upset about the grant and teaching. That has nothing to do with us. Why are you carrying on? It's not like you."

"Apparently it is. It's the new me."

"You couldn't stay in one place. You had no interest in domestic things."

"I knew something about domesticity. I learned to make bread. Don't you remember? And I knit you that sweater."

"Sweater? What sweater?"

She wiped a tear from her eye and continued with drunken sincerity. "How could you forget the sweater?"

"Betina! That was decades ago."

"I did a damn good job of it. What a bore it was. Knit and purl, knit and purl. I hated every moment of it. But what would you know about the tedium of knitting? You never tried it. Don't you remember? It had two arms and a turtleneck. It was perfect. Do you still have it?"

"Good Lord, Betina."

That was always Andrew's favorite expression.

"Good Lord, Andrew!" Betina mocked. "How could you throw away that sweater?" She wiped away a stream of tears.

"Don't imitate me and give me the scotch. You get so weepy when you drink."

When he reached for the drink they somehow ended up in an embrace. He momentarily forgot himself and they kissed. When he pulled away, she tried to keep him close.

She ran her fingers down his chest. "I remember how you used to cry when we made love. You were so much like a woman, mourning the end of our relationship when we were just at the beginning. We were so much alike."

"I don't remember you ever being like that...I knew one day you would leave. And you did. You were gone," he said.

"I never left you," she said. "You left me."

"You went off to Greece."

"I got a fellowship. You wouldn't come with me. I begged you to. I remember how you said to me, 'I'm holding you back, keeping you from spreading your wings so that you can soar.' I considered what you said, never knowing quite what to think. Perhaps, at the time, I thought there was generosity in your words...but now I know it was your way of pulling out...hoping I wouldn't really notice. Everything you said was in reverse. It was you who wanted wings to fly! I remember how courageous we thought we were, breaking up before we sank to a level of mediocrity in our relationship. Now I know we had no courage. And now you have, what's her name?"

"Leslie," he said with a bored expression, as if he'd told her a million times.

"I hate that name."

"She adores me."

"Oh could you stop it, please." She grimaced and mimicked him, "'She adores me.'"

"She calls me her god," he said tentatively, wondering if that comment would set her into a rage.

"Oh, have some pity," she moaned.

"I'm sorry," he said with sincerity.

"Adoration," she said, "it leads you in the wrong direction. It says yes, yes, and yes. Indiscriminate. Blind. Ignorant. I could've given you a puppy if I'd have known you wanted adoration. Why do you need adoration? You're beyond that. You're sure enough of yourself."

"Apparently I'm not...I've never been sure of anything," Andrew looked worn out. He stopped her from pouring more scotch into his glass.

"Let's go into the bedroom," she said.

"Good Lord, Betina. I'm engaged to be married. I'm trying hard to be faithful."

"Well if it's so damn hard, get out of that trap. Be who you need to be. Be with me tonight my love."

"I can't be toyed with by you anymore."

"Anymore?" she said, "When did I ever toy with you. Sometimes I changed directions. I got confused. But it was never to toy with you."

"I guess I knew that." He thought for a moment. "I didn't mean that." He leaned back in his chair and crossed his legs. Then he turned to her and said, "I've never seen you like this."

"Well maybe I've never felt this way. You've never really told me...do you believe in my work? Tell me truthfully!"

"I've always been your biggest fan. Some of the perspectives and directions you have now seem...maybe a little hokey."

After a long silence she looked at him and repeated the word "hokey." She tried to stay calm. "Yes. I see. My theories are hokey."

He got up to leave. "I have to go." Her lingering kiss good-bye made him smile with both pleasure and irritation.

"What are you doing tomorrow?" she asked.

"We're going to Leslie's parents' house for the holiday."

"How quaint, you're meeting her parents for the first time?"

"It's not the first time. I know them quite well and have grown very fond of them."

"How cozy," she said, trying to conceal the pain she felt from this new piece of information. She closed the door behind him and looked out her window as he got into his car and drove off.

Hokey. Andrew had called the subject of her research hokey: That was not something she would forget. The word played over and over again in her mind. She was shocked that the person she had loved most in the world and whose opinion she regarded so highly could have felt that. Weeks later, he tried to deny that he had ever used that word.

"Betina," he said. "I support everything that you do, you know that. Besides, that's not a word I use. It must've been one of your other boyfriends. Maybe it was that Peter what's-his-name."

It was true, it was an unlikely word for him to use, but she was certain that he said it and nothing he could say could convince her otherwise.

Betina poured another drink and listened to the echo of voices from the street. She heard the beautiful cathedral bells ringing outside. Sitting by the window, she hiccuped while watching a woman put a vase of Easter lilies on her dining-room table, in an apartment across the street. She thought of how this flower became associated with Mary, Mother of Jesus, because it represented qualities of modesty, purity, devotion, and virgin beauty. She watched a small crowd enter a church, going to midnight Easter mass. Deciding to join them, she put on sneakers and a sweater.

While locking the front door, she wondered why Leslie was even drawn to Andrew. How could Leslie have desired or understood his brilliance? Perhaps there was more to her than she imagined. Leslie had been her student for three weeks before dropping out of her class. Betina remembered her conservative cardigans with beaded floral designs and her manicured appearance. Leslie hadn't said much during the three weeks she was in class, but she did ask Betina about the purpose of archaeology. Betina remembered how this question irritated her. Instead of answering it, she reflected the question back to Leslie. Although Leslie was unable to offer even the simplest response, it caused her no embarrassment. After waiting a few moments, Betina said, "Archaeology is more about reshaping the present and creating the future, and less about understanding the past." It was an off-the-cuff remark that incited a heated discussion from several students who found this definition utterly irresponsible. To Betina's surprise, Leslie had the final word. She said that the comment was 'enlightening.'

As she walked down the street, she recalled with both delight and remorse the comments she had written on Leslie's paper. She had called her thinking immature and suggested that she consider doing graduate work, since this was a graduate class. Even after drinking a bottle of wine, she managed to refrain from telling Leslie to find a good husband and to stick to typing his manuscripts, (one could be taken to task for such a politically incorrect comment), though clearly that was already Leslie's plan. Betina didn't see her again in any of her classes after that. Nor did she see Andrew much after that either.

The last time Betina saw him, before this evening, was the most beautiful and the most terrible. Betina was overwhelmed with a kind of ambivalence about life and teaching at the university. It was another low period and she had drunk too much that night. She remembered how Andrew gave her a bath and washed her hair. She hadn't given a second thought to that night until now. Perhaps she had drunk herself into a stupor. She couldn't remember. But there he was, kneeling over her, rinsing the suds out of her hair and drying it like he was her mother. She had felt more peace in those moments when he held her in his warm arms then she had ever known in a lifetime. Afterwards, she felt, with the greatest of certainty, that she only wanted to be with him; but he slipped away from her and began his affair with Leslie. Perhaps her certainty brought out his ambivalence, or perhaps it was her drunkenness that caused him to flee. She wondered if she had lost Andrew forever. She knew she had been terrible to him, but she also believed he had been terrible to her. He retreated into himself, for days on end, burying his feelings, devoting himself to his work with single-minded focus.

As she entered the Greek Orthodox Church, she thought about how Andrew had been an extraordinary collaborative resource to her, shifting her perspective on things so effortlessly. When she mentioned that the creation of the sphinx seemed to have occurred thousands of years before the time currently accepted, he confirmed her view, without hesitation. He told her that the evidence of water erosion on the sphinx's body, signified that it was created at a time when the land around the pyramids was fertile and not desert. This off-the-cuff remark pointed to a miscalculation that volumes of academic archaeological work had been based upon.

She had lost Andrew and now she had lost her job. Where her life would go, from this moment forth, she did not know. Betina only knew that she could not be a puppet or a parrot of orthodox thinking. She could not spend her life regurgitating everything that she was taught, as if her education was nothing more than programming and a shutting down of the creative process. She had to move beyond theory, and risk finding her own voice and her own truth, even if it meant losing herself for a time on some strange tangent. Maybe, somewhere along that journey, she would find *gnosis kardias,* 'the knowledge of the heart.'

The church was packed, but she managed to find a seat in the back. Red eggs were passed around, symbolizing the blood of Christ, the shell symbolized his three-day entombment, and the breaking of the egg was his resurrection. She thought about the beautiful tradition of the egg, as the primordial beginning of life—even Aphrodite, Goddess of love, was said to have been born from an egg in Phoenician mythology. Betina watched the service from the perspective of seeing an ancient myth reenacted. She longed for a spirit of communion, but the holding of hands with the person on either side, in a moment of prayer, left her cold.

"We are believers, not looking at this as a myth, but participating in it. Christ the Lord has taken on your sins and through him, you can have eternal life." Listening to these words, she wondered why a person should receive redemption vicariously—weren't we all on a journey of personal growth, expansion, and discovery? Betina left the church, unfulfilled by her scholarly approach to all things, yet unable to believe. She was once again a wanderer in a shadowland. Unable to connect, she could only see featureless faces and gray figures, drifting in slow motion through the night. She was underwater, navigating her way along the murky ocean floor, her vision obscured by lack of light. Her footing was threatened by seaweed that entwined around her legs and entangled her in its knots, preventing her from surfacing.

Betina began thoroughly cleaning her house, wanting a new beginning. She scrubbed the kitchen floor, washed all the curtains, and moved the furniture around in the living room. She even converted a storage room into a guestroom. She wasn't certain why she chose to do these things—it wasn't as if she was expecting anyone to stay there. Her mood was too imbalanced to tolerate visitors and too unpredictable for anyone to bear her company. But, nevertheless, she spent several days fixing up the guest room. She hung light floral curtains on the windows, put new sheets and warm blankets on twin beds, tacked colorful prints on the walls, and brought out a small collection of antique toys from the basement and arranged them on the bureau.

That night, sitting at her desk, staring at the blank pages of the mysterious book, she wondered why Wolfgang thought it was so significant. She was soon distracted by the soothing sounds of flowing water coming from a beautiful fountain, which stood in a small enclave above her desk. Hiding amongst the stones and miniature trees were tiny frogs and wood nymphs. Jane had given her this fountain as a thirtieth birthday-present, and it always reminded Betina of the peaceful world that her friend lived in, set apart from the busyness of city life.

Beside the fountain was a kaleidoscope, a gift that Andrew had given her soon after they first met. As she twisted the ring that wrapped around the slender tube of the kaleidoscope, she saw new patterns of color in shifting geometric formations. Enjoying the magic of this simple toy, she began to feel the now-familiar sensation of rising wind—a signal of transition into other worldliness. She always loved the Navajo belief that the wind that entered a person when they were born was the one that would guide them through life. She wondered if the wind that she felt now was a female wind that came from the east. Giving the kaleidoscope a final turn, she saw entoptic patterns, like living arabesques of sparkling swirls of light. The world began to spin as she felt herself sucked into the shaft of the kaleidoscope. She entered a tunnel—one tunnel led to another and soon she was in a catacomb.

A howling wind blew through the underground chamber and brought with it distant voices singing a melody. Then she heard an old woman's voice that seemed to come out of nowhere.

"At last, you have come."

It startled her. "Who said that? Is there somebody here?"

"I'm here."

Betina recognized the voice, since it was the same one that she heard when she was flying home from Europe. This time, there was more than just a voice—she also saw an old woman, perhaps in her sixties, who stepped out from an alcove in the cave wall. She wore a medieval-styled garment—a sleeveless tunic over a long gown. A wimple framed her face, covered her hair and was drawn into folds under her chin. A small woman with a slender build, she had luminous skin, and sparkling eyes. As she spoke, she moved her hands with grace and elegance. Betina realized she was a nun, but was perplexed by her manner and tone.

"My name is Marletta."

"Why have you brought me to this place?"

"To tell you things you have forgotten. There is so much to share. I wrote it all down for you, knowing that one day you would come to this underground world. You were meant to hear this story. Like finds like." She looked directly into Betina's eyes and continued, "Like you, there was a time when I was deeply unhappy. I couldn't think as the others. I had my own world, which had nothing to do with those around me. I felt stifled by their thoughts so that I could not breathe. I felt misunderstood—I was unlike anyone I knew. My mother never spoke a cruel word, nor did my sisters. But nothing I said, no thought that I expressed made sense to them. Alone in their company, I began to shun intimacy and no longer wanted to communicate my deepest thoughts.

"I was always apart as a child, writing stories, keeping diaries. My father read a segment of my journals and found it quite unusual. He showed it to a monk, who frowned on it and said my thinking was unorthodox. He questioned the source of my inspiration. After months of persuasion, he finally convinced my kind father to put me in a nunnery, to discipline my mind. When more journals were found in the nunnery they were taken from me and I never saw them again. I became very sick from this, and could no longer find the will to eat or drink…even to attend to my chores."

Betina looked at a series of remarkable sketches of plant leaves and vines that Marletta held in her hand. As the old woman spoke, Betina realized the loss it was to posterity that her reflections recorded so diligently in her journals were destroyed.

Marletta sat down on a stone bench and motioned for Betina to sit next to her, as she continued her story. "Though I was weak and thought to be demented, I slipped away from the cloister as often as I could. I prayed that I would find a haven, and I was led to this place, this underground world, where I came to write. This was my retreat, the womb in which I found comfort. In this place my heart came alive and beat with a new spirit." Marletta spread her arms wide, embracing the holiness of this deep, damp underworld. "I was no longer the dying Marletta, I became a new me, filled with possibility. In this dark cavern I found light."

"Didn't your family and the nuns search for you?"

"They did, but I was nowhere to be found. I needed so little to survive, just a crust of bread, a wedge of cheese, an egg, an apple, a pear. Each morning I found all this waiting for me at the entrance to my cave. I didn't know who left it…but it allowed me to live apart so that I could dream my dreams. I also found trinkets, flowers, seashells, and paper and pens at the cave entrance. This went on for years."

"Did you ever find who left them?"

She nodded. "One night I lay in a half-dream state on my little cot, and I heard rustling at the entrance to my cave. There he was, a monk named Fogarth. He had known about the cave before I discovered it and had seen me come and go. But once he realized I considered it my secret retreat, he chose not to disturb my privacy. He knew who I was from the beginning. The nuns sent out word that I was missing and they even went to his monastery with hope that someone there might be able to provide a clue as to my whereabouts...or whether I was dead or alive. He never gave away my secret…instead he took it upon himself to provide for my needs…"

"Did you…love him?" Betina asked, surprising herself with this question.

Marletta took a deep breath, before responding. "I was in love with him the moment my eyes laid sight of him. He read me books...his voice calmed the fierce pounding in my heart and stilled my nerves. Other times it set my blood on fire. He taught me Latin and read Lucretius to me. When I told him about the destruction of my writings, he created a code language for me to use."

"What kind of code?" Betina asked.

"He discovered a technique by chance, while working on stained-glass windows, at his monastery. He explained to me how he made glass from river sand, beech wood and potash. He was most excited about working on the rose windows, which faced the west and were circular in design. One evening, shortly after installing his stained-glass window, he noticed that when the moonlight shone through one of the panels in the heart area of the Magdalene, it illuminated a few words on a page where he was writing. You see, he had been experimenting with a pigment that seemed to have failed and left no mark, but in the moonlight the words were illuminated.

"Although his stained-glass rendering of Magdalene was not appreciated and was destroyed by another monk, he had discovered a new pigment. He said, 'that which was invisible, would be made visible.' He was so impressed with this discovery that he spent the next few years refining the stained-glass filter, which illuminated this special pigment that could not be seen with the naked eye. It was through this filter, that I wrote and illustrated my manuscript without fear that it would be destroyed, as was the case with my previous writings. Fogarth…he could create anything."

Just as Betina wondered if they had become lovers, Marletta read her mind.

"One day he put aside his experiments and turned to me with such intensity in his eyes. He said, "*Tui tangere possum*?" Can I touch you? It was the first time I had been touched by a man. First he touched my hand, like a silk veil sliding across my palm. Then I felt the heat. My subterranean world became an alchemical study. We were the elements that mixed together to become gold…this was our sacrament. We were inseparable."

"Did he leave the monastery?" Betina asked.

Marletta nodded. "Fogarth had become too bold in his secret codes of expression, despite the flaming pyres that threatened to silence all dissent. At first his messages were disguised, but eventually they inspired discomfort. The more the church tried to silence him and control his artistry, the stronger became his desire to leave the order. We were two heretics who made up for a lifetime wasted in abstinence. And it was in those ecstatic moments together that we came to know the fullness of that which is divine. Our love brought us to new heights of vision. He called me his rose, his Illuminatrix, his lightspark—the one who longs for the light."

Marletta looked deep into Betina's eyes with a seriousness that caused her body to vibrate. She said, "I offer you...I offer you...a return to yourself. Become your truest self. You are a lightspark... return to the light. Do you not know that you are god?"

The image of Marletta and the underground chamber vanished completely and Betina found herself back at her desk, in her Cambridge townhouse. She wondered who Marletta really was and why she revealed so much of herself. Betina had read essays on medieval women and mystics and knew something of the life of Christina of Markyate, Clare of Assisi, and Catherine of Siena. One of her friends had even written and directed a play that showed Off-Broadway, and was staged at a playhouse in Cambridge. It was popular among the students at Harvard and depicted the life of Hildegard of Bingen. In her many discussions over dinner with the director, they often spoke of the limited ability that women in the Middle Ages had to express their beliefs without being considered subversive. Many, like Mechthild of Magdeburg, feared burning; others were imprisoned; and some, like Marguerite Porete, were burned for heresy, when they refused to renounce their visions and beliefs.

Betina thought about Marletta, who was unlike other nuns in the Middle Ages, in that she didn't seem to have an interest in experiencing Christ's agony—there were no references to stigmata or flagellation. Instead, it seemed that Marletta had chosen a path of pleasure and ecstasy through union with a man who became her lover. This was their religion, their pathway to *gnosis*—a pathway punishable by death. The love that Marletta and Fogarth held for each other brought to mind stories of Abelard and Héloïse. Betina wondered if Marletta knew this tragic tale, which was required reading for most English majors at Harvard. She hoped that the story of Marletta and Fogarth did not have a tragic ending.

Betina wanted to write down everything she had seen and heard, but before she could set a pen to paper, she felt the words and images slipping from her consciousness in the same way that dreams dissolve, leaving only the faintest trace, when one wakes up. Despite her efforts, she could not retrieve all the pieces of the vision.

Her hand trembled as she lit a cigarette and carefully dialed Andrew's number. "I don't know what happened," she said. "I need you to come over."

"I was just there!"

"But this is urgent, you don't understand. I had the strangest experience. I don't know what's happening. Now there's a medieval nun talking to me…I could be going mad."

"Do you have any idea what time it is?"

"Why do you concern yourself with time? There is no such thing as time! You were here an eternity ago, not a few hours ago. I wouldn't have bothered you except that I need to talk to someone. You're the only one."

"Good Lord, Betina."

She looked at her clock, which said 4:37 AM. "Okay," she said. "I'm sorry I disturbed you." She hung up the phone and picked up her cigarette. "Good Lord," she said to herself, "I must be losing it."

She finally fell asleep, clutching the phone in her arms, and slept soundly until the phone rang in the late morning.

"I couldn't stop thinking about you," Jane said. "Something told me to call. I'd like you to come for a visit. We haven't talked in so long. I want to know how you are."

"A visit…now that's an idea. You always have perfect timing," she said.

"There's something else. My son wants to show you a cave. We had some vagrants camping on the north part of our land. They made some curious designs on the cave wall. They'd been traveling across the country in search of a missing girl. The mother, Eartha Mae, has been in a terrible depression since her separation from her daughter."

Jane went into great detail about the squatters and about the unusual properties of the cave. After she hung up the phone, Betina thought about Jane's invitation, but had mixed feelings. She didn't know whether it was a good time for her to visit anyone, since her emotions were so close to the edge: She didn't want to risk snapping. But for some reason, Betina could not stop thinking about the description of Eartha Mae. The more she thought about her, the more her story took on mythic proportions. Betina thought of that mysterious mother and daughter bond characterized by Demeter's recurring search, retrieval, and loss of her daughter Persephone—a cycle represented in the change of the seasons from summer, to fall, to winter, to spring.

As Betina drifted in and out of a dream state, she asked herself: Can this search ever end? Can a daughter ever find her true mother? Can a mother ever find her true daughter without always wanting her to be more than she is? She thought of the endless tug-of-war with her own mother; and of Frances's longings for the dutiful daughter, who would accept the desires of her guiding hand without protestation. Not a daughter who drifted from her and became an atheist at fourteen, a pagan at sixteen, and a half-dozen things after that.

Lost daughters, lost mothers, lost lovers, lost sons, lost children. Lost childhoods, lost paradise. Voices of the lost children in Bosnia blended with the voices of children from the streets of Calcutta and Rio, and joined the whispers rising above the streets of New Orleans. Voices filled with longing. Her longings blended with theirs, taking the forms of swirling vapors that surrounded Earth in a heartfelt cry, echoing throughout the solar system and spiraling galaxy, and into distant regions of the universe.

CHAPTER SIX

CATACOMBS

Evangeline leaned against a magnolia tree illuminated by a dim street lamp that flickered on and off, revealing elaborate grillwork on a second-story apartment, whose balcony was overgrown with a hanging garden. She stood there like a lone actor on a stage, motionless in the pulsing spotlight, uncertain of her next move. She listened to distant sounds of the city like hollow sound effects, placed haphazardly in a sound track: a dog howling, a gang of boys quarreling, the din of a distant radio, the mournful voice of an old man singing about love and heartbreak at a blues club down the street. Though there was no wind, the magnolia tree suddenly showered its petals upon her, as if to embrace and comfort her with its gentle touch and calming fragrance. This communion with the spirit of the magnolia tree carried her into a place of silence and stillness.

The spell of this enchantment slowly faded when a car pulled up to the curb. Evangeline watched as Salome stepped out of the passenger side of the car. After tucking a few bills in her pocket, she straightened out her short tight skirt and tube-top, while the elderly red-faced driver closed the belt buckle on his pants and drove off.

Salome shrugged. "I couldn't do it, so he gave me $40.00 for watching. It's more than we ever made in a week, singing. What about you?"

"Men stop, but I can't do it either. I tell them to move along. I say I'm talking to this magnolia tree..."

Salome nodded, sharing her reluctance, then noticed Julian crossing the street, walking in their direction. She whispered, "I told you about him. He owns that club."

Julian, a middle-aged Italian intellectual with stylish wire-framed glasses and an intense look, had impeccable taste and style. He wore a black suit with a white silk scarf around his neck. Every hair in his long black ponytail was in place. Sometimes he even wore a light layer of white powder on his face, etched with blue, to bring out the vein lines. His lips were painted red and his cheeks were lightly colored with rouge. He often used makeup in a flamboyant manner, reminiscent of the style of eighteenth-century Europe, when both sexes preferred an artificial appearance. The only thing missing was the powdered wig.

He held his arms out to Salome and hugged her, and then introduced himself to Evangeline. "The street is not the place for such divine creatures as the likes of you. Come with me, my seraphim. There's a party at Catacombs, like no other." A group of transvestites passed by on the other side of the street and Julian whistled at them. "Good evening ladies." Then he put his arm around Salome and Evangeline and shouted out to the transvestites with a joyful cry, "New Orleans, the American Babylon, where decadence reigns supreme in the face of economic despair and social misery." He clapped his hands.

"Hip. Hip. Hooray. Hip. Hip. Hooray," one transvestite shouted back. "It's been a helluvah good time!"

Evangeline and Salome walked with him to his club and followed hesitantly down a set of stairs to a basement that was boarded up on the outside and appeared abandoned. Evangeline studied the writing above the door, buried under layers of city dust. Slowly, she made out the words, 'Sons and Daughters of Babylon the Great.'

Leo, a bald-headed man, with an overly developed muscular torso, that was bursting out of a tight tee-shirt, opened the door and said, "Enter and be damned," He nodded to Julian, winked at Evangeline and Salome and ushered them in.

They stepped into this living theater of fantasy and of the absurd, which had endless levels and secret rooms, and a style that was both ancient and futuristic. The brothel had Roman architecture with mirrors on the walls and ceiling. Men were dressed in wigs and jewelry, with garish makeup and flamboyant dresses, and some spoke in harsh womanish voices. The walls of this mysterious world were covered with early Christian and Coptic images. Scarlet curtains were tied in place by gold braided ropes, and scrotal grape clusters hung from the rafters. The residents of this exotic world—made up of writers, artists, dancers, and directors—reclined on couches that had large velvet pillows with silk-screen images of ancient Coptic faces bordered by elaborate fringe.

A young boy approached, who was both masculine and feminine, with finely curled red lips and a delicate bloom. Julian turned to the young Adonis, catching wind of his flowery fragrance. "Oh, my sweet *cherubino,* always a delight to see you." The young boy sent a lingering kiss to Julian who graciously caught it and held it in both hands against his heart. Julian pinched his buttock and watched as he walked off, keeping an eye on the red mark, left by the pinch, which soon faded to pink. "Doesn't he have the most exquisite ass. He's a girl on top, a boy below. We call him a *him* when we could easily call him a *her*. Maybe the creator was drunk when he fashioned this darling hermaphrodite."

"Or maybe the Creatrix enjoys variation," Evangeline playfully suggested, wondering how the word had come to her, since she had never heard it before.

"Yes, of course. Well put." Julian laughed as he straightened the hairs in his ponytail and adjusted his gold ring and watch, so that everything looked in perfect order.

"Perhaps your sweet *cherubino* was once two people…a man and a woman whose love was so deep that they merged into each other becoming one," Salome offered.

"Astonishing…though really I shouldn't be surprised that you could think such a thing, my beloved Salome. The truth is, I saved him from a murderous mother. She forbade him from playing with her perfumes and lotions...almost strangled him when she found him wandering the streets in her Balinese sarong. She ripped it from him...that's when I found him. He was naked...huddled under a stairway, not far from here. He's stayed ever since. Isn't it tragic, my sweet, that not everyone appreciates variation. How can anyone be so dull and narrow-minded? It's the spice of life."

Julian led the two girls past a series of rooms in which couples, threesomes, and foursomes were engaged in various sexual acts. Silently communicating their shock, Evangeline and Salome watched a man wearing a donkey mask enter a woman from behind. In another room, a man dressed as the pope whipped a naked man chained to a cross. Julian noticed Evangeline's confusion and said, "It brings them to a kind of rapture...heals their wounds. Trust me when I say it's their only hope for therapy."

Parting a bamboo curtain depicting Shiva and Shakti in an erotic position, Julian motioned for Salome and Evangeline to pass through. They entered a room decorated like a courtyard in an ancient near-eastern palace, with a marble fountain at the center, large overstuffed couches along the walls, and dozens of satin pillows on the floor. The two girls took a seat on a couch and listened to a man with a turban playing a drum, while a middle-aged belly dancer shook her hips and clicked cymbals between her fingers. Julian made himself comfortable on a chaise lounge and sucked on a water pipe. He watched as an elegant middle-aged German woman, Greta, studied herself in a mirror while applying sparkling eye shadow and dark lipstick. "Greta always fixes herself up so exquisitely," said Julian. "Actually, she *is* a woman, but at Catacombs, she's often mistaken for being a transsexual. Nothing here is ever what it seems."

Greta noticed Salome and Evangeline staring at her as she painted her face. "Come my darlinks, I vant fix you up."

Salome stood still as Greta put eyeliner and mascara on her eyes, and glitter on her eyelids. Then she carefully placed sequins above her eyebrows and a ruby in the middle of her forehead, which she stuck on with glue. Opening a drawer that was filled with scarves with fringe made of beads, Greta took out a diamond tiara and set it on Salome's head, then handed her a coin-ladened costume to put on. She held up an outfit made with elaborate beadwork for Evangeline. When Evangeline undressed, Greta noticed that she had two extra nipples on her body.

"I was born this way," Evangeline explained. "I'm a throwback, same as my mother. Only...I think...she might've had more than me."

"I too haf secrets," Greta said as she put finger cymbals on both Salome's and Evangeline's thumb and middle finger. "I vas born vid tail, only I had removed. All I haf left is zis tiny scar."

Julian ran his hands up and down Evangeline's back as she played the finger cymbals and swayed to the music. He told her that belly dancing was one of the oldest dances on earth, and that it once was a fertility rite.

Greta looked over at her and smiled, "Vat a natural you are." Then she sifted through a tray of jewelry and took out a small jewel and set it in Evangeline's navel. "You haf buuu-te-ful navel…it's so deep. It's za point of contact...vere energy flows from mother to child. All belly dancers celebrate zis sacred place."

Evangeline held the ruby in place with her finger, as she realized the truth of what Greta was saying. From that moment on, she touched her navel when she called out to her mother, hoping that somehow an invisible umbilical cord would link the two of them and guide them back together.

Greta pulled a cobra out of a basket and held it in her hands. She explained that the serpent represented vitality, wisdom, and fecundity, but that eventually it became a symbol for Satan. Salome and Evangeline looked into the snake's eyes and then at each other, certain that the snake was talking to them. The snake explained that he always remained strong in dignity, despite the commonly held perception of who he was—he suggested that they do the same. Unfortunately, they didn't understand the significance of his message since they had little awareness of the trials that awaited each of them.

"Now you must dance for us." Julian said.

Salome looked at Evangeline, uncertain of what to say.

"You'll be well paid...and well appreciated...not like the brutal and ignorant treatment you find on the streets. It's a permanent job opportunity…worth considering, I should think." Julian turned to look at the musicians and nodded his head.

Picking up Julian's cue, a dark-haired, bearded musician, holding a tamborine-like instrument in his hand, joined the drummer. A third musician picked up a long-necked fretted string instrument and played an emotive melody. Several other drummers started playing as Salome became a waveform of serpentine energy. More and more people poured into the great hall, attracted by the rising level of energy. Even the pope and the man with the donkey head came in to watch. Greta also began dancing and Evangeline followed, matching her flamboyant movements, but soon Evangeline withdrew from the dance. She was reluctant to have so many eyes on her and was more intrigued with watching Salome's ecstatic movements.

Salome danced with a lavender veil that she held over her head and waved in the air like a banner. She had danced this dance before in voodoo ceremonies in the bayou. She retained the memory of pounding the black earth with her feet, absorbing the comforting warmth of the Earth Mother. Her body could also recall the footsteps and movements she made to the powerful beat of master Yoruban drummers in ceremonies to Shango. She even remembered ecstatically dancing in secret among women, participating in a universal dance of the spheres.

But something inexplicable happened while dancing at Catacombs. She fell into a pattern of footsteps and movements from a time before dancing in the bayou, and before the ceremonies to Shango. In the midst of this private celebration, she stumbled upon a memory of dancing in an ancient hall, with a glorious fountain that stood in the center, and geometric-patterned tiles on the floor, similar to the hall at Catacombs. The music of the court musicians faded as new harmonies descended from the heavenly spheres, creating an explosion of joy within her spirit. The air around her became the fifth element—a living fluid that shimmered in the sunlight. She left behind a haze of dense structures and cacophonous thought forms and moved into this realm of light.

As Salome danced late into the night at Catacombs, Malcolm wandered through the streets, preaching on every street corner. "Nation will rise against nation; kingdom against kingdom. There will be famines, earthquakes and nuclear destruction. Don't ignore the warning signs. Perverts are looking for your children to sodomize. They're even selling pornography in Nazareth and Bethlehem. It's a world of degenerates."

Malcolm walked up to a group of Japanese tourists who politely smiled and nodded their heads as they hedged away from him. "Hitler's concentration camps will look like a ladies' tea-party compared to what is to come." When the last of the Japanese tourists discreetly shuffled away, Malcolm moved to a different street corner and imposed himself upon another unsuspecting crowd. "Look at the movies they make, filled with carnality, corruption and sacrilege! And they keep turning them out. Turning them out. Why? Because they're greedy and want money…and money is the god of the corrupt. Hollywood Babylon! Well watch out boys and girls. For many will come, claiming to be the Savior and many will be deceived."

Malcolm soon became distracted by a strange looking group of rebellious teenagers who ripped down the street on motorcycles, wearing helmets with jaguars leaping through the air—the tribe's totem. They parked their bikes at a short distance from him and descended. Their style of dress was both primitive and futuristic. In addition to body piercings and tattoos; some of them wore leather, spiked neckbands, black leather belts with chains, and large boots. The faces of the boys were tattooed with animal spots and geometric designs.The youngest in the group was a sixteen-year-old with dark skin, a cat-whisker tattoo circling his lips, and large epicanthic folds around his eyes. He also had three scars running down the sides of his cheeks and a thick chain around his waist. He mimicked Malcolm's gestures.

Malcolm squinted at him, "Get off my street! Devil worshipper!"

Another Indian with large feather earrings and spiral tattoos on his face grabbed Malcolm and held a knife in his nostril.

Malcolm shoved him away, "Agent of the darkside. Worshipper of Satan. Filthy pervert...ruining the land."

The Indian slit Malcolm's nostril while the one with cat whiskers and facial scars mocked him with the wild guttural and fricative sounds of an outraged crow. Malcolm screamed and shouted as the young thugs surrounded him and punched him. When they knocked him down his glasses fell off and the right lens shattered.

"It's always the good that are persecuted," Malcolm raged as he groped for his glasses, struggled to his feet, then broke away from them. The incident pushed Malcolm over the edge. Looking more crazed than ever, he decided in that moment to leave New Orleans with his daughter. He staggered down the street, calling out Evangeline's name. Hearing the pulsing of drums and enthusiastic applause coming from Catacombs, he looked through a window that had not been completely boarded up, and made out the larger-than-life shadow of Salome dancing. He looked away for a moment and began walking in the opposite direction. Then he came back to the same spot and stopped again to look more closely through the window. Squinting and staring, he soon felt certain that he saw Evangeline in the background.

Malcolm circled the building until he found the entrance. The door was not guarded, so he made his way inside. He quickly moved through the foyer and the lounge, and down the hallway. He glanced into the small rooms that lined the hallway, horrified at the shameless décor, appalled by the odors of sweat mixed with stale cologne. Fighting off waves of nausea, he felt close to fainting at the sight of lewd paintings on the walls; nevertheless, he carried on, determined to find Evangeline.

Evangeline watched as Salome lost herself in her dance, and in her lightness moved beyond the veils that separated dimensions. Never had she felt the potential of her divinity as completely as in this moment. The enormous marble hall was flooded with the brightness of the light she brought. She succeeded in raising every person in that room to greater and greater heights of illumination, leaving behind the dense matter of the earthly plane.

During that sacred dance, she discovered that this was her purpose—to remove the veils of deception that obscured awareness of higher realms. But just as quickly as she experienced that moment of blissful insight, it shattered like glass pierced by a bullet. A wormhole suddenly connected the present moment with a parallel one on her spiraling galactic soul-journey. She had the shocking memory of a time, when she danced before Herod. Remembrance of that moment was both a blessing and a curse. She recognized that gossip, rumors and political intrigue had used her name as a scapegoat by twisting her ancient dance of cosmic celebration and revelation into a dance of seduction and a grab for power.

When Salome retrieved this ancient story, which captured the minds of writers and painters throughout the centuries, she stopped dancing and leaned against a column. Losing all cause for celebration, she felt only the desire to waste away. While the audience applauded enthusiastically, Salome became faint and began to lose her balance. The snake, alerted to this sudden crisis, beamed thought-forms reminding her to embrace her inner knowing and to believe in herself. She was unable to integrate the gift of his wisdom and her life came to a halt.

Just as Evangeline was about to approach Salome and offer her assistance, Malcolm burst into the room. When he grabbed Evangeline by the elbow, Salome fell to the floor, unconscious. Possessed with rage, he called Evangeline the daughter of a harlot, and demanded that she come with him.

Stunned by his behavior, Julian realized that Leo, the Guard, had abandoned his post at the door to watch the dance. Julian screamed at Leo, "Get this lunatic out of here. This is a private party. It's for members only."

Grabbing Julian by his ponytail, Malcolm shouted with odious breath, spitting with every word he uttered, "You're right. I'm not a member of your infernal club...but neither is my daughter." Veins bulged in Malcolm's neck and temple as he clenched his broken black teeth. His whole body shook as he said, "She's sixteen—I'll have you arrested!" A fight broke out between them in which Julian shattered the left lens in Malcolm's eyeglasses so that he could barely see at all. Leo joined in, dragging Malcolm to the room of atonement that had whipping instruments laid out on one of the tables. They tied him down with ropes, but just as Leo raised the whip in the air, Evangeline ran into the room and stopped him. She said that he was really just hot air, and hardly worth the trouble of so much attention. She untied him from the table, but the moment he was free, he jumped up and started screaming.

"The Endtime is upon us. Cataclysms will prevail. You must repent." He grabbed Evangeline by the arm and dragged her down the hall, out the front entrance and out into the street. "This is the end of life as we've known it," Malcolm cried. "Take a stand for righteousness, girlie. Don't you see, he's turning out the lights. It'll be Good Night ladies. Good night." Malcolm carried Evangeline to his truck, which was covered with Biblical Proverbs. She struggled, but could not free herself. Images of their life in the cellar flooded her mind and she wondered if he intended to take her back there.

The wheels screeched as he sped down the deserted street with one hand gripping the steering wheel, the other holding her down. "I will not have you spending time with that ringleader of a satanic cult."

Evangeline was hysterical, "I'm not going to the cellar again, I'd rather die." She struggled to get out of the truck but Malcolm held both her wrists with one hand, and when she tried to open the door to get out, he pulled her back by the hair.

Evangeline glared at him, saying, "Cast the beam out of thine own eye; and then shalt thou see clearly to cast out the mote of thy brother's eye."

Malcolm strained to see through the shattered lenses of his eyeglasses and finally threw them out the window. In spite of being legally blind without his glasses, he managed to make it to Ravenford Psychiatric State Hospital. He parked at the emergency entrance and pulled her out of the truck, dragging her to the admitting office.

"I'm leaving her in your hands," he said to an ER doctor who was on call. "I can't fix her. I've tried. Teenagers these days. They roam the streets like animals. They have contempt for their parents. They're the lost generation."

"I'm not staying here. I need to be with my family," Evangeline insisted.

"I'm your only family, you have no other," Malcolm replied.

Evangeline might have been able to prove her sanity to the medical staff, if she hadn't fallen into a tirade against Malcolm. All the years of rage over Malcolm's abusive behavior reached a fever pitch, so that she did indeed seem momentarily insane. Two orderlies were called in to restrain her. When she wouldn't calm down she was given an injection. As the sedative began to take effect, she touched the jewel in her navel and whispered, "Now, more than ever, hear my voice. Find me. You who are no ordinary being. Come! Now! Without hesitation." The North Wind surrounded her with compassion and carried her voice along its course, to Eartha Mae.

PART TWO

CHAPTER SEVEN

THE TRANSFORMATION

It had been some time since Eartha Mae had had a warm meal and a hot bath, so she insisted on checking into the Ho Hum Bed and Breakfast that she noticed from the deck of the houseboat, as they made their way down the Mississippi. It was surrounded by a colorful garden that bordered the waterfront.

After docking the houseboat, Eartha Mae, Virgil and Oakie made their way to the entrance of the charming cottage. Eartha Mae was intrigued by the families depicted in the Rockwell paintings that hung in the office, though the images had yellowed and were obscured by watermarks and spider webs. She was also drawn to the odd assortment of American kitsch in the dining room and secretly wished she had a salt and pepper collection as colorful as the one in the display case.

Virgil admired several large shells on the counter and purchased a conch shell. "It calls out to me," he said to Oakie. Then he blew into it, making a deep tone that sounded like it came from the depths of the earth. He looked pleased with the sound and said, "Someday soon, I'll be needing this. You'll see."

The three of them enjoyed eating off plates with images of Lincoln, Washington, and Carter that were part of a presidential collection. As they ate, they studied their paper placemats, which had a central image of the American flag waving in all its glory. There was a list of questions about the presidents and they quizzed each other on American history. Oakie knew the name of the most honest president, and he also guessed that the color of George Washington's white horse had to be white, but he had no thoughts when it came to naming the current president. Virgil expected as much from Oakie, but ridiculed Eartha Mae for not having an answer. For Eartha Mae, the present had been consumed by her quest, while the happenings in the world around her had long been a blur. The truth was—she didn't want to know about current events.

"When there's a president that cares about me, and stops wreaking havoc on the land...well, then I won't forget that person's name. And some day soon...I just know, that's gonna happen. In fact…I can see her face before me, as we speak." She saw the image of a woman who held a vision for the future and a dream that would not be defeated. She smiled peacefully as their fields of loving energy connected. With that perfect thought, Eartha Mae finished dinner, went to her hotel room, and fell into a peaceful sleep.

In the early morning, Eartha Mae settled into a soothing bubble bath and hummed a song that she used to sing to Evangeline. While sponging herself, she thought of how she used to bathe and nurse Evangeline. She remembered how Evangeline had two faint nipple marks below two fully formed ones. She wondered if Evangeline's second set of nipples were attached to mammary glands so that one day they would secrete milk. It amused Eartha Mae that her daughter had this same abnormality. Even her own mother and grandmother had this distinct feature, though her mother's second set of nipples did not appear until she was pregnant with Eartha Mae. Unlike Eartha Mae's mother and grandmother, who had only one extra set of nipples, Eartha Mae had several rows, located ventrally and laterally along her midline.

Developing an interest in mammary glands at a young age, she perused books on the subject in a library near her home. She learned that whales and other ungulates had posterior glands, while primates, elephants, sea cows and bats had anterior glands. Examining the funnel-shaped teats on a neighbor's goat, she wondered why they were larger than the cylindrical teats on his sheep. She discovered, for instance, that pigs nursed every hour, while cows nursed every four to six hours, and rabbits nursed once a day.

As Eartha Mae continued sponging her breasts in circles, she thought of how she adored her large body. During the years that she lived a sedentary life with Malcolm, she loved to cover her skin with mixtures made from avocado, coconut, olive oil and rose water. She thought that her skin was still soft from those nightly applications. Running her hands down her warm and fragrant body, she caressed her breasts and noticed that the rows of nipples were beginning to develop. Each one now had an areola set upon buds of fatty tissue, which she sensed were connected to nerves and glands, since the area was acutely sensitive.

"How curious," Eartha Mae whispered. "My body is changing before my eyes." She didn't know how to react to this strange development, but when she touched the swollen mounds, she sighed with pleasure at the warm and tingling sensation. Eartha Mae reflected on these developments and whispered, "I'm not what I seem. I'm not what I appear to be. I am so much more—and my body knows that."

The white lace curtains on the bathroom window began to billow as she lay back in the tub to enjoy the gentle fingers of the wind that caressed her body. Soon she heard a voice whispering her name.

"Eartha Mae. Eartha Mae. Come to me," said the voice in the wind. "Come now in your magnificence and splendor. I beg of you."

Eartha Mae got out of the tub and looked around but couldn't discover the source of this voice. She sensed a great urgency in the tone, but couldn't be certain, and though she strained to hear more clearly, her efforts were in vain. Distracted by the loud snoring of Oakie and Virgil, who were sleeping in an adjoining bedroom, she clapped her hands and cried out, "Rise and shine! Rise and shine." When neither one responded, she called out even louder, "Wake up you lazy rascals!"

Oakie rubbed his eyes, then slowly rolled over and groaned.

Eartha Mae pulled the covers off of him and shoved him out of bed. He fell to the floor and scratched his head, then got up and sat down on the bed in a daze.

Eartha Mae noticed her reflection in a mirror on the closet door and was once again drawn to her image. She ran her fingers down her cheek then looked at Oakie's reflection. "Tell me. What do you see when you look at me?" she asked.

Oakie was not interested in her question and tried to ignore her.

She was insistent, "What do you see?"

Oakie scratched his belly, closed his eyes and squeezed them for a moment. When he finally had an answer, he opened his eyes and slowly said, "You're like everything soft. Like the clouds…like feather pillows." He paused and then frowned, "then other times you're like everything scary…like thunder and lightning. You're like a lion that sneaks up on me and shows its fangs. You get this fire in your eyes. I think I like you without the fire."

"But the fire is my destiny," she said. "Don't you understand, I have a powerful destiny."

"You're not always the only one with a destiny," Oakie pouted. "Don't I have one?"

"Most certainly," said Eartha Mae. "And now we must be on our way, to fulfill *our* destiny. I hear a voice urgently calling to me."

While Virgil guided the houseboat downstream past towns in Iowa, Eartha Mae relaxed in her hammock braiding a wreath of wild flowers. Still steering the boat, Virgil picked up his pen and notebook and looked off in the distance. He wrote a few words, crossed them out, tore the paper out of his notebook and crumpled it up.

Oakie watched him closely. "Will you read me a few lines?" he asked. Virgil ignored him, so Oakie stomped his feet and said, "I've made up more poems in a day, than you have since we started this trip. Gees! You're the one who's s'posed ta be the poet."

Oakie had hit a nerve. It was true. Virgil had not written one line of poetry that he was proud of since they started their trip. He threw away everything he wrote—frustrated and disappointed—because he had a vision in his mind that he couldn't express. Virgil moved his face close to Oakie's and glared at him. "If you'd spend a little more time doing your share of the work instead of bothering me with your ditties, I'd have time to finish something."

Oakie pouted for a moment then said, "That's not very nice to say...they ain't ditties."

Virgil was fuming and closed his notebook. Without explanation, he steered the houseboat in the direction of the shore and docked it while Oakie watched him suspiciously, out of the corner of his eye.

It was during a six-month stint in prison that Virgil developed an appreciation for literature. He spent a few hours each day in the library, shelving books on prisoner's rights, manuals on English as a second language, and guides to getting a high school diploma by mail. One day, as he was scanning the library shelves, a book fell off a top shelf and hit him on the head. It was a book by the great Roman poet, Virgil, whose name he shared. He felt it was divine providence and immediately sat down to read *The Aeneid*. After reading just a few chapters, he was convinced that since his name was also Virgil, he would write unforgettable epics like his namesake. Because of that, he participated in a poetry workshop, led by a Quaker volunteer who hoped to expand the minds of the prisoners and offer them new directions in life. After joining with Eartha Mae, Virgil realized the most important thing that he could do with his life was to honor their journey with an epic poem, just as the Roman poet had honored the Trojan refugees by recording their story for future generations. But he had not expected his heartfelt desire to cause him so much unhappiness, and it infuriated him when Oakie so innocently, or not so innocently, rubbed salt into his wounds. He wanted to write his own *Aeneid*, but sometimes he couldn't seem to write at all.

Virgil never wanted to repeat the aimless wanderings that led him so close to starvation and death in the Mexican highlands. That crippling sense of purposelessness left him the day that he met Eartha Mae. But now he realized that he had swung to the other side of the pendulum. Having such a severe sense of purposefulness, he was incapacitated and crippled by a fear that he could not live up to the mission he had set for himself.

Virgil understood that the journey Eartha Mae imposed upon them was an opportunity for spiritual renewal. He was more than a voyager—he was a pilgrim, seeking answers to his deepest questions. He was traveling to his own private Mecca, his Jerusalem, his Mount Meru, his Glastonbury, his Canterbury, his Santiago de Compostela. His writings were not meant to be a log of the things they had seen, but were meant to lead him to a new way of seeing. Now he was troubled because he had not perfected a new way of seeing, he couldn't feel a sense of the sublime in watching the moon rise over the mountain tops, or in the wild flowers blossoming alongside the riverbank. Sometimes he couldn't seem to feel at all.

He had accumulated several more books on the journey, including *On the Road* and *Huckleberry Finn*. He treasured the writings of these renegade pilgrims, who explored the American highways and rivers, and read both books with great care and attentiveness. He hoped that he would learn from them, so that he could write, in his own way, the story of their odyssey.

Oakie and Eartha Mae ate a late lunch around a bonfire while Virgil gracefully executed a series of powerful martial-arts movements. They watched as Virgil pulled a charred stick from the bonfire, and made lines on his face with the charcoal. Then he colored his face with juice from strawberries and blueberries. For a finishing touch, he put leaves in his hair for a mane and feathers for a headdress. Eartha Mae and Oakie joined him in a dance around the bonfire. The men danced with so much abandon that they did not notice when Eartha Mae, distracted by a distant voice that called out to her, wandered off on her own. Eventually, they began to tire and when they paused to rest, they realized she was gone.

Oakie called out to her in a forlorn voice, while Virgil's tone was sometimes commanding and other times irritated. They walked through the woods, searching for her behind every tree and shrub until they heard her moaning and sighing.

Virgil shook his head and said, "She gets stranger and stranger every day."

Oakie looked up at him and nodded. It seemed that this was the first time they agreed on anything and they both secretly savored this brief moment of understanding.

They stopped in their tracks when they saw Eartha Mae in the river, held in an embrace by what looked like a spirit coming out of the water. Perplexed by this strange interaction, they decided not to disturb her.

Determined to focus on writing his 'Ode to Eartha Mae,' Virgil returned to the campfire. Oakie joined him and within minutes completed a poem of his own. He cleared his throat and danced on his toes as he read it to Virgil. "I sings a song of praise, to the forest and the trees. To the ocean and the whippoorwill, but mostly I sings for me. Oh, I love to watch the river flow, and to see the fishies swim. I love to watch the flowers grow, and I can hear the pansies sing."

Virgil groaned. "Enough! Why do you torment me. Can't you do something else? I need quiet! I'm working on my Ode!"

"What's an O-De'?"

"You're such an ignoramus," said Virgil.

Stomping his feet, Oakie moved to a tree stump and sat down. After kicking over a few rocks, he picked up a large worm before it could disappear into a hole. Just as he was about to throw it at Virgil, he noticed Eartha Mae approaching them. Breathing deeply and rapidly, her bright and sparkling eyes focused on Virgil.

"What ya been doing?" Oakie asked in a confused tone, trying to get her attention.

"Consorting with the water spirit," she answered, still focused on Virgil.

Oakie looked even more perplexed, then he jumped up and said, "Wanna hear me do a frog?"

Eartha Mae didn't respond but moved closer to Virgil, stroking his head and neck.

Oakie stepped between them and imitated the soprano trills and raucous tenor barks of a bullfrog.

"Very nice. Very nice. That's quite enough," Eartha Mae said. "Sit in your place."

"Why does the frog puff out its throat like a balloon? And why does the firefly have a light? And why does the woodpecker have red feathers on its crest? Why are there mosquitoes? And why does a river flow? How did all this come to be? How? Why? Tell me? Tell me! You're not listening! You never listen to me! Nobody cares about me!"

"I care," said Eartha Mae in a dreamy and intoxicated voice as she struggled to shift her focus from Virgil to Oakie. She sat down and patted the ground next to her, inviting Oakie to lay beside her. Then she took a deep breath and said, "It was thousands and thousands of years ago, maybe millions, or billions of years ago, that I created this river and taught it to sing. And from the river, I created the cypress, the milkweed, the inkberry shrubs, the redroots, the wild orchid, and the Spanish moss."

Oakie studied her face, then with an annoyed look he said, "You didn't."

Eartha Mae was surprised by his comment. "Did too," she said.

"Didn't," said Oakie.

"Well do you want me to answer your questions or not?" Eartha Mae asked.

"Go on, but at this rate it'll take forever," Oakie mumbled as he snuggled closely against Eartha Mae and touched the lumps on her chest. "How come you're sprouting teats all over?"

"I'm not sure," said Eartha Mae. "Maybe I'm the mother of all creatures, the Crea…Creatress…Creatrix of all things!" said Eartha Mae, as if a light had suddenly gone off in her head. "Yes that's it. Maybe I am all things…I'm the foliage, the root, the bark, the fallen leaves, the lichen. I'm the apple blossom and the rock of granite. I'm the pebble on the beach, the fleet-footed fawn, the roaring brook. I'm the soft billowy cloud in the sky, and the fir tree in the pale moonlight. The morning mist, the dewdrop, the breeze over still water. I'm the eagle soaring above the land. I'm the purple mountain capped in gold. I'm a bee gathering nectar, the crack of lightening in a clouded sky, the frog on a lily pad. I'm the hawk that flies above the ocean, which spreads its wings above the fields and the mountain tops. I'm the mountain, I'm the desert, I'm the ocean."

"How did you come to be all these things?" Oakie yawned.

Eartha Mae did not have an immediate answer for Oakie. She thought of the weeks she spent sleeping in the cave overlooking Lake Itasca, away from the world, like Buddha who lived in the depths of the forest, and like Jesus who spent forty days in the wilderness. Eartha Mae was alone and apart for forty days and forty nights, and in this time of separation, her mind was flooded with inspiration. She was tired of the person she had been in her life, up to that point. She had lost interest in her misery and desperation, and was bored with recurring periods of helplessness and despair. She had reached the depths of darkness and could not go on the way she was. Something shifted in her—it was as if she stood back and looked at herself and in that detached stated of mind—she let go. Her mind became still and was no longer cluttered by heavy thoughts that block the light of truth. In this place of emptiness, her silence became her prayer—it was a place of infinite potential.

A spring peeper jumped on her foot and hopped onto her opened palm.

"Did you make that too?" Oakie asked.

Eartha Mae nodded. "I created things that were mighty and filled with glory…I also tended to small things that creep and hop, slither and swish, peep and tweet. I wanted a little peeper that loves the moss that grows on the rocks," Eartha Mae said as she gently placed the spring peeper in Oakie's hand.

Oakie brightened up and exclaimed, "I'm a creature that loves the furry moss! Can you make it grow under my armpits and in my nostrils? Then buttercups could grow out of my ears. I got lots and lots of ideas, just ask me. Things you never dreamed of."

"You can create your own dreams."

"No one lets me."

"Puffff! Who's stopping you."

Oakie was filled with wonder at this idea, which had never occurred to him before. He became silent, considering this inspiring thought from all angles.

Later that evening, Eartha Mae put the finishing touches on a bed in an abandoned shack in the woods. She hung long flowing veils from the skeletal remains of a canopy that once graced the antique bed. Through a broken windowpane, she watched Virgil as he stretched in the moonlight and practiced various martial arts maneuvers that he learned from his manual. He tied his hair back in a ponytail, then assumed a horse stance with his hands on guard. He moved one foot into the air, striking his invisible opponent in the groin. Then he pivoted and delivered two circular jumps. When he completed his series of exercises, he sat down by the river and closed his eyes in deep meditation to clear his mind. He focused his attention on the bottom of the river, and saw himself there, breathing in the oxygen, watching the air bubbles.

Eartha Mae lit a few candles and anointed her skin with oil. She studied the precious buds that grew beneath her fully developed breasts. Had they grown larger overnight, she wondered, or was she imagining this strange transformation. She couldn't be certain. Her flowing nightgown gently flapped in the breeze that came through the open windows and cracks in the walls of the hut. She turned very slowly and watched Virgil when he walked through the door. He looked radiant from hours of meditation, and was quickly taken in by her otherworldly sensuality.

"This will be no earthly union," she whispered with serious intent. "Tonight you are my consort. My Sky King. Let us unite in a little heaven and earth magic. You be the heaven and I be the Eartha."

She lay back on the bed and he approached her and knelt before her.

"This'll be cosmic…transcendental. Come to me, my fire-breathing stallion."

Virgil was powerless under her spell.

Oakie was disturbed by the deep orgasmic sighs and moans that came from the shack. Peeking into the window, Oakie gasped when he discovered Virgil and Eartha Mae wrapped around each other. His confusion grew as they shifted into every conceivable position. He tapped his fingers on the windowpane and weakly cried out to them to stop, but their moans buried his sad and lonely pleas. He studied them with his mouth and nose flat against the only remaining window that had a solid pane of glass. In moments, the moist vapors from his breath covered the glass and obscured his view. He wrote the words *Stop* in the vapors and watched some more, until tears streamed from his eyes and blurred his vision. He added a dozen exclamation points after the word *Stop*, then smeared the vapors with his hands as if to obliterate the image of the two of them together.

All creatures in the surrounding area were aroused by their passion. A spring peeper heard them and began to serenade his beloved with a love song. Two owls that watched from the branch of a nearby tree moved close together. The male barn owl hooted and danced before his mate, his third eyelid moving from side to side on his ghostly heart-shaped face. A deer mouse with big eyes and ears was busy grooming its fur, when it noticed another mouse holding a berry between beautiful white-gloved paws. He moved close to her to enjoy the warmth and comfort of her tiny body and was soon intoxicated by the silkiness of her fine fur. A goose looked into the eyes of his life-long partner and expressed gratitude for all they shared in their thirty years together. They recalled their endless adventures migrating north, they spoke of the magnificent sunsets they had shared, and of the goslings they had raised. Their eyes closed half way, and soon the peeps, hoots, squeaks, and coos mixed with those of Eartha Mae and Virgil, creating an unforgettable ecstatic symphony.

For Oakie, it was no symphony at all but a painful reminder of his loneliness. He was inconsolable and covered his ears as he ran back to the campfire. He crawled under an abandoned overturned canoe, kicking the ground and punching the sides of the canoe with his fists. He tore out handfuls of grass and dirt and threw it at images of Virgil that he held in his mind's eye. How could Virgil take Eartha Mae from him? How could he claim her as his own? How could she like his ugly face? The questions flooded his mind till he scrunched up into a little ball, put his thumb in his mouth and rocked himself to sleep.

At dawn the next morning, Eartha Mae gathered her things together and looked at the houseboat, which seemed particularly inviting in the early morning sunlight. She thought it was a beautiful looking boat—so festive—with colorful scarves hanging from the rafters, and bright lanterns and tinkling mobiles. "You're like a dancing star," she said. "That's it, that's your name. Dancing Star! Be our guiding star and take us to Evangeline."

No one said anything as they put their gear back on the houseboat. Virgil untied the ropes and they began another day on the Mississippi. Dancing Star floated cheerfully downstream and Virgil fanned an utterly contented Eartha Mae who smiled peacefully from ear to ear.

As the hours passed, she could no longer avoid noticing Oakie's heavy sighs. The weight of his pain began to pierce through her bliss and settled in like a heavy gray cloud, obscuring all light. Although she was not eager to awaken from her rapturous state, Oakie would not let his suffering go unnoticed. Eartha Mae said in a dreamy voice, "I have always traveled down highways and rivers. But now, I am no longer the ship without a rudder. I am the river and the flow."

Oakie took out his slingshot and frowned, "Blah, blah, blah. I'm not interested in what you think you are…you're not what you think...and you don't even make sense when you talk." Then he shot an acorn at Virgil's chest. Virgil brushed it away, barely noticing. After Oakie shot several more, Virgil began to get annoyed.

"Knock it off, retard!"

When Oakie refused to stop, Virgil got up and tried to grab the slingshot. Oakie pushed him and he lost his balance and fell back into the water. Eartha Mae chastised Oakie and struggled to get out of her hammock, but Virgil pulled himself back on deck without too much effort, before she even managed to get one leg on the deck floor.

Oakie pouted and picked up Boots, then he lay down on his bed and stroked him. "I hate everyone and everything. 'Cept you, Boots."

Virgil looked down at him, with water and seaweed dripping from his head, onto Oakie's face. "Did I ever tell you about the time I met this woman, in a little village, in the mountains in Baja?"

"No, and don't bother telling me now."

"Well, she had a terrible pregnancy; should'a killed her. I helped with the delivery, 'cause she was all alone. Her baby had a cat's head. That's 'cause she'd been cavorting with the devil. Some cats are really the devil in disguise."

"You're the devil in disguise...and Boots is an angel. Why he can almost fly."

"Give him a broomstick, then he'll be able to fly."

Oakie stuck out his lower lip and pouted, and when Eartha Mae wasn't looking, he jumped off the houseboat and swam toward shore. Boots gave Virgil a dirty look and followed after.

Virgil didn't have Eartha Mae's sympathy or appreciation for Oakie's innocence and vulnerability. Nor could he understand why Oakie lacked the ability to defend himself, and always needed protection from others. Still he felt moments of remorse at filling Oakie with thoughts that scared him.

Eartha Mae called out to Oakie, begging him to come back, but he didn't turn around. She watched as he reached the shoreline and disappeared into the woods, holding Boots in his arms. Then Eartha Mae glared at Virgil, "Why do you say those things?"

"He needs to toughen up. You're too soft with him...he'll never grow up."

"Take the boat to the shore," Eartha Mae commanded. When Virgil refused to listen to her, she pushed him aside and took over the steering. "What is your job?" Eartha Mae asked in an infuriated tone.

"To steer this boat, down this river, to the destination of your choosing," Virgil answered matching her anger.

"And you think that's all?"

Virgil shrugged, unable to grasp what she was getting at.

Exasperated, Eartha Mae explained that Virgil was divinely ordained, to lead the three of them to Evangeline. It was up to him to skillfully navigate their craft, whether it was through the darkest regions of hell or the brightest regions of heaven. Most importantly, he was to do this with bravery, piousness, and impeccability. He was to come into the fullness of who he was meant to be and to lead them down this river, and all rivers, offering protection to them, and to all in need of his guardianship. He was to be all that and more.

At first, Virgil resisted these ideas, but eventually he felt inspired by her words as he recognized the nobility of his mission. He considered what it meant to be a protector and guardian. He also thought about what she meant when she said that he could be all that and more—but what was the more?

After reaching the shore, Eartha Mae hurried down a path that took her through a heavily wooded area. Soon the path divided in two and she stood at the intersection, uncertain which direction to take. After asking the wind to show her the way, she saw the leaves on a tree that stood on the path to her right, quivering in the wind. She took that as a sign that she should walk down the right-hand path. After a short distance, that path divided in two, and she stood at another crossroads and again asked for guidance. As she stood there, waiting for a sign, an acorn hit her on the shoulder and she heard a voice coming from above her head. Eartha Mae looked up and saw Oakie sitting on a branch, halfway up the tree.

"I remember the day I found you," said Oakie to Boots. "You were sitting in a little birds nest, trying to be like the other birds. I don't know how you got in the nest. Maybe you got lost in the forest and the mama bird took pity on you, and wanted to care for you. But I remember watching you trying to puff up your little legs like wings...trying to be like your brothers and sisters. I know what it's like to try to do things, but not to be able to. And you know what? That's why I love you...cause you always try so hard. And no matter what...no matter what anyone says...I'm never gonna leave you."

"Oakie? Is that you?" asked Eartha Mae.

Oakie stroked Boots's cheek and ignored her. "How would you like to go home to Lincoln," he said. "I'd give you warm milk every morning. Then I'd dress you in a royal cape and hat and we'd go for walks." He looked down at Eartha Mae and frowned, "I don't know why I let her convince me to leave home and go on this stupid trip. That Virgil is meaner than mean."

"Oakie," cried Eartha Mae. "Oakie, come down from there!"

"Go away!" Oakie moaned. Then he ignored her and continued to talk to Boots. "Mostly I miss my tiny trucks and cars. Did you know that I built a model of Lincoln? Some days there'd be earthquakes, other days there'd be tornadoes and atomic bombs. But my little cars would always make it across town. You could always count on them."

"Who are you talking to?" asked Eartha Mae.

Oakie held Boots close to his heart. "I'm talking to Boots, since he's the only one who has time for me. He's my only real friend in this whole wide world."

"Don't fret. I'm coming up." Eartha Mae tried to climb up the tree, but fell to the ground when the branches cracked under her weight.

Oakie snorted and threw a twig at her. "I'm tired of you telling me what to do, 'n bossing me around. You think so much of yourself and so little of me." He wiped away a tear. "I'm not coming down. I'm gonna live up here forever. This tree's my friend. I'm staying here, with the birds and caterpillars."

Eartha Mae steadied herself as she tried a second time to climb up closer to him. When she reached a branch below him, the tree swayed so far to the left that she nearly fell to the ground. Moving to the other side, the tree leaned so far to the right that they both nearly fell out. Finally she managed to position herself in a central place.

Oakie ignored her, his eyes intent on a butterfly struggling to emerge from a cocoon. Then he said to Eartha Mae, "Sometimes I think you make things up. You think I'm just some dumb Oakie from Fenokee that'll believe anything you say. He grit his teeth and looked at her through squinted eyes. "Some days you're nice to me...and other days…you forget me. I can't keep track of all your sides."

"I know...it's true I have many sides. Sometimes I'm lazy, I move at a sluggish speed when my light condenses to matter. I am what you see here." Eartha Mae embraced Oakie, looked into his eyes then spoke with great compassion. "Sometimes I'm just regular, other times I come into my power and I'm transported."

"Huh? Whatever." Oakie spoke softly of his frustrations. "I thought you loved me. But now I know that Virgil's always been your favorite. You went off with him and didn't even think of me."

Eartha Mae struggled to find an answer. "Maybe you could say I need several consorts. That's how I create so many different kinds of things."

"Can't you just think these things into being?" Oakie offered.

"Sometimes, not always. I prefer variety—that's the nature of creativity." Eartha Mae paused and thought for a moment, then said, "When I was sleeping in our 'Cave of Voices and Dreams', I had all kinds of memories. I could see myself...dancing. Swirling. Spinning. Drifting. I could see landmasses exploding out of the seas. Rising. Falling. Splitting. Volcanoes erupted out of the lands. Bursting. Cracking. Bleeding. The sea was dark and deep. Twinkling. Sparkling. Gleaming. The land was breathing, with greening power. And then came the rivers. Winding. Branching. Shifting. Then the vegetation and the animals. Creeping. Crawling. Clinging. Maybe that's how it happened, then again maybe not. My memory is not quite what it could be, and there are so many ways to tell it."

"But where am I in all this? That's all I care about. Me…Not you. Let's talk about me!" Oakie poked at the cocoon with a twig, trying to create a little hole for the butterfly to emerge.

Eartha Mae held his hand and said, "Let it make its own way, in its own time. If you try to help it too much, its wings won't develop and it won't be able to fly." She was silent for a moment and thoughtful. "Even though I created so many things, there was something missing. I thought and I thought, and finally I realized that I needed a creature that would press his cheek against the moss that grows on the underside of a rock. Someone who delighted in its softness."

"Yes, That's me," Oakie exclaimed.

Eartha Mae nodded and continued, "Someone who would play with the dragonfly on a lily pad, who would kiss the buttercups, dance with Boots, and chase after ladybugs and fireflies. Someone who would wonder about the workings of all things. After days and days of thinking and searching I realized what I needed."

"You needed an Oakie!"

"Yes, I needed an Oakie to sing the praise of these small creatures. When that thought came to my mind, that's when you came to be. My Oakie. Pinnacle of creation."

Oakie's face lit up. He was so pleased by the story that a flood of tears swelled in his eyes, and he rubbed them with his soft pink fists. "Pinnacle? You mean that?"

"Most certainly," said Eartha Mae, as she winked at him and reached for his hand, and led him down the tree. "You are the pinnacle, the brightest light of all creation. Wherever you go, you fill everyone's hearts with joy and happiness. You are pure sweetness."

Oakie's eyes grew wider and wider as she sweet-talked him all the way back to the boat. "Is that what I am? Pure sweetness?"

"Of course," said Eartha Mae. "Like the finest honey. Like the perfume of the most beautiful flower. All that and more."

Eartha Mae held his hand and guided him back onto the boat, never pausing for a moment. "Like the softest puppy, like the loveliest kitten, like the brightest angel. All that and more." She steered the boat back out into the middle of the river, and watched as Oakie lay down on his bed, smiling with contentment.

As the days went by, Oakie let go of his resentment toward Virgil, and the two of them began to enjoy each other's company. They worked together harmoniously cooking dinner, building campfires, and tidying their living quarters. In idyllic moments they played chess or cards. After Virgil let Oakie win at checkers, Oakie danced a jig. Finally the subject of Virgil's liaison with Eartha Mae came up.

In a soft voice, Oakie asked, "Can you tell me something? What were you doing that night, with Eartha Mae?"

Virgil hesitated then said, "Just a little heaven and Eartha magic."

"That's what I thought," said Oakie. Grateful for the answer, he jumped up and down then hopped away. Then he slowly spread his arms and imagined he was a butterfly, emerging from a cocoon. Now was the perfect moment to be born anew.

Virgil looked at Eartha Mae, recognizing his strange new alliance with her. Telling himself to have faith in the new direction of their relationship, he picked up his pen eager to begin writing.

Eartha Mae was moved by the seriousness of his intent and the sincerity of his struggle to find words to speak of the changes occurring in their lives. She regretted that she had been too self-absorbed to reach out to him in the past few months, and had spent all her time wallowing in self-pity. Now that he was once again her consort, she wondered if he could accept sharing her with all the mysterious and ethereal earthly forces.

Virgil crossed out a few words in his poem and closely studied Eartha Mae. He thought of the Virgin Mary and the story of her virgin birth. Part of him wished Eartha Mae could conceive without other lovers, but then that would also mean he couldn't be her lover. Though it was hard to accept her as she was, he knew he didn't want her to be like Mary. He told himself, it was nothing he'd have to worry about—they were so different. While Mary created Jesus, Eartha Mae was creating the world—or at least her own crazy world. Still, he wished she was focused on him alone, the way Dido was committed only to Aeneas, in *The Aeneid*. Even though Dido died of heartbreak and madness in a pyre, and called out to the Furies to avenge her betrayal, at least she was faithful to Aeneas and never needed anyone else. But then again, Virgil preferred Eartha Mae alive rather than dead, so if it meant that she would take other lovers, he knew he would have to accept that.

He wondered if she was simply deluded, or if she really was transforming before their very eyes. He knew little of the compassion of Kuan Yin; he had never heard of the fertility powers of Inana or Ishtar; or of the destructive powers of the ten-armed Goddess Kali; nor did he know anything about the modern day compassionate hugging saint, Ammachi. But from his careful reading of his namesake, Virgil, he knew something of Roman Goddesses. He thought about how Eartha Mae had Venus's passion, Juno's unpredictability, and moments of Minerva's warrior spirit and wisdom—all this blended with the irrationality of a Fury. Maybe she *was* becoming more like the Goddesses he had read about in Virgil's masterpiece. He watched her absorbing the warmth of the sun with a look of complete contentment and surrender. In a flash, her contentment changed to irritation as she shooed away a dragonfly. In the next moment, she admired her swelling breasts and popped a few chocolates into her mouth. He reconsidered. Since she had a style that was like no other, Virgil decided that she couldn't be compared to any of the Goddesses that the Roman Virgil celebrated. She had called herself a Creatrix, and now Vigil began to believe it. Somehow she was reshaping her own body with originality and inventiveness, and at the same time, passionately restructuring her world.

Virgil wondered how someone as ordinary as Eartha Mae, had such certainty of who she was and what she could be. Maybe she had never been ordinary, he thought—maybe she had always been remarkable. But how had that happened? He recalled the things she said about her parents. Her father ran a barge up and down the Mississippi, while her mother worked as an aide in a hospice. He remembered that she spoke of her mother's and her grandmother's healing abilities. Eartha Mae said that her mother assisted catatonic patients who had lost the means to communicate. Often she was able to awaken them to life. It took a bit of time for the hospice staff to understand that miraculous healings were happening through her, since she was so quiet and unpretentious. Eartha Mae's mother even brought Malcolm's father back to life at the hospice, after a heart attack. Shortly after he was healed, Malcolm met Eartha Mae, and it was love at first sight. At first, he saw only the highest potential in her, and believed she had her mother's gifts. Eartha Mae flourished in the portrait that he painted of her. She also admired his gifts for envisioning the future. But even after Malcolm's vision of her shifted, it couldn't shatter her sense of self. Virgil decided that her sense of purpose was something she was born with, not something that her mother, father or husband gave to her.

In thinking about Eartha Mae and how she was tapping into the fullness of her creative potential, he thought of himself and like Oakie, he also felt left behind. She said he was their protector and guardian, and much much more. He knew that the secret of becoming more than he was lay in the power of his intention, but that is where he differed from Eartha Mae. She possessed the gift and power of *focused* intention that so overshadowed his limited ability. Yet in accompanying Eartha Mae on her journey, and aligning himself with her intention, he sensed he was changing in subtle but important ways.

CHAPTER EIGHT

ON THE ROAD

Betina studied a few maps and marked a route from Boston that took her through Cleveland, Toledo, Chicago, and Madison, ending in Lake Itasca, where Jane lived. Hitting the road was something Betina liked to do whenever things fell apart.

On the way from Boston to Cleveland, she felt like every decision she made in life led to this place of desolation. "Hokey." Once again she heard Andrew's comment in her mind, the one he claimed he never made. Why was she pursuing such a "hokey" course of study, one that no one would fund? Why did she choose such controversial subjects? Why hadn't she become a psychiatrist, a marine biologist, or an interior decorator?"

Nothing in her life was working. She felt like she had been asleep for the last ten years, wearing blinders that prevented her from seeing other choices. Steering with one hand, she opened her purse and took out a bottle of Percodan and popped a few pills in her mouth, hoping it would help her relax.

Andrew had said, "It's not like you to doubt yourself." She remembered thinking, "but it's like me now." She thought of Andrew in their early years together. He had never been charismatic with women, perhaps because they couldn't imagine the depth of his devotion and passion beyond his clumsiness and absent-minded professor posturing.

Betina lay in bed in a dreary hotel off the interstate in Toledo and clicked on the eleven o'clock news. It was a turbulent time; violence breeding violence, shifting allegiances between countries, paranoia, propaganda, passionate protests against war spreading throughout college campuses and around the world, arousing countless incidents of police brutality. She lowered the volume and returned to thoughts of how she first met Andrew. On the day of Harmonic Convergence, when a number of her friends were meditating on global peace, Betina attended a lecture at MIT. Andrew's associate discussed a theory that he called a Magical Mystery Tour of the universe—later called the Mother of all theories. He considered concepts of space and time to be primitive and artificial. He dismissed Einstein's theory of gravity and general relativity, as well as the quantum mechanical view of the universe. His theory seemed brilliant to her, but he had gone off the deep end in developing it. He disappeared into himself during the lecture, and everything he said began to sound like gibberish.

At the reception that followed the lecture, Betina entered into a casual conversation with Andrew. He was disturbed at seeing his friend cross the thin line from genius to madness. He spoke with dismay about another associate who sold out by accepting a high-paying job with a government nuclear weapons project. Years later he committed suicide leaving a note explaining how he regretted using his creative genius for such destructive purposes.

In his despair, Andrew spoke to her in a self-absorbed but completely honest manner about how his pursuit of a theoretical understanding of all things had cut him off from connecting to day-to-day events in his life, and particularly from most human relationships. He didn't want to end up like his associate: brilliant but out of touch, disconnected, and socially impaired. Betina watched as tears swelled in his eyes when he told her he was lonely.

When they met after that, he would immediately erect a wall when a moment of connection arose between them. She plotted against his defense strategy. Her eyes scanned his body as he rambled on about the collapse of the predictable Newtonian universe, then moved into a monologue on Chaos Theory.

"Yes," she abruptly interrupted. "It's all so random, isn't it? Our lives going so clearly in one direction…then being shifted by a random event. Our destiny is forever changed. Or was that intersection part of our pattern?"

That got Andrew going on a monologue about deterministic chaos, using pinballs as an example. "There are 1,024 different paths that a pinball can take from the top to the bottom, when there are 10 layers of pins and…."

"I see," Betina cut in. "And to think, every moment in our life brought us to this point."

"Yes, it would be most interesting to calculate how many movements that entailed," he said as he loosened his tie and wiped away perspiration forming on his forehead.

"Yes, and how many revolutions around the sun, and how many heartbeats," she said with exasperation.

"Well, let's see...one million heartbeats equals approximately thirty years..."

Betina interrupted his mental calculations. "I'm more interested in knowing what's in your heart."

He looked at her, like a deer caught in the headlights of an oncoming car. In a weak and parched tone he said, "In my hhh…hhhearttt?"

At last he was silent, Betina thought. Frozen really, but quiet. She handed him a glass of water.

He had been an altar boy as a teenager. When she visited his mother's house in a small town outside of London, she saw a picture of him in a procession. She knew she would have been drawn to him, even as a teenager. There was an earnestness in his countenance as a young boy that he never lost as a grown man.

Betina watched as he took a handkerchief from his pocket and again wiped away beads of sweat that were ready to roll down his cheek. Then in a voice devoid of hope she asked, "Andrew, what are you thinking? What are you feeling?"

"Who me?" he said hoarsely, then finished off the glass of water.

"Yes you. I just wondered..."

As tears welled in his eyes, he struggled to speak though his throat was completely dry. "I am close to suicide."

"Why suicide?" Betina offered him another glass of water.

"Because I am making such a bloody ass of myself. Because being me is utterly unbearable. Because I don't know how to behave any differently. I live in a straightjacket."

"I don't know what happened that made you so afraid." She paused and her voice became a whisper. "Andrew, please assert yourself with me!"

Instead of seizing the moment, Andrew retreated to the subject of time travel and rambled on faster than the speed of light. It was a favorite subject of his in those days, when he felt the freedom to pursue the study of controversial subjects. "Did you know that gravity normally bends or warps space," he said, "however torsion twists and 'pleats' space. This pleating can lead to the ability for a particle moving through space time to jump forward, constituting a form of time travel." She remembered how he mentioned the alleged US Navy 1943 Philadelphia Experiment in this context. He had just read a paper that showed how a large mass of iron or steel might induce a torsional effect: the result of this was the possibility of time travel.

"You completely changed the subject," Betina remarked.

"What was the subject, then?" he asked sheepishly.

She stroked Andrew's arm and ran her fingers down his face. Like a pinball shifting to a new path on its deterministically chaotic course, he started rambling on and on about how the brain releases dopamine and norepinephrine, which contribute to a rapid pulse and a heightened sense of awareness. When he began to speak about the increased production of the neurotransmitter serotonin she put her hand on his mouth to shut him up and he looked at her, helplessly, his hands shaking, his lips trembling, his eye twitching.

That was enough. Her sympathy shifted into intense annoyance. She quickly put on her coat, grabbed her purse, and went home. Placing a bag of ice on her head to relieve a headache, she told herself that a relationship with him would be out of the question. But in the middle of the night, Andrew came to her apartment and frantically rang the bell. She was half asleep when she opened the door. He looked possessed, but she said nothing, not wanting to break the spell as he carried her into the bedroom. He undressed her, pulling off her ragged Harvard T-shirt and ink-stained running shorts. He kissed her neck and breasts. They made love until their bodies were worn out with exhaustion. She didn't sleep at all that first night together. She watched his eyelids flutter as he dreamed and circled his nipples with her fingertip, marveling at the perfect ring of silken hairs. She brushed aside the hairs that covered his face and wondered where this blend of terror and hunger came from. He was unlike anyone she had ever known.

Now alone in a hotel, miles away from Cambridge, she was uncertain what her new life would bring. She regretted that Andrew decided not to be part of it. Tossing and turning, she wondered if her future would contain the emptiness that she felt in this room, where hundreds of people before her had slept, many weary of life, with little faith in their journey. Sitting by the window at the Toledo Roadside Hotel, Betina's thoughts jumped to another subject, as she watched the cars whiz by on the highway. She wondered if her vision of the medieval nun was actually an experience in time travel. Maybe she had called them dreams: Now she wondered if they were pleats in time.

CHAPTER NINE

THE PAINTING

Leaning against a cement pillar, Evangeline looked around the dreary communal room in the hospital, which was sparsely furnished and thoroughly devoid of beauty. Her head ached from the on-and-off buzzing of the fluorescent lights and the deadening hum of an old television. Frieda, Rose, Sylvie, Dimitri, and Vlad sat in a far corner of the room watching *Young Amazons*. Although nearly all the patients at the hospital had been born in Louisiana, or neighboring states, these five elderly patients often sat together since they shared a Russian heritage. They also had a fondness for this action-adventure about Penthesileia, Queen of the Amazons, and her battle to preserve the privacy and power of her tribe of female warriors.

Vlad watched enthusiastically when Penthesileia—wearing a short, cleated, leather skirt; a leather boustier; and sandals that laced up her muscular calves—pinned a young English Explorer against a tree and told him that he would be taken captive since he had invaded their secret campground in the jungle. "I know why she wants to take him captive," Vlad shouted, disturbing those that weren't heavily sedated. "She wants him."

"That's what you men always think. *Mouzhik*," Rose shouted.

"You're the peasant," Vlad yelled back.

Evangeline watched as a parade of ants marched across the worn-out linoleum, making their way through a cracked windowpane to the lawn. Eager to follow them, she asked one of the orderlies if he would allow her to take a walk on the lawn. Nathan, a large man, who was slightly cross-eyed, dressed in a short-sleeved white shirt and white pants, agreed to supervise her walk. Although she wasn't comfortable in his company, she was tired of the oppressive atmosphere in the communal room, and was grateful to get some fresh air. The lawn was hardly more enticing since the grass was dry and there were large patches of dirt, where no grass would grow. No birds flew overhead, there were no flowers or bushes of any kind, and an unpleasant odor came from a dozen garbage cans stacked outside the back entrance. Evangeline cringed when she heard a particularly blood-curdling scream coming from a patient in a room overlooking the lawn.

Celestina noticed how miserable Evangeline looked and motioned for her to join them. She was a short plump English woman who wore a pillbox hat with a small net veil and a delicately flowered dress adorned with a strand of large white beads. "A spot of tea should cheer you up," Celestina said.

Evangeline took a seat next to Celestina and her son, Ethan, who sat in a wheelchair. He was in his mid forties, balding, with a potbelly, short arms and unusually small hands and feet. Celestina nodded to Nathan who sat at a distance, with his eye on Evangeline. Then she lifted a teapot, filled three mugs, and offered one of them to Evangeline.

"Thank you," Evangeline said as she took a sip.

"I wish they'd let me brew my own. They're ignorant about making tea. 'Tis a fine art, you know. In Japan…making tea is a sacred ceremony. Lovely. If you can make a good cup of tea, dear...you can do just about anything." Celestina looked distressed as she examined the thick white mug, which had a couple of chips on the rim and tiny cracks in the handle. "To think of the tormented people...who've held this mug in their hands. I feel their pain...I feel the insanity. Do you think I'll catch their madness if I drink from it?"

"I couldn't say," Evangeline answered.

"Next time, I must bring my own teacups and my own teapot. I have a set that Grandmother gave me. It was treated with such great care. Not one teacup from that set was broken or even chipped. It was passed down from Great Grandmother...through a pure line of descent."

Ethan rolled his eyes and in a painfully slow voice said, "That's where all the mm...mmm…madness comes fff…fff…from...the lady's ppp…pure line of ddd…descent."

Celestina looked pained, "I'm not just any lady, Ethan. I'm your mummy." After taking out a handkerchief from her purse, she wiped away the drool that was sliding down the side of Ethan's mouth. Turning back to Evangeline she said, "He never used to be like this." She cleared her throat, smiled at the orderly, and took hold of Evangeline's hand. "Let me tell you how to make the perfect cup of tea, my darling..."

Just as she was about to explain the procedure, the orderly excused himself for a moment, to tend to Sylvie, who was having convulsions in the communal room.

"Thank goodness he's gone. I've been wanting to speak to you alone," Celestina whispered. Her manner of speaking changed completely as she let go of her gentle Englishwoman facade. She spoke quickly and intensely, trying to squeeze in as much information as she could, in the few moments she had alone with Evangeline. "Anyone can see that you don't belong here. You have to be careful how you behave, if you want to get out. I'm telling you this, because my son's mental health has deteriorated so severely over the past year. My efforts to have him released have only made the situation worse. Dr. Hoagland resents my interference and insists on increasing my son's medication. Each time I visit him, he becomes more and more confused and forgetful." Celestina shook her head. "I should never have listened to the guidance of his doctor, who said he would be helped here. My son attempted suicide, several times. But enough about Ethan, that's my problem. I want to talk about you, while we have the chance. Please listen carefully."

Evangeline cleared the hair away from her face and nodded, eager to commit every word to memory. She looked at Celestina with eyes as clear as glass.

"Number one. Don't show any anger or resentment to Dr. Hoagland. Show that you respect his judgement and that you appreciate his efforts in helping you. You *must* play along. Number two. Say only good things about Ravenford and about the staff here. Number three. Say that you want to put in the work to recover and that you trust Dr. Hoagland's guidance. Make eye contact. Number four. Say these things with the utmost sincerity, not with sarcasm or cynicism…but don't overdo it. Number five. Say that you're changing as a result of Dr. Hoagland's therapy. Say that you feel optimistic about your future and…"

They watched Nathan and another orderly lift Sylvie from the ground and roughly tie her down in her wheelchair with wrist and leg straps. She sat crying in her wheelchair, unable to wipe her nose or the flood of tears that streamed down her face.

Celestina whispered, "The way they handle her…she broke a rib six months ago and last year, she ended up with a broken wrist after one of the orderlies tended to her. She came here for depression after losing her husband and home. Look at her now…she's nearly a vegetable."

Evangeline watched as Sylvie was wheeled away, down the corridor.

Celestina rushed to finish giving Evangeline final words of advice, when she saw Nathan approaching. "Say that you feel you are beginning to understand how to become a productive member of society. That's always a winning line."

When the orderly returned, he announced that it was time for group therapy.

"Thank you for your efficiency," Celestina said politely. "You can always count on Nathan, isn't that right, Evangeline."

"Yes," Evangeline said tentatively and then again with conviction. "Without a doubt."

Evangeline followed along as Nathan wheeled Ethan through the doors that opened into the communal room. She turned and looked back at Celestina who nodded to her with approval, then the three of them disappeared into the hallway. They passed through a number of long dark corridors, to a dingy room in the west wing of the hospital. Dr. Rex Hoagland, a psychiatrist in his early forties, sat at the head of the group, wearing a traditional white doctor's jacket. Hidden behind large glasses and a carefully manicured red beard, was a narrow face that had the bone structure of a fox. Evangeline and Ethan joined Frieda, Rose, Vlad, Dimitri, and several others. They watched with surprise as Sylvie was wheeled in, strapped in her chair, with her arms dangling by the wheels. Mucus ran out of her nose, her hair was disheveled, her head hung limply on her chest.

In a deep and serious voice, Dr. Hoagland studied each one in the circle and asked, "What do you want?" No one answered so he spoke more slowly and clearly. "I mean just what I said. What do you want? It's a simple enough question. Not a trick question."

Tears welled in Rose's eyes.

"Why are you so emotional?" Dr. Hoagland asked.

"Because I can't think of an answer. And I've never known the answer to that question. It's been a lifetime of not knowing." Rose rocked back and forth as she began to cry.

Ethan began to tremble uncontrollably, until Evangeline put her hands on his shoulder to calm him.

Vlad spoke out boldly, "Well, I know what I want. I want to go back to Tbilisi, and spend holidays in the sulfur baths with father and mother."

Frieda responded next, "Yes. And I want mama."

Ethan cried, "Mummy. Mummy."

Rose wiped away a tear, "You have a mummy…you have it all. I have no one." She suddenly stood up, "I want my sisters back alive. Millie, Gertie, Trudie, Sissy. I want my son to forgive me and take me home to live with him. I want to get out of this prison. I want to get rid of this arthritis. I want to move my arms with ease. I want to dance again, like I used to. I want to dance the tango."

Frieda cried, "I want to hear my mother's lullaby one last time."

Finally Evangeline responded, "Yes, I miss her lullabies."

Evangeline preferred group sessions to the one-on-one biweekly therapy sessions that she had with Dr. Hoagland. She hated the way he studied her face and took notes, even when she said nothing. After a long period of silence, he asked "What are you thinking?"

Evangeline had a million raging thoughts but held back on all of them. Answering politely, she said, "I'm feeling some real changes. Getting a clearer understanding of things."

"Have you had any dreams that you want to share?"

Evangeline had so many dreams she could share: enchanted dreams of talking flowers in her secret garden; magical dreams of her childhood with Eartha Mae; healing dreams of being comforted by the compassionate wind; dreams of her future where she traveled through distant lands; even dreams of the future of the planet as it sang a bright song and danced through the heavens. Sensing that she should try to convince him of her mental health, she strained to think of what a normal dream might be. "I dreamt that I was home with my father and mother, the home we lived in when I was a child. You visited us. I showed you photographs of our life. Of simple activities…eating dinner around a table, holidays with relatives, sitting on the porch telling stories…I'm sure that day will come someday." She became silent, wondering if he knew that this was a life she would never have, and was not even a life she longed for.

Dr. Hoagland pressed his index finger over his lips and watched every move she made, making her feel even more uncomfortable.

"Don't you think I'll be back home again soon?" Evangeline asked. Though she struggled to find the key that would lead to her release, she was at a loss. She didn't know how to manipulate this situation. Hardly knowing how to create a persona of normal, she realized at the same time that pretending to be normal wasn't going to help her get out of Ravenford.

"When I see that you've adjusted and can handle life outside this hospital, then you'll be allowed to return home," Dr. Hoagland replied. "You have to start putting in the work…changes don't happen on their own."

His words sounded as flat and unauthentic as the dream she related, since Evangeline knew he had about as much interest in normal as she did. Nevertheless, she continued with the pretense that returning to normal was her desired destination. "You're right. I want to put in the work. I want to tell you more about my dreams. I could express them by painting. I have a hard time finding the words to say what I feel, but if I could draw the picture that's in my mind, it would answer your question. We'd have so much more to talk about."

Dr. Hoagland stared at her, his eyes running up and down her body. Then he got up and stroked her cheek and soft hair that fell to her waist. Since the session was over, Evangeline slowly got up to leave, hiding her nervousness, wanting desperately to get away from him. When he pressed himself against her Evangeline swiftly ran through Celestina's advice in her head.

Though she didn't want to, she looked him in the eye. She inched away from him, as she said in a soft but clear voice, "I've appreciated your concern about my mental health. I look forward to being a productive member of society again." He was entranced by her lavender eyes and began to calculate how he would have her.

She struggled to find a strategy that would keep her safe from him. "When you decide that I've improved sufficiently to return to society, I will have so much to say about the excellent treatment I've received." Evangeline knew that much of what Celestina had said was on target, but more importantly, she knew she had to come into her power if she was going to survive Dr. Hoagland.

Dr. Hoagland sucked in his lips and let her pass out the door. He stroked his pointed red beard as he watched her walk down the hall with an orderly.

The next day, Evangeline attended her first art therapy class. Standing at an easel, Evangeline squeezed a tube of canary yellow and one of rose red, onto a palette. After mixing the colors with a fine-tipped brush, she sketched the outline of her mother with a halo of roses. Rose and Frieda nodded with approval at Evangeline's sketch. Evangeline was pleased that they appreciated her work and said, "All my life, the scent of roses has sent shivers down my spine."

"Yes…I know what you mean. A shiver memory," Rose responded.

"That happens to me, but I thought I was the only one," Frieda added.

Other patients gathered around Evangeline as she continued working. Even those who were the most disturbed found comfort in gazing into the gleaming eyes of the woman in the painting. The woman became more than Evangeline's mother, she became mother of them all.

Frieda dipped her fingers into Evangeline's palette and painted roses on the walls. "I hear her singing to me," she said. "It's my favorite lullaby.

Rose, Dimitri and Vlad joined the others and the walls were soon filled with red, pink, lavender, turquoise and golden roses, of all different sizes. Frieda ran after one of the roses that came off the wall and floated around the room. Even Sylvie and Ethan found the strength to get up out of their wheelchairs. They chased after other roses that came off the wall and sailed past them. A woman who hadn't moved in a decade came to life, catching a beautiful yellow rose that danced before her. She laughed for the first time since she had been placed in the institution. Many others began moving around, shouting and dancing amidst the magical spinning roses.

Celestina, who worked one day a week at the hospital, as a volunteer, arrived just in time to witness the joyful scene. She secretly carried a small camera, hidden in her pocket, to document some of the disturbing events that took place in the hospital. Without any of the orderlies noticing, she took several snapshots of this most unusual sight.

The excitement startled Nathan who had been napping in a corner. Jumping out of his seat, he yelled, "Everyone. Everyone. No painting on the walls! You must stop immediately. Put down your brushes and paints, now! Sit down in your chairs." Those that heard him paid no attention to his demands. They could not contain their excitement and continued running around the room.

Frieda squeezed Evangeline's hand, "This is my dream, how could you know?"

"It's my dream as well," said Ethan as he held out his hand to dance with Evangeline and Celestina.

The laughter and excitement traveled through the hospital corridors alarming Dr. Hoagland and the entire staff. Dr. Hoagland got up from his desk and started down the hall to the art therapy room. "What's going on here? What's causing this hysteria?" he asked, appalled at the spontaneous and uncontrolled behavior of the patients.

Nathan responded helplessly, "I don't know what's happening. It's the painting. It's alive."

"What do you mean, alive?" Whispering in the orderly's ear, Dr. Hoagland ordered the removal of the painting. Other aides rushed to take the patients back to their rooms, but they refused to budge. They had to be dragged out.

Celestina stood in the background, committing every detail to memory. She tried to calm Evangeline as two of the orderlies wrapped the painting in sheets and tied it up. She whispered sternly, "Remember what I said, dear. You don't know what they can do to you if you lose control. Hoagland will not tolerate disobedience."

But Evangeline could not contain herself. "Why are you taking my painting? It's not yours to take!" She grabbed onto the orderlies to stop them from covering the painting, but was held down by Nathan. When she turned to Dr. Hoagland, she screamed, "Don't you want to heal? My painting is healing…isn't that obvious? What kind of place is this? Why are you trying to destroy us?" When Dr. Hoagland grabbed onto her wrist, she bit his arm.

He looked at her with rage and bit his lips till they were bloody, so that he would not explode in front of his entire staff. Shaking from head to toe, he turned to Nathan and said, "isolation," in a controlled tone.

Frieda, Vlad and Ethan also had to be restrained and sedated as they tried to follow the trail of dancing balls of light that the painting left as it was taken down to the end of the hallway.

Celestina cried silently as she watched this most miraculous moment dissolve into chaos and torment for all. She held in her anguish while promising herself that somehow, she would tell the world about the cruel treatment toward patients that was practiced on a daily basis at Ravenford.

The orderlies took the elevator to the basement, walking down several dark and dusty corridors until they reached the storage room. Making their way past stacks of old chairs, tables, and beds, they placed the painting between old oxygen tanks and antique equipment used in shock treatment and lobotomies. Before leaving, the orderlies peeked under the sheets, taking one last look at the painting, confused by the enchanting power it held over them.

Although Evangeline did not receive chemical injections, or electric shock, she became a prime candidate for Dr. Hoagland's personal study of sensory deprivation and was put in a black cell that lacked natural and artificial light. He was certain that since there would be no physical trace of this emotional torture, no one would know. Dr. Hoagland expected that by the fourth day, she would begin hallucinating and in the days after that she would most certainly begin to break down. But that is not what happened.

As she sat in the darkness of that black cell, day after day, Evangeline told herself that she had been through much worse. In the underground shelter, she was a prisoner of Malcolm's madness. In this black box, she had the freedom to open completely to the dream of Eartha Mae. She realized that losing control and biting Dr. Hoagland after he stole her painting was not necessarily a mistake. She could survive this isolation, in fact, she could sink more fully into her dream without distraction. The lack of fresh air could have been devastating, but Evangeline dissolved the walls, in her mind, and merged with the universal consciousness.

Although Dr. Hoagland came to her cell several times, Evangeline had called in the protective, nurturing energy of her Great Mother. She also moved into her personal power, and each time she looked at him with her clear, piercing, other-worldly eyes, he felt inexplicably weakened and always left without violating her. This miracle of faith sustained her through two weeks of isolation, offering her protection from Dr. Hoagland's most sinister agenda. She wasn't breaking—she was growing stronger. The radiance in her eyes and face grew with each passing day. Her darkest hour provided the greatest opportunity to transform herself and her world.

CHAPTER TEN

A COLOSSAL MONSTROSITY

Eartha Mae dangled her feet in the river as they sailed past the town of Sauget, Illinois. She stroked the side of the houseboat with affection, certain that the vessel had a personality of its own and that it needed to be honored with respect and gratitude. She whispered, "Dancing Star, Dancing Star take me to my daughter. Do not forget the seriousness of your mission. We trust in you to lead the way." Her mood of contentment diminished as she noticed that this great river, born in the Pleistocene Period, named Missi Sipi by the Ojibwe Indians, seemed particularly sluggish and forlorn. There were problems at every turn. The locks and dams that spanned the upper Mississippi had changed the free-flowing waters into slack-water pools and even the gulf was starved of oxygen and covered in algae.

They passed an ominous sign with a skull and crossbones. Eartha Mae read the warning to Oakie and Virgil: "Fish from this river are contaminated with dangerous levels of or-gan...or-gan...or-ga-no-chlorines and dioxin, a poison causing cancers, birth defects and miscarriages. Consumption of fish or shellfish from this river should be avoided." She noticed that grease covered her feet like black boots, and she was overcome with sadness. In a soft voice, she whispered to the river, "What has become of you, my beloved consort?"

Along the river's edge, a tall lean woman, with wild gray hair that hung below her waist, sat in a dried-out eucalyptus tree that creaked and cracked in the wind. She looked down at the warning sign as she beat on a drum filled with crystals and stone, painted with images of Grandmother moon in all her cycles—full, half, and crescent. She wore a long black dress with a rope tied around her waist and a black-lace veil and mourned the desecration of the land and water. Once known as a painter and performance artist in her younger years, she had transformed into Estrella Estevez, the *curandero,* in her later years. After wandering the world for a decade, following an inner calling, she made her way to the shores of the Mississippi River. She returned every day to the same spot, mourning the poisoning of that once great river of life, and praying for its return to health.

Eartha Mae, Virgil and Oakie nodded to her as they passed by, wondering who she was. Then their attention shifted to the peculiar color of the sky, which was smeared with pink from sulfur dioxide gases. Virgil was so distracted that he did not notice a pole jutting out of the water, and accidentally steered right into it. Boots was thrown off the deck into the black water, causing fluorescent rings of green to appear. To their horror, he burst into flames.

Oakie jumped up and cried out "Boots. Boots!" He wanted to go in after his cat, but Virgil stopped him.

"You can't go in there! It'll burn you too!"

Estrella noticed the commotion and shouted, "There's phosphorous in there. Danger. Danger."

When the flames finally died out, there was no further sign of Boots. Still, Oakie called out to his cat with a piteous cry. "Boots, please come back." Despite his pleading, he could not resurrect the cat.

Eartha Mae was saddened by the loss of Boots, and heartbroken by the poisons in the water. She cried out "Pearls before swine. Look at what they've done to my river. They've turned it into a sewer."

Oakie looked at Eartha Mae as if she was nuts, then sat with his head in his hands, whispering Boots's name over and over like a mantra. "You were my only friend. The only one who ever really cared about me. I know you'll come back. I know you'll find a way. You have nine lives. Remember that, Boots. You have nine lives…nine lives."

Soon Dancing Star passed a monstrous apparition that loomed in front of them, obscuring all light. It was a nuclear power plant, a godless city unto itself, made of soot covered towers and steel tunnels that encircled the odious structure. Like a vampire, it sucked the life force out of everything around it, robbing animals and vegetation of health and vitality, turning a once vibrant river, which thrived in an endless celebration of life, into a watery wasteland. There was a second sign that said "Car windows should be kept closed—this region is contaminated by poisonous fumes." The smell of decaying fish, mixed with fumes, was overpowering. Oakie's eyes began to burn and Virgil couldn't stop coughing.

Surveying the industrial complex, Eartha Mae was beyond herself in despair. "What is this colossal monstrosity?" she whispered in horror.

They steered the vessel to the shore and the three of them got off and walked along the shoreline. In the distance, dozens of state prisoners in light blue uniforms were scooping up thousands of dead fish. Eartha Mae picked up condoms and plastic soda bottles, then she examined a slimy plastic hose. Knotted around it were pairs of sneakers, nylon stockings, a toaster, and several other objects too corroded to identify.

Oakie held up a two-headed fish that was in a state of partial decay. "Poor Eartha Mae," he said. "She worked so hard and look what she gets."

Relishing Oakie's pity, Eartha Mae's expression changed to one of an injured child. Her eyes widened, her shoulders slumped and she began to pout. She sat on a large rock and in a voice that resembled Oakie's hurt child voice, she cried, "Why do they do these things to me?"

Oakie patted her back. "Poor Little Eartha."

Eartha Mae hung her head, "Why is everyone so mean?"

Oakie agreed, "That's what I'd like to know."

She leaned her head on Oakie's chest and he rocked her like a baby. Virgil approached them and suppressed a smile, as he looked at Eartha Mae in this ridiculous position. He had never seen her look to Oakie for comfort.

Opening one eye, Eartha Mae studied the look on Virgil's face and resented his amused expression. She jumped up, reclaiming her regal posturing. Her moans and groans turned to rants and raves. "I am overcome with sickness. The gifts that I have given are trampled on. A pristine world turned to muck. How can I go on? My love is unrequited. My joy is turned to sorrow."

Hearing Eartha Mae's heartrending cry, which resounded throughout the land, Estrella climbed down from the eucalyptus tree and made her way along the shoreline. Virgil watched as she approached and hoped that she might offer Eartha Mae words of comfort.

Sitting beside her on a log, Estrella extended her hand to Eartha Mae. "Yes, you have suffered deeply, that I know." The more Estrella comforted her, the more tears seemed to flow.

"No one understands," Eartha Mae moaned.

Estrella gently wiped away the tears on Eartha Mae's cheeks and wrapped her arm around her shoulder. She suggested that Eartha Mae spend the night at a hotel in town, where she could relax in luxury and pamper herself a bit.

Volunteering to get her a room, Virgil and Oakie wandered through the streets that bordered the river looking for a suitable place to spend the night. It did not take long for them to find a hotel run by an elderly couple, who showed great concern when Oakie told them about Eartha Mae's condition. They made sure to give her their best room, one overlooking the Mississippi, and in no time at all Virgil was tucking Eartha Mae into bed. He covered her with a down comforter and sat beside her, putting his hand to her forehead.

"What is this sorrow in my heart that grows deeper with each new day?" Eartha Mae asked. "Why do they assault my beauty?

What will it take for them to understand that they are destroying me?"

Virgil whispered to Oakie in a worried voice, "She has a fever. It must be very high."

Oakie thought for a moment then jumped up. "I'll take care of it." Running out the door, he did not hear Virgil shouting at him from the doorway to come back. He made his way to a local pharmacy and stood outside for a few moments, then slowly opened the door and walked in, setting off a buzzer that announced his entrance. The pharmacist was filling a prescription in the back behind a glass partition, then glanced over his reading glasses to keep an eye on Oakie.

Oakie looked at several shelves then grabbed as many bottles as he could without looking at the labels. When the pharmacist wasn't looking, he slipped them in his pocket and under his shirt. At the cash register, Oakie held up a bag of cherry cough drops.

"Just the cough drops?" the pharmacist asked.

"Yes," said Oakie in a guilty voice.

Eartha Mae tossed and turned in bed, her stomach rumbled and her cheeks were flushed from a high fever. Sitting beside her, Virgil stroked her forehead with his fingertips, until he heard Oakie pounding on the door. Virgil let him in and stood back as he bounded into the room, tripping over a luggage rack. The stolen items spilled out of his pant pockets, from under his shirt, and from inside his jacket.

Picking up the bottles, Virgil read the labels. "This one's for warts. This is for poison ivy. And this one's for roaches! What were you thinking?"

"I didn't think. I grabbed what I could," cried Oakie.

Exhausted by Oakie's uselessness, Virgil turned to the television as a broadcaster read an urgent report. "We interrupt our regularly scheduled program to inform you of an unusual heat wave that is spreading across several European countries including Germany, Denmark, and Finland." They looked at clips of Germans on beaches and of Danes fanning themselves and wiping their foreheads with handkerchiefs. In another clip, a Finnish family was seated directly in front of a fan, eating dinner. The broadcaster continued, "At an English resort, the warm waters lured a dozen killer sharks into the sea off of Brighton." There were pictures of the giant shark, followed by the body of a seven-year-old boy, torn apart by its attacker. "In Mexico, fifty gray whales were found dead on the Baja Peninsula due to sudden temperature changes. In Jerusalem, thousands of people from apocalyptic Christian sects have gathered to witness the raising of the dead, the resurrection of Jesus and the battle of Gog and Magog. Most are dressed in white and many believe themselves to be prophets. It's messianic mania and there are rumors that there will be a confrontation between Muslims and Jews."

Eartha Mae continued to toss and turn in bed. When she suddenly sat up, the volcanic rumblings of her stomach caused her to emit an explosive burp. This was followed by an image of a sudden burst of waves overflowing a dam.

The broadcaster continued, "Twenty-nine locks and dams and miles of levees on the Mississippi can do nothing to prevent the flooding that is taking place. Desperate men and women are piling sandbags along the banks of the river in a futile attempt to keep the raging river from flooding the town." Against a map of the Mississippi, which showed the stretch of tributaries from the Appalachian Mountains to the Rocky Mountains, the broadcaster continued, "The towns of Bemidji, Brainerd, St. Paul, Bay City, La Crosse, Rock Island, Hannibal, St. Louis, and Memphis have all been flooded."

Another broadcaster stood in front of an animated map with flickering arrows showing ocean currents. "The ocean currents have changed directions. The Humboldt Current, at the tip of South America, is moving east. The Alaska Current is moving in a southern direction and the Canary Current is moving northwest."

A third broadcaster pointed to another map. "Even the wind patterns have shifted from their normal circulation patterns. The usual cool current that sweeps up the West Coast of South America and the westerly winds have shifted to the east. El Nino has brought floods to America. The polar front, the southeast trades and the doldrums are all changing directions."

Eartha Mae sobbed, "I'm at a breaking point."

The broadcaster spoke with great distress, "Earthquakes are occurring in all parts of the world. In the past hour there has been a 7.5 magnitude quake in the Kuril Islands; an 8.3 magnitude South of Sumbawa, Indonesia; a 7.9 magnitude in Southern Alaska; an 8.8 magnitude in West Virginia; a 6.0 magnitude south of Honshu, Japan; a 9.9 magnitude in the border region between Chile and Bolivia; and an 8.9 magnitude earthquake in the Solomon Islands. Military ships in the Persian Gulf are being smashed to smithereens by violent waters, and the neighboring countries of Iran, Iraq, Kuwait, Qatar, Saudi Arabia, and the United Arab Emirates are experiencing earthquake activity throughout the region."

Oakie held her hand, "You gotta keep your temper."

Eartha Mae looked annoyed, "And why is that?"

Oakie thought for a moment, "Because look what's happening!"

Virgil nodded, "All hell's breakin' loose!"

"And you think that's my fault?" Eartha Mae asked.

Oakie and Virgil looked at each other in complete confusion, believing both that it could not possibly be her fault, but also sensing that the destruction was indeed the result of her pain and torment.

The television broadcaster pointed to red triangles on a world map that marked eruptions taking place worldwide. "Scientists of the *Instituto Internazionale di Vulcanologia* are monitoring the Strombolian activity on Etna. Explosions can be seen up to forty miles away. Three main flows of lava were reported coming from active vents. Gas plumes from the eruption are being driven to the south and a new fissure is developing. Scoriae and ash are showering local villages, and reports of damage and injuries are currently being estimated." A spokesman for Indonesia's Mines and Energy Ministry released a warning about the Krakatau volcano. "A new island, near Anak Krakatau, is emerging, and spectacular displays of volcanic lightning are passing over the cone. Explosions can be heard up to sixty miles away." A broadcaster in Mexico reported that, "Popocatepetl erupted violently, showering ash on Mexico City. The blast caused a number of houses and several bridges to collapse. The ash plume reached ten miles into the air and authorities are preparing to evacuate villages within a twenty-mile radius of the volcano." The list went on and on, and included eruptions as close as Yellowstone Park and as far off as Fernandina in the Galapagos.

Virgil clicked the remote. On another station a broadcaster showed pictures of enormous hailstones. "In Auckland, thousands of homes were damaged as hail, the size of watermelons, smashed through roofs, windows, and skylights. Cars were completely leveled by this strange natural phenomenon. People are being treated for cuts and lacerations, and there have been more than 30,000 calls for urgent help." Virgil changed channels again. "In Mexico, a freak snowstorm in the Mexican Mountains killed 270 million monarch butterflies. They migrate annually from Canada, to Mexico—a distance of 3,000 miles. The butterflies arrived in Mexico on the Day of the Dead and are thought to be the spirits of the ancestors. Now their frozen bodies litter the ground in pine forests west of Mexico City."

Oakie muttered, "Guess it's not always worth coming out of the cocoon."

Virgil looked at Eartha Mae hesitantly, "What are you thinking now? Tell me. What's on your mind?"

Eartha Mae responded, "I'm considering a little collision."

"Little. How little?" asked Virgil with alarm.

"Maybe a little cosmic one. Like a collision of galaxies." Eartha Mae said with an agonized expression.

Virgil was quiet for a moment then said, "Can I get you something to calm your nerves?"

"Bring me clover, chaparral, Pau de Arco, burdock, sarsaparilla, chlorella, ephedra, fenugreek. That's just for starters. Maybe it will heal my heartache," she said.

Virgil tried to write everything down, then paused. "Where can I find these things?"

"I'm sick all over. It's hopeless." Eartha Mae dropped her head and closed her eyes.

Tears streamed down Oakie's cheeks at the thought that he could lose her.

They heard a woman's voice calling out to them from outside their second floor window. "Hey! What's going on? How's she doing?"

Oakie looked down from the balcony and saw Estrella standing there. "Not so good. Can you help?"

In moments, Estrella made her way to their hotel room. Sitting down beside Eartha Mae, she immediately understood the seriousness of the situation. She turned to Oakie and Virgil. "I need you to play a rhythm. It helps me to get into a deep state."

"What's a deep state?" Oakie asked.

"Just do what the lady says," Virgil responded.

Virgil tapped on the back of a tray that he found in the kitchenette and Oakie grabbed a tin wastebasket and imitated Virgil's rhythm.

"That's perfect," said Estrella. "Just keep it steady."

"Why are we doing this?" Oakie whispered.

"Just play the drum steady. I need to hear a rhythm that will set me on my voyage," said Estrella.

"What voyage? It doesn't look like you're going anywhere," cried Oakie.

"It's an internal voyage. Ssshh." Estrella closed her eyes. "I enter a tunnel. The wind blows around me. I am sucked through the tunnel."

Oakie asked, "What tunnel?"

Estrella ignored him, "I spin through a black void."

"What void?" asked Oakie.

"I move at a frightening speed," said Estrella in a louder voice, hoping to block out his questions. "I see streaks of light. Red, green, blue." Her voice began to fade as she entered into a trance.

"Where? Where?" asked Oakie impatiently.

Estrella opened one eye for a moment and glared at him, "Sssh. No talking allowed. Just play the drum!" She returned to her trance state. "I call out to you, spirit world, spirit world. I am on my way. On my way. I entreat you. Illuminate my mind. I am the whirling of the spheres. I am the spinning of the stars. I am the wise woman who brings a cure. Let this sickness be washed away. Let the bad air be purified. Let the cleansing wind wash over this woman and surround her with healing. I ask for the remedy. I ask for the cure. I ask for the healing."

Estrella spoke in a singsong voice—sometimes laughing, other times imploring. While chanting, she saw a flux of light patterns and her body began to sway. Her eyes sank back in her head as she clasped her hands together, holding them tightly to her breast. Estrella watched as Eartha Mae radiated an aura that changed from violet, to red, to yellow, to orange, to green; like a light that was rapidly brightening and dimming. Soon Estrella realized that she was dealing with no ordinary woman, and she called for a council of spirit guides.

Estrella continued softly, in a voice that slowly began to build. "I call out to eagle, who dwells in the clouds. I call to you hawk, messenger of the gods. I call to you turtle, steadfast, determined, and trustworthy. I call to you light-footed deer, so tender, gentle and kind. Come to me bear, leave the comfort of your cave, bring to me your wise council. Come crawling to me snake, oh sensual one. Oh butterfly, emerge from your chrysalis. Fly to me on wings so light, so bright, so luminous. Wolf bring your medicine. Raven spread your black wings and bring me your magic. Oh lion, awaken from your slumber, come running to me, bring your fierce roar, bring your courage. Do not fail me. Lynx bring your secrets. Buffalo, so solid and steadfast, hear this prayer. Owl, spread your wings and bring your wise council. Frog, cleanse us of this sorrow and pain. Whale, ancient one, star child, bring your wisdom and your primordial call."

She stood there for hours, maybe days, reciting the names of angels, entities, devas, even fairies. She whirled around in a circle with her arms raised toward the heavens and called out to the plant kingdom. "Revitalize her. Bring your power. Bring your healing force. Carry Eartha Mae to the source so that she may be healed. Take her on your back, take her on wings, take her. Fortify her. Fortify her. I call out for her spirit to return, in the fullness of its being. I call to you wind from the east, with your white light; wind from the south, with your blue light; wind from the west with your yellow light; wind from the north with your blackness. Inflate me with your breath of life and lead me to the cure for this suffering soul."

Then Estrella took a deep breath and an unearthly tone sounded from the back of her throat that she projected into all of Eartha Mae's organs, so that it resonated in every cell of her body. She bathed Eartha Mae's body in this healing vibration, and watched as her face twitched, and her fingers and toes began to wriggle. Finally a radiant smile burst out on Eartha Mae's face, and when she opened her eyes she filled the room with a brilliant golden light.

CHAPTER ELEVEN

LEOPARD SPIRIT

Betina listened to the radio, as she drove on the interstate through a light rainstorm and headed toward Jane's house. The radio host spoke about a sudden subsiding of the winds, rains, tornadoes, earthquakes, floods, landslides, and wildfires. An intense discussion about the bizarre climatic conditions was underway in this call-in program. Everyone had a theory. For one caller it was a warning, for another it was a punishment, for a third it was a random convergence of earth disasters, for a fourth it was a cleansing. A fifth caller said that it was not the end, but barely the beginning of the cataclysms. A sixth caller said it was from global warming. A seventh call came from an environmental scientist who said the theory of global warming was unproven, if not a scientific fraud. An eighth caller spoke of solar variability.

Betina was particularly intrigued by the comment of the next caller who said that these kinds of bizarre weather conditions increased with frequency toward the end of the 1900s. She thought he was correct, since she couldn't remember a time when disaster struck at once, in countries all over the world. He also said that one-third of all natural disasters of the last century happened in the 1990s. That's three times the average number of disasters—not to mention the fact that they were far more serious. Now at the beginning of the new millennium, they were happening more often, causing far greater devastation. She considered it miraculous that there was relatively little loss of life.

Deep in thought, Betina nearly ran into several large branches—which had fallen across the road, during the heavy rainstorm—as she drove down a two-lane road in Minnesota. Turning off the heated radio discussion, she thought about the endless adventures she and Jane shared during their college days. She remembered how they went on shamanic retreats in the Mexican highlands, how they studied with local craftsmen in Oaxaca, attended gamelan concerts and twelve-hour dream plays at the Brooklyn Academy of Music.

She took a great deal of mushrooms in those days, believing they could help her understand the mysteries of life. Jane had gone on some of these psychedelic journeys with her when they dreamed of returning to that atomic level of consciousness, where form became collections of whirling energy pulses, a mosaic of vibrations and force fields. They wanted to transcend all human longings, emotions, and limitations. Betina realized that all these shared experiences stopped abruptly when Jane married.

She pulled up in front of Jane's home and sat in her car for several minutes feeling both reluctance and curiosity. She had been to Jane's Minnesota home twice in the past, but now it looked lovelier than ever. Her black lab barked and ran to the car as Betina got out. Jane waved as she finished a conversation with a handyman who was sawing a tree that had fallen across her patio. After greeting Betina with exuberance, they each grabbed a piece of luggage and made their way across the patio. Jane explained that the storms had knocked down several trees, and she was having them cut up for firewood.

They sat down in the living room, enjoying the light and warmth of the sun's rays, which came through glass panels in the ceiling. "The sun is finally coming out," said Jane. "We've had a few serious rainstorms here, nothing much to complain about...compared to the rest of the country. But don't let me start in on the bizarre weather conditions…that's all Phillip and I have been talking about, reading about, and thinking about. I haven't seen you in so long…I certainly don't want to talk about the weather. I want to hear about your latest adventure."

"I hardly know where to begin. I feel like my life has always been a straight path with no diversions. But since I quit teaching, it's opened into a wide field. I don't know which way to turn...I've lost my direction." She looked around the living room and noticed several pictures of herself on the wall, at an archaeological site in the Near East. "Sometimes I forget what it is that I searched for with such intensity."

"Isn't that what searching is all about? Finding what you should be looking for?" Jane asked.

"What if you don't ever discover what you should be looking for?" Betina muttered. She scanned the domestic world that Jane inhabited. "Are you happy in this life? Is it enough?"

"There's never an end to wanting, but it's enough." Jane paused, "Why?"

Betina sat down again. "Oh, I don't know. Maybe I regret every single choice I ever made."

"Let me show you something," Jane said. She pointed to a half-dozen books on her bookshelf: *Anima Mundis, Dance of Kali, Dreamscapes, Temples of the Sublime, Sacred Tongues,* and *Viriditas*.

"I sacrificed everything to write them, but now they've lost their meaning."

Jane led her into a warm and inviting kitchen, which had polished copper pots hanging from the rafters, straw baskets, and bundles of dried herbs in metal buckets. The framed poster of the painting by Vermeer, that Betina sent from Amsterdam, hung on a wall above the kitchen table. On the refrigerator were several drawings by her son, Petie.

Jane took a box of letters out of an antique cabinet and showed Betina postcards she sent from Damascus, Jerusalem, Mt. Etna, the Dead Sea, Baghdad, the Black Sea, Nepal, Taj Mahal, Ethiopia, Olduvai Gorge, Malta, and New Grange. "This is the most recent." She began reading, "'There is nothing like the glory of this place. I am moved to tears to be at this sanctuary on Malta. I have seen more than thirty temples, and a number of these have floor plans in the shape of the goddess. I write to you as I sit in the temple of Hypogeum. In moments like this, I have no doubts about my life or the path that I have taken.'"

Later that evening, Betina sat on a kitchen stool sipping a glass of Chardonnay while Jane made paella. Jane spoke of the joy she found in raising her son and mentioned that breast-feeding him had been so exciting to her, even more arousing than sex had ever been with Phillip. Betina found the comment curious but didn't have a chance to ask what she meant since their conversation was cut short when the phone rang. Jane chatted for a few minutes while Betina looked at photos of Petie fishing and canoeing.

"Good news and bad news," Jane said as she hung up the phone. "The good news is that the phones are finally working again. The lines have been down for days. The bad news is that Phillip will be working late…it seems that he's always working late these days."

"Well, maybe it's not so bad. It'll give us time to ourselves," Betina offered. After dinner, Petie snuggled up to Jane on the couch in the den, while she read aloud from a book Betina had given him; an adaptation of *The Quest for the Holy Grail*. As Jane read, Betina looked at a rug that Jane had been weaving on a loom. Admiring the emerging pattern of mountains and evergreens, she smiled with appreciation at Jane's love of nature.

When she finished the chapter and closed the book, Petie asked, "But how do you get pure enough to see the Holy Grail? What do you have to do?" Jane turned to Betina for an answer.

She was pleased by this perfect question from such a young and remarkable boy. "You must be strong in faith and action. You must be committed…you must let nothing distract you from the course of your quest."

Jane looked at her watch and before Petie had a chance to ask another question, she said, "Time for bed, because tomorrow...you have something very special to show Betina."

Betina looked surprised when Petie gave her a loving hug before running up the stairs.

Jane laughed, "You're a heroine in his eyes. He often asks to hear stories about your adventures, so I tell him about your discoveries in Greece and North Africa. You're his Indiana Jones. Thank you for the book, I'm sure he will be reading it over and over."

Flipping through the illustrated book, Betina was reminded of the importance of asking the right question, when beginning a quest. She remembered how Perceval asked: 'Whom does the Grail Serve?' and wondered if that was what she was missing in her own lifea perfect question. She said to Jane, "I guess the question that drives me right now is 'What is it that I desire?' I think I've been traveling in a maze, because I have lost track of what it is I'm looking for. What about you? Do you have a question?"

"I guess mine would be, 'What is it that everyone desires of me?' That's what I ask all day long, when every moment I try to steal for myself is interrupted by a PTA meeting, Boy Scouts, or driving Petie to a lesson of some sort."

She pondered Jane's comment and was sharply reminded of their different lives. "How old is Petie now?" she asked. "Ten, eleven?"

"Ten! Eleven! He's fourteen. Can't you tell? His voice is changing, he's getting facial hair. He's entering puberty."

"Fourteen! Puberty…I remember when I was fourteen," she said in a dreamy manner. "We were living in Africa. That was the year I first menstruated. To celebrate, my mother gave me a necklace that had a leopard's tooth on it. She also gave me a small bottle of perfumed oils and a brilliant colorful batik shawl made by a !Kung woman. I put on the necklace, perfumed my body, and wrapped the shawl around my shoulders. I felt so sensitive. I took a long walk and wandered farther from our house than I ever had before. I climbed a hill, and beyond it saw a beautiful sparkling lake. I remember taking off my clothes and walking naked down a dirt path, over several hills, till I reached the ochre sands surrounding the lake. I heard distant baboons scampering through the brush, and the screech of a reedbuck that might've been fleeing from a lion. I felt so much a part of nature.

"Across the lake, I saw a leopard, sniffing the air. I was certain he had followed my trail of blood and had been shadowing me. I calmly watched as he circled the lake." She became silent as she remembered how he disappeared from her view, but suddenly reappeared, looking down at her from the top of a craggy cliff. His gold coat, patterned with black rosettes, shimmered in the sunlight; his spotted black limbs were particularly muscular. His face was morphing between that of a black African man and that of a leopard. "I lay still and soon I saw him standing above me. I dreamed he was upon me, that I lost my virginity to a leopard. That I was impregnated with its spirit."

"You were given leopard's power, a leopard's nature," Jane commented. "You've always been determined, swift, unswerving."

Betina thought to herself that she was no longer feeling like any of those things.

That night, Betina slept in Petie's bedroom. As she put on her nightgown, she glanced in the mirror and noticed that she had lost even more weight. She could see the entire length of her spinal column and even some of her ribs. Her hipbones were jutting out and her neck looked longer than it ever had before—even her cheekbones were more prominent. She had never been so skinny and her nightgown hung loosely on her 5′ 10″ frame.

While looking through Petie's rock collection, she noticed that he had carefully hand-numbered every rock. The numbers corresponded to a master list that described the places where he found them, their age, and mineral composition. There was even a tray of fossils and a box labeled lunar rock samples, which had lunar lava, lunar soil, and lunar breccia from the Apollo mission.

Lying in bed, Betina looked at a poster on the wall of a mother gorilla and her offspring, and fantasized about studying gorillas. It wouldn't be so hard to get a second degree in primatology, then she could live in the jungle, away from people. Thinking of the remarkable existence that Dian Fossey must have had, Betina remembered that she was mysteriously murdered for defending gorillas. Reconsidering, she thought about how she could buy land in the United States and breed the last remaining pairs of gibbons, since their natural habitat in the treetops of the Malaysian rainforest had been cut down. Or, she could live near the ocean and spend her days swimming with dolphins. Anything but the life she had.

These fantasies were interrupted when she heard the muffled voices of Jane and Phillip coming from their bedroom. He had just come home and they were talking about scheduling a contractor to finish the new wing of the house. Would it be best for him to come on Monday or Wednesday? Their tone became argumentative, but she could not decipher anything else that they said.

On her way back from the bathroom, Betina crashed into a corner table in the hallway, knocking the box of letters off the table, which Jane had looked through that afternoon. She picked up the box and made her way back to Petie's bedroom. After lighting the scented candles on her bedside table, she looked through the letters she had written to Jane—they were in chronological order and several were written in code.

Betina remembered how her interest in cryptography began when she was a little girl. She even concealed a message to her mother within a hard-boiled egg. She made a kind of ink from a mixture of alum and a pint of vinegar and wrote on the shell. The solution penetrated the porous shell leaving a message on the hardened egg albumen. When her mother removed the shell on Mother's Day, she read the message, 'You are the perfect mother.'

Betina had read everything on the subject of cryptography, including the stories of alchemists who used it to keep their discoveries secret. She was even interested in the scandal surrounding Mary Queen of Scots, who wrote secret letters by using a kind of alphabetic substitution. It occurred to her that her love for cryptography led to an interest in reading all that she could on the decipherment of ancient languages. That led to her study of archaeology and the interpretation of ancient cultures.

She took a letter out of an envelope that she had written on a trip to Cyprus, when she was sitting on the beach where Aphrodite was said to have been born from the foam. She remembered that she had written the letter in code, because she was reluctant to speak honestly and openly about Jane's plans to marry Phillip. It took Betina a bit of time to crack her own code, and she wondered if Jane had ever taken the time to decipher the contents. She had written a short story that described her feelings about the capricious nature of love, represented by a rebellious teenager, Eros, who recklessly shot arrows into people's hearts, creating more havoc than happiness. His mother, Aphrodite, was unable to exert any control over her son's whimsical behavior and was beside herself because she could not find a way to console the wounded victims of love. This story was Betina's way of telling Jane not to marry Phillip.

Putting the old letters away, she felt comforted lying in Petie's bed, holding his stuffed leopard in her arm. Sleeping in Petie's room brought back memories of her childhood. She looked at the illuminated constellations of the Northern Hemisphere, that Petie recreated with great care on his ceiling. She could see the constellations of Leo the Lion, Virgo the Virgin, Bootes the Herdsman, as well as the constellations of Lyra, Aquilla and the Northern Cross. She also spotted Orion, Canis Major, Auriga and Taurus. She remembered how differently Orion looked from the Southern Hemisphere, since it was turned upside down. On moonless nights, in Africa, she could see the Large and Small Megellanic Clouds—two satellite galaxies of the Milky Way. She never found the North Star in the Kenyan night sky, but her mother taught her to recognize the eleven circumpolar constellations and their six brilliant stars.

In Dreamtime explorations, she went back to the lake, where she had her mystical experience with the leopard, at fourteen. She wondered if he would find her again, as she moved through the surreal landscape. Sitting by the shore, she listened to the familiar night sounds. There was the shrieking and bloodcurdling howls of hyenas that hunt in the night in packs and the maniacal laugh that so tormented her, when they were attacked.

Just as it happened more than twenty years earlier, she saw the leopard standing above her on the jagged cliff. This time she watched as it leapt toward her in slow motion and came to her larger than life, engulfing her momentarily in its vastness, with the leopard spots becoming constellations of stars in a glistening galaxy. Moments later, the leopard reappeared standing firmly before her with piercing eyes and an unwavering gaze. She watched as various body parts morphed back and forth from leopard to human. She was also shapeshifting—her face growing long whiskers, her hands morphing into leopard's paws. Soon she was running with this leopard at lightning speed, through the Savannah, their muscles rippling with every leap.

Reveling in her newfound grace and agility, they leapt high into the air, soaring over jackalberry trees growing atop ubiquitous termite mounds. They passed over a pack of warthogs communing around a muddy shallow pool of water. Dancing past a mirage of pink clouds, made of a throng of flamingos, they were soon soaring over the Rift Valley. Floating through impressionistic patches of emerald green, crimson, and gold, Betina caught an occasional snapshot glimpse of a redheaded weaver, pygmy falcon, and a night heron that distinguished itself in the haze of colors. Then they made their descent, near Lake Nakuru.

They followed after a herd of swiftly-moving gazelle until they returned to the very spot where they had made their encounter. Staring into each other's eyes, the powerful leopard spirit re-ignited Betina's dying flame.

CHAPTER TWELVE

ADORNMENTS FOR A QUEEN

"Providence," Virgil exclaimed, as he carefully steered the houseboat between boat fragments, roof beams, displaced bedposts and mattresses, front doors and pieces of picket fences. "That's the only way to explain why Dancing Star remained intact."

"It's like we were in a bubble," Oakie said incredulously.

"Yep. Tore through homes from Sauget to Memphis," Virgil added.

Eartha Mae leaned on a railing in a daze and watched an odd assortment of items float past her. Stunned and confused, she wondered if her misery had anything to do with creating this nightmare of destruction. How could someone who had been ignored by her father and battered and abused by her husband have any influence at all? Feeling ineffectual and powerless, she asked herself why she had ever proclaimed herself to be a Creatrix.

Oakie lay on his stomach holding a pole with a hook. He reached into the water and was thrilled when he pulled out a lunchbox of Snow White and the Seven Dwarfs. After several attempts he managed to snag a little toy truck on his hook. He showed these things to Eartha Mae, but no matter how long he dangled them in front of her eyes, they remained glazed over—traumatized by the wreckage that lay before her. He sighed and pulled away, tired of her unpredictable mood swings and exhausted by the complexity of her nature.

Although the houses and businesses along the river had all been ravaged, there was one restaurant with brightly-lit, colorful paper lanterns that seemed untouched by the storm. They noticed a sign announcing that a free dinner would be served to all those who had endured the hurricane that devastated the region. It was their way of sharing their blessing and expressing sympathy to the people of their community.

After docking Dancing Star, they wandered into the restaurant. They were warmly greeted by the owners at the front door. The old Italian couple explained that they didn't understand why they had been spared, when every building around them had been damaged or even destroyed. They told them of the hardships others had suffered from the violent hurricane—many had lost everything they owned. Eartha Mae looked embarrassed when they offered their sympathy for any troubles they might have endured. They encouraged the three of them to order anything on the menu.

In no time at all, a waitress set a plate of baked turkey hash and garlic cheese grits in front of Eartha Mae. Her appetite returned in full force and the world and its problems slipped away. Unfortunately, these precious moments of happiness were soon interrupted when Oakie opened a clamshell and splattered grease on her best dress. She ignored him at first, but when he hit her in the eye with a clamshell, she glared at him with disdain. "Why did I ever take up your company?" she asked as she tried unsuccessfully to remove the grease stains with a napkin.

Oakie shoved a handful of French fries in his mouth and said, "That's what I ask myself...What am I doing...following after you on this journey to the ends of the earth. When I first met you, I thought it was the luckiest day in my life. Now I don't know."

"I remember that day," Eartha Mae said sadly. "I had reached the end of my rope. Virgil's motorcycle had died of exhaustion and old age…and there we were...stranded in Lincoln...till you came along to save us. I liked you the moment my eyes laid eyes on you."

"Well, I liked you too," said Oakie, as he struggled to crack open another clam. "You were nicer than anyone I ever met. But sometimes

I miss Aunt Olive. Maybe she misses me. Sometimes, when she was sleeping…I'd play in her wheelchair. I'd take it around town and go grocery shopping in it. People were nice to me then. They'd reach for things...off the top shelf. I had friends everywhere who'd help me."

"You pretended to be crippled?" Virgil asked.

Oakie frowned and said, "Maybe it's time for me to go back to Lincoln. Maybe I'm just in the way..."

Virgil nodded his head over and over until Eartha Mae kicked him in the shins, under the table.

Since Oakie wasn't quite ready to part ways, he ended up tagging after the two of them as they wandered through the main streets of town. Impressed by some of the outfits displayed in the store windows, Eartha Mae told Virgil that she no longer had anything to wear. Since Oakie had ruined her only good dress and she had outgrown all her other ones, she decided to have a dress made, though she had no idea how she would pay for it. Virgil and Oakie followed after her as she entered one of the shops. A timid young woman approached them and offered to be of assistance.

Eartha Mae took hold of her hand and said, "I'm looking for something elegant. This ol' potato sack has had its day. I need something that expresses the real me..."

"You've come to the right place," Chloe said enthusiastically. "I design clothes for people of all different sizes and shapes. I even design clothes for the country music stars." Chloe Johnston was in her thirties, delicate as a heron, with a long elegant neck and thin blond hair that hung past her shoulder and veiled her face.

Oakie piped up, "It'll need a real special design...she's got more teats than a pregnant dog."

Virgil grinned, "Yes, her breasts are a mighty and wondrous thing. There's at least a dozen—and they are so sensitive. A stroke of a feather and they stand alert. One small kiss and they blossom like rosebuds."

"They are my eyes. They are my ears. They are my everything," Eartha Mae whispered with pride.

A flush appeared on Chloe's cheeks as she looked with embarrassment at Eartha Mae's body. Suppressing confusion and refraining from asking questions, she timidly measured Eartha Mae's bustlines, then she showed Eartha Mae a dozen different fabrics and dress designs. Eartha Mae studied all of them and carefully settled on three different patterns—which would need extensive alterations to accommodate all her breasts.

Humming a cheerful melody, Chloe labored over the dresses on her sewing machine, while Oakie watched. Virgil tapped out an energetic rhythm on a table, improvising to the sewing machine rhythm.

Eartha Mae nudged Oakie, whispering in his ear, "How very talented she is, see how she sews. Look at all the different things she can do. Isn't she tidy. And what beautiful flower arrangements she creates. Listen to her sing…just like a canary."

They returned to Chloe's the next day, and the day after, and watched with eagerness as she carefully worked on the dresses and sewed in breast supports to hold each breast in place.

Eartha Mae whispered to Oakie, "Isn't she pretty? Isn't she sweet? She is so capable and kind." Then she left the two of them alone, hoping that her hints would inspire Oakie to approach Chloe and get to know her.

Chloe turned to Oakie and in a shy voice said, "I hope you don't mind my asking…but when did this happen...the breasts," she whispered. "Has she always been this way?"

Though he sensed her embarrassment, Oakie responded enthusiastically since it was a subject of great interest to him. "They started growing on the houseboat. We didn't know what was happening. I thought, maybe they were mosquito bites. But each day they grew a little more...and a little more."

Chloe blushed, confused by the story.

"Your dresses are beautiful," Oakie offered. "I like to watch you work on your sewing machine." Touching her hands for a moment he said, "You have the prettiest hands I've ever seen. They're soft, just like the furry green moss...Do you know why I was created?" Before she could respond, Oakie continued, "I'm here to celebrate all soft and furry things! Eartha Mae says that's the meaning and purpose of my existence."

Embarrassed by the way he looked directly at her, Chloe turned her back and opened several drawers, picking out a pair of elbow-length gloves and a crown. While examining the gloves, she wondered if she was close in age to Oakie. In some ways he looked about forty, but sounded like a boy of twelve. She decided, in that moment, that she liked him just as he was, and that he was the one she had waited for all her life.

Eartha Mae tried on the finished dress made of red velvet, with cups that uplifted her many breasts for all to admire. She was pleased with the accessories that Chloe had chosen for her. While carefully studying her appearance in the mirror, she asked "But what shall I wear around my neck?"

A second later, Chloe's twin brother, Ewald, came into the shop carrying a pet boa constrictor around his neck. Ewald was thin and wiry, and was always running around Tennessee, pursuing one lead or another. As a tabloid journalist, he was known all over Memphis for stories on flesh-eating bananas, Elvis sightings, and alien-abductions. He even wrote a story on his pet boa, claiming that a beautiful princess was trapped in the snake's body after a curse was put on her by a Voodoo Priestess.

Eartha Mae looked at Ewald and reached out to touch the smooth skin of this primordial creature. "May I hold her?"

Ewald nodded and put the boa around Eartha Mae's neck. Standing back to study her, he was stunned by her many breasts which were featured in the new dress. He decided in that moment that she would be his new feature story.

While looking at her face in the mirror, Eartha Mae watched as the snake nuzzled its head close to hers. "It's better than a feathered boa," she said. "See how she likes me."

Never one to pass up an opportunity, Ewald said he'd rent it to her, if she would pose as a model.

••• ♛ •••

Preparing for the photo shoot, Eartha Mae slipped on her new gown and tied a satin sash around her waist, then she put on the long-sleeved gloves and the crown. After taking her place on a makeshift throne, she wrapped the boa constrictor around her neck, and Ewald began taking photographs.

"I had a girlfriend once—name was Laurel Lee. She had three breasts." Ewald exclaimed. "A lil' one grew betwixt the other two. At first she wouldn't let me touch it. Thought I'd make fun of her, tell her she was deformed. Seems her pappy done the bestial thing with a cow named Lucy. See…Lucy was her real mother. Point is...it don't really matter none how it happened, cause I thought them three breasts was the most beautiful thing I'd ever seen…until now, that is. I never even imagined there could be a twelve-breasted lady!"

"There's more than twelve," Eartha Mae noted with pride, as she watched Ewald with growing suspicion. Eyes glazed with desire, he took one photograph after another, rubbing against her at every opportunity. The more he rambled on about Laurel Lee and Lucy the cow, the more she tired of his company. And when Ewald called Eartha Mae his favorite cowgirl and proposed marriage, she told him there had to be more to a relationship than breasts—beautiful as they might be.

In the evening, Chloe entertained Oakie in a cottage that she shared with her brother. While eating gingerbread cookies and sipping mint tea, Chloe asked, "Who is Eartha Mae. Why do you travel together?"

"I ask myself the same thing," Oakie sighed. "Sometimes she makes me so mad. Once I hid out in a tree to get away from her. I was thinking about leaving. But when she found me, she told me stories...I changed my mind."

Oakie enjoyed talking to Chloe about life in Lincoln, and about his journey with Eartha Mae down the Mississippi. He followed her into her bedroom when she went to get a sweater. "I've needed someone to talk to. Someone who could understand me. I get so lonely…Did you know I can do a gold thrush? Listen to this," he said and began chirping.

"Guess what this is," Chloe said as she began trilling.

Oakie jumped up and shouted, "I know, I know. A nightingale!"

She nodded with delight.

Flapping his arms, he spun around the room while buzzing. When he could go on no longer, he collapsed on the bed, trying to catch his breath.

Chloe clapped her hands. "It's a bumble bee!" she said and sat down next to him. He touched her index finger with his pinkie and held it there until she moved her hand away.

"I've been so alone," she said, trying to prevent a tear from rolling down her cheek. "I'm so misshapen. Everything about me is wrong. I'm dull and plain."

"I think you're perfect the way you are," Oakie exclaimed.

Chloe looked up at him with a smile, "No, you're perfect."

"People always make fun of me, 'cause I have no whiskers. But Eartha Mae says this is the way I'm s'possed to be...Do you believe that?"

"Yes...It makes you soft…I love things that are soft," said Chloe.

"Why I used to be soft all over, but now I have some calluses. They're rough and hard. It's from the journey down the river."

She marveled at his hands and looked at him with tenderness.

Then he showed her a black and blue mark, "I got this from wrestling a grizzly," he said, hoping to impress her. "I'm very strong...but the truth is…what I want most, is to be big and round and create things—just like Eartha Mae." He looked closely at the quilt on the bed, "Did you make this?"

"Yes," she said shyly. "Each square tells a story. It's nothing special."

"Oh yes it is." Oakie curled up on the bed and thought about the strange feelings that grew within him when he was close to her. Then he took a toy truck out of his pocket. "I found this in river," he said as he ran it across the bedspread.

Cutting a small square from a roll of white cloth, Chloe began planning a new design. Trilling like a little nightingale, she watched as Oakie fell asleep. Entering into Oakie's dream, she sat beside him in the toy truck that was now life size. Like a small bird, she nuzzled her head under his chin and pecked at his cheek. Soon they were both singing like two lovebirds.

Eartha Mae was pleased that Oakie was getting to know Chloe, since it gave her time alone with Virgil. Strolling arm-in-arm through a seedy part of town, they were intrigued by the cheers and applause coming from a club called Lola's. A short chubby man, wearing checkered pants with suspenders, stood at the entrance and invited them in. He ushered them to a table in front of the stage.

They watched a tall blond-haired woman with broad shoulders and wide hips, parading up and down the runway in platform shoes. She seductively slipped off a cowboy shirt and unzipped her shorts, revealing a fringed G-string and pasties on her breasts. After raising her long and shapely leg parallel to a pole, she hugged her foot close to her head and twirled around a few times.

"Isn't she luscious?" exclaimed Eartha Mae.

Virgil nodded, surprised by her enthusiasm.

Two middle-aged brothers, Hickey and Dickey, sat at a table next to them. Born only a year apart, they were almost identical in their looks. Both had broad grins, revealing large gaps between their front teeth, and heavy stubble covering their face and neck. They wore baseball caps, faded flannel shirts, and khaki pants—held up by a rope—that were many sizes too big for their slim bodies.

Noticing Eartha Mae dancing in her seat in rhythm to the music, Dickey leaned over and whispered, "Why don't ya git up there. You kin shake it like the best of 'em."

Bored and worn out from performing every night for months, Lola was intrigued when she noticed the interest the men had in Eartha Mae. Offering her center stage, she motioned to the drummer who played a long drum role. After refusing several times, she finally accepted the invitation. Certain that Eartha Mae would have something most unusual to offer, Hickey and Dickey jumped up to help her onto the platform.

Looking out at the men sitting before her, Eartha Mae wondered what she could give them. Holding the pole with one hand, she spun around and around. She tried several times to raise her leg against the pole like Lola, but could hardly keep her balance. The men grew impatient and groaned with disappointment. Lifting her leg a few inches off the ground, she pointed her toe, imagining that she was a ballerina. She could still recall some of the movements practiced in a ballet class that she watched through a window as a child. She tried forming a "V" with her heels together and toes pointed outwards. Then she touched the heel of her front foot, with the instep of her back foot. While attempting to spread her feet apart, and pull them back together—so that the heel of the front foot touched her toes—she lost her balance and nearly fell off the stage.

"Enough of that," screamed a regular.

"Give us a show we'll never forget. We know you can do it," another man shouted.

She stood before them, frozen, afraid, and uncertain about what to do, or how to move. She knew they were used to a kind of eroticism that she couldn't deliver. She couldn't rotate her hips like Lola, nor could she bend over like her, so that her head touched the floor. But she knew that she had other talents and gifts. After hesitating for a moment, she slowly opened the buttons of her dress, revealing row after row of breasts to an astonished crowd. Soon there were hoots and hollers coming from all directions. But more than showing them her breasts, she wanted to share a vision of what they meant about who she was. Holding a picture in her mind with the fullness of her intention, she attempted to project images to the men in the room. One person after another began to see more than Eartha Mae's body before them—they began to see in her the origins of all things. This story had so many themes and variations, but the way that she decided to tell it that night at Lola's was to show how her breasts became volcanic, spewing fire and smoke, creating mountains and canyons, hills and valleys. Then she showed how her large belly gave birth to the forests. From her vulva came the rivers and oceans. From her fingertips came small creatures. From her feet came the desert sands, the great plains, the grasslands of the Savannah. From her toes came all manner of large creatures. From her mouth came the howling winds and the soft summer breezes. Eartha Mae had become the life source from which all things flowed.

The men were stunned by these images and wondered how they were entering their minds. They didn't hear Lola when she announced it was closing time. They didn't notice when she flicked the lights on and off; they remained motionless in their seats. Finally

Lola went around the room shaking each one of them in an effort to clear out the club. Most were reluctant to leave. Others did not know whether to tip or not, since this was not the kind of striptease they were accustomed to. Some held out ten- twenty-, even fifty-dollar bills, which Virgil collected, while others rushed to help Eartha Mae off the stage. Though they were drawn to her, they were shy and intimidated at the same time.

The men slowly stumbled out of the club, scratching their heads in confusion, uncertain how to respond or what to say to each other. Eartha Mae, Virgil and Hickey and Dickey were the last to leave.

"What happened in there?" Virgil asked.

"I don't know exactly. I know I touched them…Guess you could say I spoke a kind of truth." Eartha Mae shook her head, amazed at the power she had tapped into. "Well, I know one thing…all that dancing's made me hungry."

"I can fix ya up some'in mighty fine. Our camp's jest down by the water. Won't be no trouble," Hickey said.

"We'd sure enjoy the comp'ny," added Dickey, as he limped along after them, leaning on a crutch for support.

Accepting their invitation, Eartha Mae and Virgil followed the brothers along an abandoned railroad track where many homeless people camped. Hickey and Dickey knew everyone's name, since they had often shared meals as well as life stories. They waved to a toothless man with a long black bushy beard who was lying beside a campfire, with his scraggly-haired girlfriend tucked in his arms.

"Evenin' Gov'nor," Hickey nodded.

"Care to join us?" the bearded vagrant asked.

"Can't right now. Gots me a catfish to cook fer my friends here." As they continued walking, he added, "Me 'n Dickey usta live unda' a bridge. It were jes a stone throw from Graceland. That was 'til we was run off. Usta see Elvis dere on 'casions. Only saw da fat Elvis though," said Hickey.

"I knew da skinny one. And oncest I saw him houndog," Dickey said gleefully. "Da King lives on! Yes siree bob, da king lives on!"

They settled into their little hideaway beneath a bridge. Hickey pulled out a cast-iron pan from a makeshift shelf, hidden by shrubs and tall grasses. "Ya know," said Hickey to Eartha Mae, "I kind'a likes campin' unda' dis ol' bridge…'n I loves listnin' to da water at night…'n countin' dem fallen stars. I been happy here. We always stays unda' bridges. We gets da best a both whirls." Putting a toothpick in his mouth, he threw a catfish and some shrimp on a grill that he set over the fire. "We likes to see Lola Fridays, but Mmm Mmm, tonight was some'in else. You was beau-tee-ful up dere. Won't never forget it."

Eartha Mae blushed, "Why thank you," she whispered. "I been blessed."

"You surely have," said Virgil.

"I seen things in you…things I never seen before," Dickey said. "Never know'd a lady like you…We's honored to share dis meal wid y'all." He reached for a whiskey bottle, hidden in a crack in a concrete post. "I always says dat a day wid'out whiskey, is like a day wid'out sunshine. Here's to you." He took a few sips, then held up the bottle, offering her a swig. "Care for a lil' sunshine? It'll make ya sing a song a cheer."

Eartha Mae shook her head.

Dickey laughed, "Guess you don't need none. You are sunshine! Sunshine 'n moonshine. You gots a glow 'bout you. A loomnescence." He started humming and soon he was singing in a very loud voice that echoed under the bridge. "Ya gotta keep da devil way down in da hole."

When Hickey smiled, his face became a delta of wrinkles. "Mmm. Mmm. I don't know what kings or queens eat, but dey oughta eat dis. I been livin' off da fish from dis here river all my life. Mmm. Mmm. Back in late summer, when da air is heavy and still, 'n da gulf water is warm, swarms of shrimp, crabs, ‘n deep-sea fish ‘peer in shallow water. We calls it jubilee, ‘cause we can scoop ‘em up by da bucketful.”

Dickey turned to him, “Yup...But it ain’t no jubilee for dem fish.”

Hickey shook his head, “Nope, not for dem. We used ta have crawfish every night. We'd pinch off da tail an eat da meat, 'n suck out da fat. Some of dems gots two or three tails.”

Eartha Mae looked troubled, “Three tails? How’s that?”

Hickey explained despairingly, “At’s cause we’s on cancer row. Sorry ta say, that cancer took Dickey's leg. Went down to da bone.” He shook his head sadly, then added in a cheerful voice, “Maybe he can't run none to well, but damned if Dickey's dick ain't got wings.”

Dickey looked down, “Yup...Seems ta have a mind of its own. Peoples in these here parts call me Winged Dickey.”

Hickey laughed, “I tel’ ya, keep it on a leash.”

Dickey shook his head, “It ain’t kind to cage God’s critters.”

Hickey stretched out his arm, “Pass me da holy water, will ya Dickey?”

Dickey was reluctant, “Maybe dat's why you's always seeing things, like dem three-tailed crawfish, ‘n two-headed crabs. Ya goes too heavy on da holy water.”

Hickey looked insulted, “What I sees’s real!”

Dickey poked him, “Tell em what you seen last week!”

Virgil perked up, “Yeah, tell us.”

Hickey was pleased to be asked this question and looked to the sky, re-experiencing a sense of wonder. “I seen a spaceship, hoverin’ over dis bridge. Must’a seen da campfire ‘n decided ta pay me a visit. Dey lowered a door an’ a little feller, say four-feet-high stepped out. His eyes was curious. Sad. Trusting, you could say. It give me dis eerie feelin’...but also I felt a kinda love. I think dey give me gifts, yup, dat’s what I bleav. Mental gifts. Dey open my mind ta seein’ things. Dey had messages to share.”

"Reckon you was chosen," Dickey said.

"You think?" said Hickey with a hopeful smile and tears in his eyes. "Or maybe it's like I chose ta see."

"Where was the creature from?" Eartha Mae asked.

"From the Pleiades, I reckon," Hickey responded.

"The Pleiades. I'd like to know that place." Eartha Mae said longingly.

"It's up there." Hickey pointed, "Dem stars in..."

When they looked up they noticed two policemen standing over them, shaking their heads. "We got reports that you been disturbing the peace," said the short and fat one, whose cheeks and neck were folded over like a Shar-Pei's. "No campin' under the bridge."

"Get us a home if you don't want us campin'," shouted Dickey.

"That's right. Something palatial'll do," Hickey laughed gleefully, then suddenly turned serious when the policeman gave him a look of disgust.

"If you don't move along, we'll haul you off to the county jail," said the tall and skinny policeman, with a face like a Pug.

"Don't mind if you do," Dickey timidly responded. "I needs a vacation."

"Look officer…soon as we finish dis here meal—we'll be on our way. Scout's honor," said Hickey.

The two policemen hesitated, then accepted his promise and walked on.

"I could send a little comet after them, one that'll dwarf all others and make the Leonids look like a fizzled firecracker," said Eartha Mae with a twinkle in her eye.

"That's kind of overreacting, don't you think?" moaned Virgil.

"I guess," she grumbled.

Dickey took a couple of gulps of whiskey and started in again, singing, "Ya got ta keep da devil way down in da hole." His voice became louder and louder, and soon the others joined in. They sang the same song into the early morning hours. Even Oakie could hear it in his sleep, on the other side of town.

Sitting up and stretching his arms, Oakie was pleasantly surprised at finding Chloe lying on the bed beside him, wearing her fuzzy bathrobe and furry rabbit slippers, holding a square in her hand for the patchwork quilt. He watched the gentle rise and fall of her breasts as she slept beside him on top of the quilt. Picking up his little tow-truck that had fallen on the floor next to the bed, he drove it over strips of white that lay between square patches on the quilt, imagining that they were the main streets through town. Then he drove the little truck around the outskirts of Chloe's body, starting at her shoulders, down alongside her arms and around the curve of her hand. Imitating the sound of an engine as it shifts into first gear, he guided the truck up her shoulder, which had become a range of mountains. From there, the truck headed down her chest, pausing at the opening in her bathrobe. Lifting the fabric, he peaked at her small breasts, then carefully drove the toy truck under her bathrobe and over her breasts.

Chloe opened one eye and looked at him.

He hung his head in embarrassment. "Are you mad at me?"

"Maybe. I'm not sure. Maybe not," she whispered with confusion as she closed her robe.

"I wish I had breasts like you."

"That's funny of you to want that."

"Guess I'm always thinking something stupid." He was ashamed and mumbled, "Everyone says I'm a dim-wit. Do you want me to go?"

Wanting to comfort him, Chloe held out the square for the patchwork quilt and showed him the embroidery. "It's the story of

Oakie. I worked on it all night. I was inspired. That's you steering the boat down the river. That's Eartha Mae on her throne."

He studied the details of fish in the water and fluffy clouds in the sky, then held it close to his chest. "It's the most beautiful thing I've ever seen."

"I would've finished it," she said, "but there was a strange creature at the window all night. It scared me a little. I didn't know what it was. It looked like a possum, but it didn't sound like one."

Oakie sat up in bed. "Where is it now?"

"It's still there," she said. "I can't get it to go away."

He looked out the window and saw a creature tapping on the glass with its paw, meowing in the particular way that only Boots meowed. "That's just got to be Boots. I thought he died in the river—he went up in a fireball. It's Boots! I know it is. I know it is," he shouted and jumped up and down. "He found his way back to me. He must've followed my scent. He does have a sixth sense and nine lives!" Opening the window, Oakie reached out for his cat and took him into his arms. He had no body hair, and his skin was covered with scabs and oozing sores, but he was alive. "Boots can live through anything. Did you know that I found him in a bird's nest, when he was a kitten. A raven kept him warm under her wings. Yup, that's where I found my wonder cat. But Virgil hates Boots. Says he's the devil in disguise."

"Oh that's certainly not true," said Chloe. "I bet he's an angel in disguise."

Tears filled his eyes as he looked at Chloe, "Well…that's nice that you know that about my cat...I like you."

In the morning, Virgil prepared the houseboat for their journey down the Mississippi, while Eartha Mae went to pay for her new dresses with the money she earned at Lola's. Oakie joined Eartha Mae at the counter, holding Boots in his arms, while Chloe folded the dresses and put them in a box. Boots was dressed in a new mantle and hat that Chloe had made for him.

Eartha Mae read the words, 'Boots the Fireball,' written on the back of the cape.

"Boots is no ordinary cat," said Chloe.

"Of course not," said Eartha Mae.

"He's heroic and majestic," said Chloe.

It meant so much to Oakie that Chloe appreciated his cat, and could see past the bloody sores that covered Boots's hairless body. She saw the magnificence in him that others could not. He knew he wanted her with him forever. At the same time, he did not want to abandon his journey with Eartha Mae until they had reached their destination. Without consulting Chloe, Oakie informed Eartha Mae that she would be coming with them, for the rest of the journey, and that would be that. Never having been so bold, he wondered if Eartha Mae would have a fit. To his surprise, Eartha Mae agreed.

"I'll need someone to help me into these fine new dresses," said Eartha Mae. "In fact, I'd like to put one on right now. I need to be who I really am—right now and forever more. It can't wait till tomorrow."

Chloe looked overwhelmed with joy at Oakie's display of affection. She was pleased to help Eartha Mae into the yellow dress that was decorated with lace around the neck and sleeves, with tiny red, blue and gold roses adorning the cups that held up her breasts. After adding a few finishing touches, she stood back to admire the new Magnificent Eartha Mae.

CHAPTER THIRTEEN

INMOST CAVE

Betina walked with Jane and Petie on a narrow dirt path through a forest of spruce, balsam, and pine trees. Petie ran ahead of them, his cheeks rosy from the cool crisp morning air, his head warmed by a hat Jane had crocheted depicting moose against jagged snow-covered mountains. He coaxed them to hurry after him, but engrossed in conversation, they continued walking at a leisurely pace. While shuffling through autumn leaves that carpeted their path, they listened to the yodeling call of a couple of loons in the distance, flying above the forest, toward Lake Itasca.

"The three of them camped out in this cave for weeks," said Jane. "Petie spent a great deal of time talking to Oakie McFokie or MacFarley, I can't remember for sure. He acted like a boy Petie's age. Maybe he's a little slow. The other fellow, Virgil, had a strong presence. He was always taking everything in, always alert. At the same time he kept apart...very solid, muscular physique, long black ponytail, part Asian. Maybe part American Indian. Eartha Mae was in a terrible depression. I think she'd been hearing voices."

Just as Betina was about to confess that she had also been hearing voices, Petie ran back to them and took Betina's hand, to hurry her along. Speaking in an excited tone, he told her that there were magical paintings on the cave wall that she had to see. He even said that he had fallen asleep in the cave, and had had very unusual dreams.

Petie led them to the foot of a cliff that had a cluster of boulders obscuring the entrance to the cave. They climbed around the rocks, crawled through a narrow crack and entered a central chamber.

Before them stood the quiet magnificence of the rock walls, illuminated by Petie's flashlight. Betina had the distinct impression that there were spinning fractal shapes in the handprints on the wall. She sensed a living presence.

"I can see why Eartha Mae called this her 'Cave of Voices and Dreams,'" Jane noted.

"Listen to this," said Petie, as he played his body like a drum. The sound that came back was like the galloping hooves of a herd of bison that were drawn on the walls above. "You've got to try it!"

Playing a rhythm on her thigh, Betina was intrigued to hear the echo of a dozen drums. It seemed that the sound was being reflected off the stones and was changed into another form in the process. She wondered if that was why Eartha Mae had chosen to sleep in this cave for so many weeks—perhaps she was connecting to a kind of memory field of coded dreams. After twenty minutes of exploration she told Jane she wanted to spend the night there to explore some of the smaller tunnels and to see what dreams would come. Petie and Jane left her alone with promises to place food and camping gear at the entrance to the tunnel, later that evening.

Slipping and sliding in the mud, Betina finally managed to reach a chamber at the end of a long tunnel. She sensed that it had been a sanctuary for thousands of years, where countless rituals had taken place. As she breathed in the clammy air, she studied her shadow on the cave wall. Switching off the flashlight, her eyes adjusted to total darkness. The silence was overwhelming and was soon interrupted by the reverberation of falling pebbles. Then there were sounds of water dripping, echoing throughout all the chambers and passageways. She thought she heard the chirping or clicking of a bat, but told herself she was imagining this, since these sounds are ultrasonic. Whatever the chirping was, it passed and was replaced by silence. Sitting in a quiet meditative state, she breathed in the cool dampness of the undulating earthen walls.

Feeling the familiar rush of wind, she became aware of a large group of women dancing and chanting. One woman played a small hourglass-shaped drum, another played a pair of cymbals, a third blew into a conch shell, while others played copper horns, tambourines, and trumpets. Betina had come to associate the spirit of Marletta with the voice that came from the ancient manuscript, but now she came to her from the deep recesses of the cave.

Taking her hand, Marletta said, "There, in the very heart of darkness, we reinvented ourselves."

Though she was dressed in a nun's habit, Betina sensed that it was a shield and disguise for the freedom, independence, and wildness within. Marletta joined the shadowy figures of barefoot, wild-haired drummers. The rhythms built to a fierce intensity and frenzied rhythm and soon the cavern became filled with dancers spinning through the air with great agility. Suddenly the music stopped and the dancers receded to the background.

Marletta turned to Betina, her eyes were gleaming with exhilaration from the dance and sweat glistened on her forehead. She motioned for her to dance. "It's your turn," she whispered.

Betina was embarrassed when all eyes turned on her, "I couldn't. I'm a spectator. I don't belong…I don't really know where I am or how I got here. I'm not a dancer."

"We are not dancers, this is not a dance, this is a prayer. There are no spectators here. You must live this," she insisted. "The drum will lead to remembering."

One of the drummers came forward and played a steady rhythm for Betina. Then a few more joined in, inviting her to begin.

Betina was mortified by their expectation, but she couldn't find a way to extricate herself from this situation. They would not let her hide in the safety of observation, nor would they let go of their request for her participation. Closing her eyes to block out the gaze of those who stood before her, she breathed in the precise rhythms of the drum pulse until it flowed in her blood and led her into a trance. The rhythm of the drum merged with her heartbeat. Her hands began moving with a symbolic sign language that opened her heart to the profound energies around her. Then her feet remembered a pattern of movements. A tall woman, wearing a tiara of feathers and bones intertwined with crystals, stepped forward, singing to the drumbeat. Other women joined in as a chorus.

In this dance, Betina's body became a fluid waveform; she weaved through the crowd like a stream. Moving past women in veils, feathers, masks, and animal horns, she noticed that she too was dressed in a similar fashion. She was releasing everything that had been pent up within her—her rage at Humbert; the struggles with her father; the sadness at her compromised relationship with her mother; her frustration with Andrew. She wanted to abandon old dramas, and dismember her old self to make way for the new. In this moment of frenzied release she knew that her true nature was not a collection of stories, events, and emotions—it was the still point at the center of it all.

She ended her dance by returning to the purity and tranquility of the fetal position. Moments later she found herself waking alone, reborn, in the healing womb of the Earth Mother.

As Betina made her way through the woods back to Jane's house, she thought about how easily she had entered a portal into a parallel world and how quickly it had closed its doors to her. She joined Jane by the fireplace in the living room and noticed that her hands had settled into a mudra of alignment—one of the hand positions that she held during her initiation dance. The cave was indeed a powerful vortex, she thought. It was a place for dreaming, just like the caves in Ephesus and Malta. She knew that the ancient mystery ritual that she had just experienced had been dreamed and danced close to the earth in secret, through all the ages.

Jane was interested in hearing about her experiences but also eager to tell Betina about a short article that appeared in a section of the local newspaper called *Weird But True*. "It's about a hunger strike at a psychiatric institution in Louisiana." After reflecting for a moment Jane said, "You know, I've heard about Ravenford Psychiatric State Hospital. Several years ago, there were reports of patients being abused. A documentary filmmaker went into Ravenford with a hidden camera and filmed some shocking material, showing drug experimentation and patient abuse. The footage was later lost—probably stolen—and the reporter mysteriously disappeared. Without the footage, there was not enough evidence to continue to investigate the practices of the Director of the hospital... Dr. Rex Hoagland."

"Yes, I've heard a number of tales about the crimes committed in some of these institutions," Betina replied. "One of Andrew's colleagues talked to us about the massive doses of electroconvulsive therapy he received for depression. When we visited him in the hospital, he couldn't even remember that he had received a Nobel Peace Prize in Physics."

"The problem is, so few people believe the stories that these patients tell. They're simply labeled insane. Some of the techniques in the twenty-first century are about as beneficial as lobotomies were in the mid 1900's." Jane said.

"Or the rack and the thumbscrew, used in the inquisition to reform the heretics. But what about the article?" Betina asked.

"Well this is the first bit of news I've seen in a few years about Ravenford. It seems they removed a painting because it was having a very unusual affect on the patients." Jane began reading, "According to a witness who chooses to remain anonymous, patients were so deeply affected by this painting that they got up to dance after being in catatonic states for years." She looked up from the article and said, "The thing that is so intriguing is that the sixteen-year-old girl who painted it, has the name Evangeline. Somehow, someone managed to take a photo. The image in the painting looks like Eartha Mae, who spoke of having a child by that name. I wonder if this could be her daughter?"

Betina carefully read the article and studied the photo of Evangeline who stood next to her painting. Although the reproduction of the painting was grainy, and in black and white, it reminded her of the fresco in the Bosnian church, of the Great Mother, whose image emerged on special occasions from underneath the superimposed portrait of the Madonna. So many isolated pieces—visions and voices in caves, living frescos, an enigmatic manuscript, a mysterious painting. Betina wondered if somehow these fragments fit together into one cohesive picture.

CHAPTER FOURTEEN

EVANGELINE'S ESCAPE

As Betina set out early in the morning for Louisiana, to find Evangeline, she thought about the fragmented and nebulous nature of the story she was trying to piece together. How could she have expected a grant for such an ephemeral puzzle? She thought of the researcher who was awarded several hefty grants to search for Noah's Ark. He had found other famous sunken ships and knew ancient trade routes. His proposal clearly laid out what he was searching for, while the object of her quest—which she had tentatively defined as an exploration of the living phenomenon of divine feminine emergence—could only be discovered in the journey itself. The direction of her journey had no map but was based more on intuition and chance encounters.

She hit a traffic jam, just a short distance from the psychiatric institution in Louisiana, where Evangeline was confined. Realizing that she hadn't spoken to her mother in quite a while, Betina took out her cell phone and placed a call to St. Mary's Home for the Aged, in Quebec. Lately, it was rarely beneficial for them to talk by phone, since Frances had lost the ability to connect a voice to a living person. This time Frances was lucid and recognized Betina without any problem.

"Where are you?" Frances asked. "You spend too much time with the natives and not enough time on your schoolwork. You have no idea how you upset your father with endless stories about talking trees and animal spirits."

Betina was taken aback when she realized that her mother was talking to her as if she was a teenager and still living in Kenya—she didn't have a chance to say that her father had been dead for more than a decade.

"I want you to come home and start packing. Your Grandmother isn't well, and we are meeting her in France."

Betina understood that Frances was talking about the year that they went to Lourdes with her Grandmother, who was nearly crippled. Only sixteen at the time, Betina recalled the confusion she felt when her Grandmother insisted that the healing waters had cured her—she said that even her silver medallion of the Virgin had turned to gold. Leaving her walker in a room filled with wheelchairs, crutches and canes, her Grandmother flew back to Quebec, healed of arthritis. Betina and Frances returned to Kenya, overloaded with bottles of healing water stuffed into their suitcases.

Although Betina believed and disbelieved at the same time, she drank the healing water whenever she felt troubled or confused. Her mother, however, was finding greater solace from afternoon and evening glasses of sherry than from the blessed water. It was clear that Frances was unhappy with her husband, Theodore. He wanted to take a hiatus from medicine and spend his time spreading 'the word' throughout the Eastern Mediterranean region. Even though Frances had no interest in moving away from her friends and their beautiful Kenyan home, she didn't think it was her place to challenge Theodore's desires.

Not eager to travel with them, Betina begged her mother and father to let her spend the year living with her grandmother. Theodore resisted his daughter's request because he was not fond of her grandmother's liberalism. Nevertheless, Betina managed to persuade him, and she moved to Quebec at sixteen, while her parents traveled through Lebanon, Syria, and Cyprus.

In Quebec, Betina began to associate Theodore's dominance in the family with his faith that celebrated a trinity that had a Father, Son, and Holy Ghost, but no mother, daughter, or feminine spirit. She never felt like she belonged in his world since she could not embrace his religion. She had read the *Gnostic Gospels*, discovered at Nag Hammadi in Egypt, and knew that Jesus had a wife, Mary Magdalene, and maybe even a child. This heretical perspective only enraged Theodore who was not about to add the feminine element to his masculine paradigm.

The year she spent living with her Grandparents had moments of magic. Betina and her Grandmother spoke mostly French on their mini-vacations around the Gaspe' Peninsula. They spent hours studying gannets through binoculars as they roosted on the cliffs of their island sanctuary. They also shared a spirit of wonder as they watched humpback whales gracefully moving through the ocean waters. On weekends they drove to Montreal for major Catholic holidays where they prayed to the gentle Virgin, in the majestic neo-gothic Basilique Notre Dame. Betina wondered if her grandmother's faith in Mary was a quiet rebellion against the male trinity.

She even persuaded her Grandmother to participate in pagan rituals that were held in the Canadian woods, during the full moon. She joined in on the freeform dancing, wearing long flowing dresses and scarves, moving with an abandon that Betina never imagined she possessed. Curiously, her Grandmother never mentioned any conflict with her own faith when they celebrated the beauty of nature in pagan rituals. She was at home celebrating both the serenity and comfort offered to her by the Virgin as well as the abandon and creativity that she found in the earth-centered rituals.

Though her matrilineal Grandmother had lived for many generations in Quebec, her Grandfather was from Scotland. He moved to Canada after meeting her Grandmother in Inverness, while she was touring the British Isles. Following a lengthy correspondence, he traveled to Quebec to marry her, settling down in the city that she had lived in all her life. After spending a lifetime as a fisherman, he devoted himself to gardening in his final years. He used to sit for hours near a little fountain of the goat-legged god Pan that stood in the center of his garden. Sometimes he played his bagpipes, other times he would sing the legends of his homeland. Betina noticed that in all his songs the clans were always defending themselves against someone. If they weren't fighting amongst themselves, they were fighting invaders like the Vikings, the Romans and the English.

He said that the plants in his garden loved to hear tales of his ancestors, who lived in Scotland's western highlands. He sang of warrior kings who lived by the sword, bravely facing the inevitability of war. He said that the flowers would lean toward him when he sang, since the musical tones had the power to soothe these sentient beings. The flowers that bloomed around him were large and lush. Their perfumes were more fragrant and their colors more radiant than those in the back of the house. The vegetables that grew along the side of the courtyard were exceedingly large and succulent. He believed that the magic of the music also touched them.

All the secrets he told her about the sensitive nature of flowers and vegetables transformed the way she regarded plants. Still, she always wanted to know how the flowers in the garden could flourish while being serenaded with such heart-breaking stories of young women, who would never see their beloved husbands again—their days of happiness together so short lived. She wondered if the sadness that was a constant and inevitable part of her grandfather's life, had taken away the gaiety that may have been the inherent nature of the flowers, or perhaps they just absorbed the music and were oblivious to the underlying message of loss and tragedy.

She stopped at a roadside café and sat down at the counter. As she ate the lunch special, she heard a television report of a devastating attack on a small Middle-Eastern village. The attackers were comprised mostly of young men and boys: some of them younger than twelve years old—many of them orphans. These boys had discovered a major underground network of tunnels, a hiding place for opposing forces. This was a promising victory for them and they set their flags on top of the highest mound in the region. The young boy who led the others said that he had received a message from above telling him to crush these infidels. The broadcaster explained that his victory was short lived, because moments later, he met his fate at the hands of a sniper bullet. The boy was now considered a martyr and was carried off by a few of the children, while the others sank into despair at the hope that had died with him. A waitress, finding the subject matter too heavy, turned to a station that had mindless repartee between co-hosts of a talk show, so Betina could not find out whether the attack had taken place in Iraq, Palestine, Syria or some other Middle-Eastern country. She said to herself that it didn't really matter which country it was—the world was beginning to look all the same—children everywhere were being indoctrinated to fight wars they didn't even understand.

She couldn't help but reflect on Samir, Vesna, and Zoran, and the other teenagers that she met in Bosnia. She thought of all the young victims of war: children who were taken by force into military service after seeing their mother or father butchered before their eyes; eight-year-old boys forced to kill using AK47s or rocket-propelled grenades. There were children in Somalia, Rwanda, Angola, Sierra Leone, Congo, Sudan, Sri Lanka, Afghanistan, and Burma, who had been used, abused, lied to, manipulated, traumatized, and ultimately discarded. And what was she doing in response to this world crisis, she asked herself. She was doing nothing more than hiding out in the comfort and irrelevance of the ruins of ancient civilizations, shielding herself from the ever-rising voice of despair. Secretly, she hoped that in coming face-to-face with Evangeline she would have the opportunity of finally doing something—for one child at the very least.

As she stood in line to pay for her meal, she noticed that the front cover of a tabloid had a feature story, by Ewald Johnston, with the title, *The Return of One Great Mama*. After suggesting that Mama was probably the product of a bestial union between man and cow, the writer asserted that she would be a perfect candidate for Ripley's *Believe It or Not*. Betina was stunned by the article and after purchasing the magazine, she ran to her car to compare the photo of Eartha Mae with the painting of her by Evangeline, that appeared in the newspaper article that Jane had brought to her attention. The similarity was undeniable. She was overwhelmed at how these synchronicities confirmed that she was rapidly connecting the dots of a story she was meant to know.

As Betina walked through the gate of the psychiatric institution, she thought of the emotional ups-and-downs of her sixteenth year—of the freedom she felt being away from her parents, of her longing to be in love, and of her fears that she was unlovable. When she entered the main lobby, she wondered if she would see anything of herself in sixteen-year-old Evangeline. She looked up at a statue of a serene-looking Virgin, then made her way to the front office where a nurse was carefully filing papers. "Can you direct me to Dr. Hoagland's office?" she asked. "I have some very important information for him."

Betina was surprised that the nurse didn't insist that she make an appointment. Instead she absent-mindedly pointed to an office at the end of a long corridor, then went back to her filing. Walking down the corridor, Betina was struck by the dismal atmosphere and wondered if the rumors of patient abuse could be true.

Dr. Rex Hoagland was staring out the window when she knocked on his door, which was halfway open. She knocked a second time and then a third, but he didn't seem to hear her. Finally she stuck her head in and asked, "Are you Dr. Hoagland?"

He looked startled, then nodded.

"My name is Betina Sharp. I've come to talk to you about the young girl who made the painting…Evangeline. I have some information about her mother that I'd like to share with her."

"Do you know her mother?"

"Not exactly…But I believe she was staying on my friend's land…Camping out, you could say."

"Is that where she is now?"

"Well I don't know where she is at this very moment. She was last seen in a boat—going down the Mississippi—and it seems there was a recent sighting of her in Memphis. I'd like to talk to Evangeline about this."

"Evangeline is a very disturbed young woman. She can't receive any visitors…it would upset her fragile state. You look intelligent enough to realize that it's against our policy to let strangers visit our patients…in fact, I really can't talk to you without an appointment. We have a new nurse, filling in today. She should've made that clear to you."

"The news I have about her mother...that would mean very much to her, I'm sure...I want to be of help."

"Let me get this straight. You haven't met the woman that you claim is her mother, and even if she was, you don't know where she is now." He paused to look her over, then continued. "Raising her hopes but having no solid information is not a help to her. I really can't discuss her case any further with you. It's strictly confidential. I have a meeting in a few minutes."

"I've read a newspaper report on the incident that took place here. I know about the painting. Have you considered that she may be experiencing a mystical state?"

"She is unable to function. She is crippled by obsessive delusions about her mother and about many other things. I'll be the one to determine her diagnosis, if you don't mind."

They argued back and forth about the difference between delusion and vision and finally Betina said, "Institutions make people sick. They put people in boxes...they label them borderline, split personalities, bi-polar, schizophrenic. The box becomes a coffin and the individual who stands before you can no longer be seen."

Dr. Hoagland raised his voice with growing impatience. "Evangeline is psychotic. She cannot differentiate fantasy from reality. She has hallucinations, she hears voices, she has delusions of grandeur. She can also be aggressive and violent.

"You took away her painting! Did you expect her to remain complacent?"

"In her extreme loneliness, she creates a world of her own...she is possessed by delusions."

"Think of all the people who have seen Marian apparitions. Are they deluded? Should they be institutionalized?"

"This has nothing to do with Evangeline."

"Evangeline had a vision of a Mother that touched all those around her. Maybe she's seeing more than her own mother, she's seeing..." Betina fumbled for words. She held back, fearing she would further alienate Dr. Hoagland if she said what she really thought. She began again, "Are you certain she is mentally ill rather than visionary? Maybe it's just that you don't like what she sees." She paused, hoping he would respond, but he remained silent. "When will you release her?"

"When she earns our faith that she can function in the world beyond this institution. Right now, she abuses every privilege that has been extended to her. The last time she was given the privilege of walking around the grounds unescorted, I found her sitting in a puddle of water, covering her face and body with mud."

Betina thought of an old movie about Bernadette, and remembered a scene where she was washing her face with the earth at the place where the healing waters of Lourdes would soon flow. She was certain that Evangeline had an equally powerful reason for covering herself in mud, and suspected that it was an intimate expression of union with the earth. But just as she was about to respond, Dr. Hoagland cut her off:

"Enough. I will not continue this discussion. You must leave now," he said, as he escorted her down the hallway toward the main lobby.

Standing by the door, she asked, "Why does her painting threaten you?"

He sighed, "End. Of. Discussion. Period." He held open the door to the main entrance of the institution and motioned for her to walk through.

He sounded just like Humbert, she thought. She took a step toward the door, then stopped and said, "These dreary walls...medication that numbs the minds and affects it in unpredictable and dangerous ways...These things don't heal. But you are suspicious of a painting?"

"I want you out of here immediately," he shouted. "This is a private hospital. You have no business interfering with our business. It's against hospital policy. I've given you enough of my time and will order security to remove you from the premises if you do not leave at once."

Running her hands along the cement walls, she walked toward her car, then stopped and looked back at the doctor. She was surprised at how she confronted him since she knew she had no right demanding to see a patient that she didn't know. Maybe if she hadn't been so aggressive, she would have had her way. Perhaps she should've been gentler. After examining their conversation from a dozen angles, she called it quits. She watched as Dr. Hoagland disappeared into the building, then she slipped through a side door. As she made her way down the hall, an old woman crossed her path and flagged down a nurse who was delivering medication to patients.

"My son won't speak. He won't eat. You have to do something," cried Ethan's mother, Celestina.

"Then he'll have to be force fed," said the nurse.

Celestina was aghast, "For heaven's sake, put the painting back! I was there, I saw my son dancing for the first time in years. That painting brought him back to life."

"That's not for me to decide," the nurse responded.

Celestina wiped away the tears that fell from her eyes. "Don't you care about my boy?"

"We are doing everything possible for him," said the nurse.

Betina approached Celestina, after the nurse got on an elevator with her cart filled with pills and needles. Celestina trusted Betina and explained that she wanted to have her son released from the hospital, but didn't have the legal right to do so, since he had tried several times to commit suicide. "Before he was an intelligent man, in great pain. Now he feels nothing. He hardly even speaks. He just drools and shakes. The only time there was any improvement was when he was in the presence of Evangeline's painting."

"That's why I'm here. To see Evangline. I saw the painting in the newspaper," Betina explained.

"I took that picture. I want the world to know what's happening here. They don't know that I was the one to contact the papers, or else they'd never let me back in here to see Ethan," Celestina explained.

"Do you know where Evangeline is now?" Betina asked.

"They put her in isolation after the incident with the painting. I tried many times to look in on her, but I couldn't get past the orderlies." Celestina wiped away more tears that fell from her eyes. "Now she's in her room, but I haven't been able to visit her."

"And where would that room be?" Betina asked in a calm manner, containing her sense of urgency.

Celestina quickly explained that it was in the east wing. She suggested a set of stairs that no one ever used, so that she would not run into any doctors, nurses, staff members, or guards. She also suggested that she hurry, since the nurses would be medicating people in that wing of the hospital, within the hour. Following Celestina's excellent directions, Betina reached Evangeline's room with no interference from the hospital staff, and tapped on her door. Where there was no response, she turned the knob and let herself in.

Evangeline was sitting in a corner of her room, holding a beautiful red rose that Vlad stole from a bouquet given to one of the nurses on her birthday. She was living inside the rose, brushing against the rich velvet petals, breathing in the heavenly fragrance, luxuriating in the rich crimson tones that swirled around her. She had a peaceful expression on her face, when she looked up at Betina.

"I'm sorry to barge in. I didn't want to be discovered in the hallway. I'd like to talk to you," Betina whispered.

Evangeline nodded.

Closing the door behind her, Betina approached Evangeline. She was surprised at Evangeline's calm demeanor. She even had a radiance about her. "I read about the painting you made. I was very moved by the story. I guess that's why I've come here to see you."

Evangeline looked surprised but said nothing.

Betina had so many questions that she didn't know which one to ask first. Finally she said, "How do you feel about being here? How do you feel about your doctor?"

Evangeline sighed.

"How was it that you were admitted into this institution?"

Evangeline cleared her throat, then said, "My father brought me here. He said I was crazy."

"Did they perform tests on you?" Betina asked.

Evangeline nodded. "The tests confirmed that I'm crazy."

Evangeline looked at Betina for the first time, as if she was trying to get a sense of who she might be. "I don't usually like to be asked so many questions… but there's something about you that makes me not mind so much…I refused to go to my father's underground shelter...so he brought me here."

"Where did the image for your painting come from?" Betina asked.

"Dr. Hoagland says it's my delusion." Evangeline slumped against the window. When she looked out at the lawn, she saw a boy climbing over a stonewall, sneaking into the grounds of the institution. Her face lit up when she saw two smaller boys follow after him. "Christian, Tex and Raider…they've come for me."

The boys approached an old door that led to a rarely used back entrance of the institution. Christian and Raider tried to kick it open, while Tex examined a small window with a shattered pane of glass. He ripped out a rusty mesh screen, broke off jagged pieces of glass that remained in the window frame, and motioned for Christian and Raider to join him by the window.

"Maybe you can climb in," Christian suggested. "You're small enough."

Tex twisted and turned as he squeezed through the tiny window then fell headfirst into a pile of dirty sheets in the laundry room. After rubbing his head, he managed to get up and unlock the door so that Christian and Raider could get in. They raced out of the laundry room, down a corridor that took them to the cafeteria. Tex came close to blowing their cover when they tried to sneak past the food-service staff as they prepared dinner. The head cook looked around when he heard Tex's heavy footsteps.

"You and those damn boots," Christian whispered, as they quickly hid behind a curtain. "Can you take them off just this once?"

Tex hated to be without his boots, since he couldn't bare being two inches shorter, but he acquiesced since it was impossible to move quietly with them on. They slipped past nurses tending to catatonic patients strapped in wheelchairs, and ran past locked doors of patients confined to padded cells.

They looked everywhere for Evangeline and circled through the corridors a second and third time. Finally they sat on a bench confessing to one another that they didn't know if they would ever be able to find her. But as they watched the patients in their hospital rooms—across the courtyard, in the east wing—Christian was certain that he spotted Evangeline standing by her window before drawing her curtains shut.

The three boys immediately headed down the corridor and tried the doors to several rooms until they reached Evangeline's room. They slowly opened her door and had no trouble recognizing her though she looked terribly thin. She still had the same remarkable lavender eyes with the dark ring around the outer edges of the iris, and a sweet and gentle demeanor. Most surprising was a luminous quality that she radiated.

Christian lifted her in the air and said, "We didn't know where you were or else we would've come sooner. I read about you...and the painting. It was in the papers."

Betina was impressed when she discovered that she wasn't the only one that paid attention to the article.

Eyeing Betina suspiciously, Tex asked, "Who is she? What is she doing here?"

"She's okay," said Evangeline.

"We hitched all morning to get here," Tex explained.

Evangeline wrapped an arm around Raider, who quickly suppressed a surge of tears and remained stiff as she pulled him close. She took Tex in her other arm, like a young mother who had been reunited with her children. Betina watched with intrigue as Evangeline comforted them like Wendy with Peter Pan and her coterie of lost boys.

While Tex and Raider studied every move that Betina made, Christian discussed a strategy with Betina for Evangeline's escape.

"You with us then?" Christian asked.

Betina nodded, amazed at herself for agreeing to be part of Christian's scheme.

Then she left the room and approached a guard in the hospital corridor. "I've just had an appointment with Dr. Hoagland and am all turned around. How do I get out of here and how can I get on the interstate going south?" She had the guard repeat the directions several times in order to distract him so that Evangeline and Raider could slip through a door behind him.

Christian and Tex had another mission to tend to; that was to find the painting. Evangeline had told them that the orderlies took it to the storage room in the basement, but she didn't know where in the room they might have placed it. Having no trouble finding the stairs to the basement, Christian and Tex were relieved to find that the door to the storage room was open. Finding the painting was another story, since the room seemed as large as a baseball field. After spending more than an hour, searching each row, they finally noticed an unusual light that came from a particularly dark corner. It turned different colors and was shining through the sheets; they knew immediately that it was Evangeline's painting.

No one noticed as they slipped out the back entrance of the hospital with the painting. After running down several streets with the painting, wrapped in sheets, they became uncertain of their direction. Leaving the painting against a wall for a moment, Tex checked one street, while Christian scanned another: Betina and Evangeline were nowhere in sight.

A fawn-colored man, short but muscular, happened to come up the alley, attracted to the luminous glow that came from the painting. Lifting the sheet, he looked with intensity at the image of Eartha Mae. Moments before Christian and Tex returned for the painting, he grabbed it and ran off. Christian and Tex screamed and shouted and ran after him, but he was too fast for them. When Betina pulled up in her car with Evangeline and Raider in the front seat, Christian and Tex jumped into the back.

"He ran off like a wild cat. He even had a face like a cat…with whisker tattoos," said Tex as he drew invisible lines around his mouth that ran to his earlobes. "He wasn't wearing a shirt, just shorts, and had spots like a leopard. He also had a heavy silver chain around his neck…looked like an Indian," Christian added.

"We can find him, I'm sure of it," Evangeline insisted. Betina tore off after the thief and caught sight of him in the distance. Christian yelled at him to stop, but that only made him run off at a faster clip. By the time they reached an overpass, he had disappeared. Though they searched the streets, he was nowhere to be found.

Turning to Betina in dismay, Evangeline said, "I wish you could've seen the painting."

"I saw a photo of it," she offered.

"That's not the same thing. It was living. Maybe you could've explained it to me, the power it had. How it was that I created it when I've never really painted anything before. Everyone felt the magic." She closed her eyes and whispered, "I have to have it back. I need it with me."

"We'll get it back...somehow." Betina was surprised by her own certainty. She was also intrigued by the man who stole it. He seemed so out of place and out of time. Where had he come from and why did he want the painting?

"He stole your dream," Christian sighed.

"You'd think he'd have a dream of his own, and wouldn't need ta be stealing someone else's," Tex angrily inserted.

"Maybe we have the same dream," Evangeline offered.

PART THREE

CHAPTER FIFTEEN

LITTLE FLICKER OF LIGHT

Evangeline, Christian, Tex, Raider, and Betina made their way through the French Quarter of New Orleans to Maw-Maw's voodoo shop, which was on a quiet street off the main thoroughfare. The name of the shop, 'Congo Square,' was written on a wooden placard, suspended by chains, and illuminated by the dim light of an antique street lamp. A gust of wind blew the last remaining fall leaves and the placard creaked as it swung back and forth, hitting the wall of Maw-Maw's storefront.

"Maw-Maw's not really related to Salome," Evangeline explained to Betina. "After I was put away, she looked after her. Maw-Maw knew Salome's mother before she died."

Christian knocked at Maw-Maw's hundred-year-old thick wooden door, intricately engraved with an ornamental design. He knocked louder and louder while Tex and Raider banged along with him, but still there was no answer. "She doesn't hear too well," said Christian. "And her apartment is in the back of the shop."

Just as they were about to give up, Maw-Maw opened the door a crack. She held her hands to her heart when she saw Evangeline and the others. After unhitching several chain locks, she opened the door all the way and took Evangeline into her arms. "Evangeline, you've returned to us!" Maw-Maw said. Then she gave a warm welcome to Christian, Tex and Raider.

Tex stepped forward to introduce Betina, "She helped with the rescue. She drove the getaway car," he said proudly.

"I guess that's one way of putting it," Betina smiled with a strange sense of pride mixed with confusion as she considered the role she had played in Evangeline's escape.

"Thank you for all you did," Maw-Maw said to Betina then turned to Evangeline. "When Salome heard that you were locked up, she made Christian go after you. Having you back is sure to be the best medicine for her."

Celebrating her Nigerian heritage, Maw-Maw wore an ankle-length skirt made of a colorful batik-print with a matching turban. She was buxom and full-bodied, and her warm-hearted smile made her eyes sparkle. She often wore little African bells that tinkled when she walked and she always smelled of patchouli. Around her neck she wore intricate Yoruban relics that had been passed down to her from her grandmother and great aunts.

The small group followed Maw-Maw into the house. The rich scents of ginger and cardamom, cinnamon and cloves permeated the long hallway. Betina took a quick glimpse at the sepia photos on the wall, depicting Maw-Maw's relatives and friends. Each room that they passed was warm and inviting, and furnished in an ornate style.

At the end of the hall was the most sensuous room of all: the bedroom. It had an antique bureau at one end, covered by an embroidered shawl with fringe that hung down to the floor. Next to it stood a dressing table with shelves filled with elegant perfume bottles and heart ornaments, and a box of lipsticks and hairbrushes. An elaborate lamp rested on the table, with a sculpture of a winged Cupid taking aim at a young girl, ready to pierce her with an arrow that would implant in her an irrepressible longing for love. The walls were decorated with copies of Pre-Raphaelite paintings that somehow complimented the Nigerian folk art that was displayed on a shelf above the bureau. There was even a statue of a stone angel, who offered protection to those sleeping in the soft and luxurious bed.

All six of them stood in the doorway and looked down at Salome, who was holding a necklace in her hand as she lay in a deep sleep, in this nest of enchantment that Maw-Maw had so lovingly created. Maw-Maw sat down and whispered in Salome's ear, but she did not wake up.

"We were working all afternoon, making this necklace," said Maw-Maw as she stroked Salome's cheek, brushing aside a couple of thin braids that fell in front of her eyes. "I guess it made her tired." Maw-Maw took the beautifully crafted necklace from Salome's hand and gave it to Betina so that she could look at it closely. "I stuffed it with herbs and incense. I only work on it on Fridays—to get help from the Venus powers." Pointing to the objects sewn inside the silk band of the necklace, Maw-Maw explained that "Lavender's for purification. Patchouli's for true love. The color of the silk is purple—for Salome's awakening." Then she pointed to a finely woven straw basket holding dozens of tiny objects. "Salome chose the charms for the talisman. She laid them in order so that I could string them together. That's how you harness their energy. It's in the binding."

Betina admired the assortment of objects in the basket and picked up several crystals, shells, and gemstones, to look at them more closely.

"This is a gift of my love. I pray for Salome in every stitch." Maw-Maw pointed to a few of the pieces in the necklace. "This is rose quartz, it's a lovestone. Imperial topaz is for warmth and abundance. Fossilized wood holds the mysterious spirit of the sacred forest. All the pieces have meaning and power." Maw-Maw kissed the necklace and placed it back in Salome's hand. "Return to us now. Wake up, Salome…remover of veils between worlds. Return to this world."

Maw-Maw had touched on a truth that sent a shudder through Salome's body. Salome's eyelids began to flutter and finally she opened her eyes. A faint smile appeared on her face when she saw Evangeline looking down at her. After kissing her forehead, Evangeline sat down on the bed beside her. Christian sat on the other side of the bed, taking her hand in his.

Salome slipped in and out of consciousness as she spoke to Evangeline. "What have I been to you? What will you say about me?"

"Say about you? When?" After thinking for a few moments, Evangeline responded, "I'll say that you have been...that you are my greatest friend. You are loyal. Kind. Good. The best friend anyone could ever have, the kind to give your life for."

Christian nervously pulled out a cigarette and lit it. When he put the matches on a bedside table, Salome reached for them.

Maw-Maw gave Christian a stern look and whispered to him, "How could you smoke in here?"

"Let him. What does it matter now?" Salome whispered as she lit a match, studied the flame and then blew it out. "That's all that I am—a little flicker of light. Soon to be extinguished."

While Evangeline continued to talk to Salome, Betina accompanied Maw-Maw to the kitchen. As Maw-Maw prepared a pot of tea, Betina studied a curious display on a shelf in the hallway, soon realizing it was a little altar. There was a small oil painting of a young woman with big hoop earrings, wearing a long skirt that accentuated a narrow waist, and long sleeves that puffed at the shoulders. She was dancing in the bayou with a group of men and women in the background.

"That's my beautiful Momi. She's dead, but never gone. She lives on, in the grasses of the bayou. In the cry of the blue heron. She used to do the *Fe Chauffe* dance, out near Lake Pontchartrain. Mam'zelle Marie was there....Those were great times. There was feasting. Gumbo. Jambalaya. Momi taught me everything I know about charms."

Betina looked at a clay pot containing different colored earth, and there were small bones in a little wooden box, next to a potpourri. On the wall above the altar were photographs of other relatives and of Salome when she was a child.

"That's my shrine to the ancestors. We call them *egun* in Yoruba. They are the souls that have moved beyond the body. Every day I ask for their guidance in helping my Salome." She poured a cup of tea for Betina and put a few biscuits on a plate. "My medicines have not been effective. She resists them," Maw-Maw said sadly. When Betina finished her tea, Maw-Maw carefully studied the arrangement of tea leaves in her cup. "Have you been traveling for a long time?"

"Well, yes."

"In the East?"

"I was just in Malta, Turkey, Bosnia and Greece."

"Wandering. Searching for things?"

"Perhaps you could say that."

"I see the disappointments of your past…but I also see that you will experience miracles in the future. You will enjoy them, but you must not try to convince others of their reality. The one who has the vision has beauty, splendors, and glory in this life. That is something no one can take away."

Betina listened carefully, sensing that there was truth in what she said. Maw-Maw took the teacup to the sink and washed away the tea leaves. Then she quickly pulled together elements she needed to make a special candle to aide Salome in her recovery.

"Tomorrow, I am going to pray at the sacred tomb of Mam'zelle Le Veau," Maw-Maw explained. "Perhaps you'd like to join me."

Betina had come across stories about Marie Le Veau, while writing a paper on secret spiritual movements in the United States. Knowing that her name was synonymous with voodooism in New Orleans, she wanted to learn more about this mysterious woman.

Betina and Evangeline met Maw-Maw at the cemetery the next morning. Maw-Maw wore a white robe over a white dress and a white headdress. Knocking three times with her left hand at the gate of cemetery number one, Maw-Maw said, "St. Peter, St. Peter, please let us in." After a moment she said, "St. Peter says to come in."

They crossed the threshold into the cemetery, turned left, then right, to Marie Le Veau's tomb number three. Maw-Maw placed flowers at her grave and spoke in a reverent tone, "We have come to ask that you help young Salome who's been suffering for so many long months." Maw-Maw walked around the tomb and Evangeline and Betina followed. Extending her arms toward the sky and down to the earth, Maw-Maw pressed her forehead on the front of the tomb. She placed seven silver dimes in the basket attached to the front, then picked up a piece of red brick that lay on the ground, making an 'X' on the tomb. Evangeline also made an 'X' next to hers.

Maw-Maw nodded her head. "Thank you Mam'zelle."

Evangeline whispered, "Thank you."

Maw-Maw took the candle out of her purse that she made the night before. She said a prayer as she lit it then placed it on the tomb. Closing her eyes and focusing her thoughts, Maw-Maw said, "Mam'zelle is speaking. She tells me that although I pray for the life of Salome, she also receives prayers from Salome asking to be taken from this earth." Maw-Maw was quiet for a moment then said, "Our efforts are in vain if Salome has no will to live."

None of them said a word as they solemnly filed out of the cemetery and got into Betina's car. They wondered how they could incite in Salome a will to live. The long period of silence was finally broken when Evangeline stunned them with a request to take a short detour and stop at her father's house.

"I want to see him," she said.

"After what he did to you," Maw-Maw asked in a startled tone.

"He had you committed, didn't he?" Betina asked, equally shocked by her request.

"Well yes…but I'm concerned about him," she replied.

"You're concerned about him," Maw-Maw repeated, turning to Betina with an incredulous expression.

Betina shrugged her shoulders and shook her head.

As they approached Malcolm's house, they saw an old man putting stacks of papers and boxes on the sidewalk.

"That's his landlord," said Evangeline, as she got out of the car and walked over to him. "Why are you throwing my father's things on the street?"

Remembering that she was Malcolm's daughter, the landlord explained, "He ain't been around. Ain't paid no rent in months. I should'a done this a long time ago, seein' as I get complaints every day from other tenants about all his eccentrics."

Evangeline looked at pictures that he had thrown into the garbage and at a book Malcolm had written. Several stacks of pamphlets and papers that Malcolm used to distribute to people he passed on the street, were piled beside a garbage can.

Maw-Maw and Betina watched from the car as Evangeline disappeared into the building. Maw-Maw shook her head and said, "Malcolm used to have a min'stry, with regular Sunday sermons till every las' one of his followers deserted him. But that didn't take the wind out of his sails. He took to the streets—preachin' to anyone that came within half-a-block of him."

They got out of the car and walked over to the boxes of papers and books. Malcolm's writing was everywhere—it was an endless stream of consciousness with spiraling and wavy lines of text describing the destruction of the world. His sentences took the shape of whirlwinds and lightning bolts, hailstorms, and volcanic eruptions. He could write twenty-two lines of text per inch and he wrote on everything. Maw-Maw studied his apocalyptic visions which covered the cross that he carved into a headboard, which was now lying on the sidewalk. "He's crazier than I thought," she said, shaking her head. "Don't know why she wants to come back here. You'd think she'd a had enough of that ol' man."

Evangeline finally came down from the apartment, carrying a book that Malcolm had written called *Manifesto of the Endtime*.

"Are you planning to read that?" Betina asked.

"Guess you could say it's a memento," Evangeline responded as they got back into the car. As they drove to the French Quarter, they passed a house that had a rose garden in front. In a dreamy voice, Evangeline recalled an early memory of her father. "I remember when we were walking down the street together, I plucked a rose from a bush. I said partly to myself, partly to Malcolm, that sometimes I felt like a rose. This made him wild and he flung himself into the rose bush and thrashed around in it. His clothes were shredded...his skin oozed blood from a thousand scratches. I stood there...telling myself that he didn't exist. This wasn't happening. I concentrated on the rose. I brushed the petals of the rose against my cheek. I had this idea that if I could fall inside of it...that its petals would surround me and love me. I would live deep in the heart of the rose. I would be cared for by the perfumed rosiness of the velvet petals. I didn't speak for weeks after that. I sat in a corner of my room...staring into the center of the dying rose. I watched the petals as they slipped to the floor one by one, till there was nothing left but a brown, shrunken center. My imagined paradise withered before my eyes and so had my dream.

"My mother brought me trays of food, but I ate nothing. Maybe that made her desperate. She sang nursery tunes and carried me downstairs to sit in the kitchen with her while she made a gingerbread house for me. She built a forest of marzipan trees and marzipan animals…she made a witch that guarded the woods. Slowly, I began to hear her songs and see the magic of the gingerbread house. She gave me a little lion to eat and I remember that moment…of finally coming back to life and drifting into this magical forest.

"Then Malcolm came home. He was wearing posters on his front and back with proverbs written on them. He looked at the candy house and started seething. He shouted and said that the witch was a vision of Satan…that it was a demonic story. My mother tried to calm him, but he smashed the gingerbread house with his hands and stomped on it. He shoved her against the wall and carried me out of the house. He threw me into the front seat of his truck. My mother ran out after us and chased us down the street, but he left her there. We drove all day and all night till we reached his underground shelter—he built it for the End Times. I think that's where he is now. In that shelter."

"Was that the last time you saw your mother?" Maw-Maw asked in a distressed tone as she took hold of Evangeline's hand.

"Yes, but I have this feeling...like I'll be seeing her again soon."

"I think you will," Betina added. She was about to tell her that Eartha Mae had camped on Jane's land but held back. She had a sense that it wasn't really necessary, because somehow their paths would soon be colliding.

After dropping Maw-Maw off, Betina parked her car on a side street in the French Quarter and followed Evangeline to a house that was boarded up. Evangeline pulled aside a large board that covered a window and they climbed into the hallway on the first floor. Shafts of light came through holes in the walls and a couple of pigeons flew off their perches, out through cracks in the roof. Large pieces of plaster and bird droppings covered the floor and several steps were missing as they climbed the stairs to the second floor. Betina heard several rats scurry out of their way and was about to say something, but Evangeline told her to ignore them.

She hated to think that Evangeline lived in such wretched conditions, but felt some relief when they reached her apartment. Her world was not quite as bleak as she imagined. She had managed to decorate the place with colorful photographs and posters of Mardi Gras, and there were a couple of old couches and art-deco sofas and lamps in her living room.

They made themselves comfortable on the balcony, sitting on wood crates, and sipping lemonade. Tex joined them while Evangeline looked through Malcolm's manifesto.

"When I look at these pages a strange thing happens," Evangeline said.

"Like it makes you sick?" Tex moaned.

"I used to think he was an angry god whose rage could destroy everything...particularly me. But now I know I'm not so easily destroyed...I see him as someone who is scared."

"Pyscho's more like it," Tex commented as he drank another glass of lemonade.

"I need to find him. Something is terribly wrong."

"Something's always been terribly wrong with him," Tex insisted.

"Well, this time...it's critical," Evangeline replied.

Tex looked at Betina, frustrated by Evangeline's concern for Malcolm. Then he offered Betina a refill on the lemonade.

After a pleasant dinner at her hotel, Betina returned to her room. Sitting by a window overlooking St. Charles Avenue, she watched the hotel staff decorating a picket fence with festive Christmas lights in front of the hotel. The seasons had changed quickly from fall to winter and Christmas would soon be upon them.

She opened a letter from Andrew. He wrote, "You were right about Leslie. I was fooling myself. I didn't want to admit that I would be bored with her. What struck me as charm became silliness. Her adoration, as you called it, was not really adoration at all, but a tiresome dependency, uncertainty, and helplessness. Even though I became tired of her fears, I wanted to keep a distance from you because I didn't want to hear your critical estimation of her—I was afraid of your influence." Pausing for a moment, she let go of thoughts of Leslie and considered whether Andrew's inability to connect and commit to her had been more a result of her independent spirit or his need for space. Her heart fluttered at the surprising last line of his letter. "Despite our struggles, I have no other will but to be with you."

She wrote back to him immediately, "These past few months have been the most difficult. I have needed the comfort of your arms more in this time of my life than ever before. I don't know what to think of myself, or of how I have shaped my own character and destiny. I don't know how to define myself now, without my link to the university. But I will pursue this research—grant or no grant. I guess you knew I would. Your faith means everything to me."

She put down her pen and picked up the phone to call Andrew. Just as she was about to dial, she heard the voice of Marletta, coming to her from a great distance.

"I've been waiting for you. I have many things to tell you," she said.

Closing her eyes, Betina heard the stirrings of a distant wind. In a moment she found herself caught in the center of a dark whirlpool—an imploding vortex. Betina took a few steps in this fluid world toward a cone-shaped structure that had a path encircling it. She began circumambulating this path that led to a platform, which stood high above the ground, underneath a domed ceiling. She was aware of the pulsing of drums and the intense humming of women in the distance. Turning her head, she saw vague figures of women holding torches, moving toward the base of the cone. Some of them followed her up the coiling path as she reached the summit.

She soon sensed that her perch, high above the ground, was meant to give her a view of events below so that she could record them. She took a seat at a very unusual desk that had spinning spiral designs carved into the desktop. A pen lifted in the air of its own accord, placing itself in her opened palm. Then pages of a book swept open until she found herself looking at a page with a partially completed mandala that had an exquisitely detailed border. As she continued working on the mandala, adding stars to the firmament, she realized that she had sat in this same spot many times in the past and had written in this same book.

The drummers wandered through the gathering—their drumbeats leading the women into trance states. Their arms and bodies swayed like branches of willow trees, blowing in the wind. Her heartbeat sped up with anticipation as a shaft of light entered the crown of her head. She felt certain that something remarkable was going to happen as the drumming and chanting became faster, building up to a climax.

Suddenly, she was awakened from her trance state by a knock at the door. Though she was disoriented, she got up and answered it. Evangeline stood before her, taking Betina's hand as she spoke with great urgency.

"I spent the evening in the garden behind my house," Evangeline said breathlessly. "I go there when I need answers. It's a magical place...filled with roses that blossom when I walk through the archway. I was lying on the stone bench and asked, 'Should I find Malcolm?' All I could hear was a big 'yes.' That 'yes' came from everywhere…from a place deep in myself…from the flowers that speak to me…from the stone angels and the lion guardian."

Betina held herself back from telling Evangeline to forget him. It occurred to her that Evangeline might be right—that instead of forgetting or burying him in her mind, she might find greater release by attempting to resolve things with him.

CHAPTER SIXTEEN

THE BAYOU

As Betina and Evangeline drove deeper into the bayou, they heard the glorious trumpeting and honking of long-necked birds, and the rasping cries that came from a raucous pair of great blue herons. One lone bird, with a six-foot wingspan, which Betina couldn't name, glided onto the water. She thought of the pterodactyl, that extinct flying reptile that once inhabited this region. The great blues stalked prehistoric swamps two million years ago, surviving through time because of their adaptability. Adaptability. It wasn't a strong element in her nature or in Evangeline's. Betina could see that they shared a fierceness to have things the way they believed they should be, rather than to accept things the way others wanted them to be. But maybe, Betina thought, that was also a kind of adaptability.

Evangeline broke her train of thought and said, "You know, I'm really glad we met. You accept my thoughts. You don't try to second guess me like the white coats. That means so much to me. To be honest, it means everything."

Mist was rising above the waters of the bayou and knotted webs of Spanish moss refracted the rays of sunlight. An alligator watched them from the side of the road, his tail swishing back and forth, until he slithered into the primeval waters as they drove by. A hawk cried out overhead, its voice echoing through the eerie swampland, fading into the distance as it disappeared behind the cypress trees. Betina shivered when a nutra rat, a giant rodent the size of a small dog, made its way across the road.

Evangeline said, "I always wondered why Malcolm treated me like he did. Maybe he hated my mother…so he hated me. He blamed her for everything that was wrong in his life...and everything that was wrong in the world. When Malcolm thought I was good, he called me Evangeline. When he thought I was morally weak, he called me Eve, and I alone suddenly became responsible for the fall of all mankind. Malcolm once had a big following—mostly women. They met on Sundays at the YMCA. There was Flora and her daughter. There was May, Roxanne, Val, and Maggie. They would've done anything for him. They moved into the shelter with us, when I was ten…when Malcolm told them the Endtime was near. Malcolm loved to flatter them; he told them about their greatness. They always fell for that."

"Most people do," Betina mumbled.

"They'd do anything he wanted, 'cause if they didn't…he'd tell them they were plain and ordinary after all...not even worth his time. He had these women to himself in a kind of marriage. They would chant, day and night, 'Out. Out. Satan. Out! Out!' Then they would fall to the floor, one after the other. They looked like guppies…gasping for air. Malcolm even got them to beat themselves, to purify their spirit.

"When Flora wasn't busy beating herself, she embroidered pillows that said 'The world's end will be / In nineteen-hundred and ninety-three.' When that final day arrived, they waited to be lifted from this world, into an eternal world of light like Malcolm promised. They waited for days...but nothing happened. The following year, Flora began embroidering more pillows…this time they said, 'The world will be no more / In nineteen-hundred and ninety-four.' But Malcolm went crazy when he realized his calculations were off. He became obsessed with the creation of a device to measure the end of the world in waves...time waves.

"The only reason I managed to escape was 'cause he worked night and day on it and finally forgot that I was even there. The other women left shortly after me. They were fed-up with Malcolm's obsession...and his lust. He even went after Flora's daughter. I heard they fled from the cellar one night while Malcolm napped...they became followers of Flora."

Evangeline's stories always astounded Betina. She imagined Flora leading the small group of faithful followers into the wilderness. She reflected on charismatic leaders of past movements who founded centers all over the world from Jonestown, to Waco, to Heaven's Gate. Betina sensed that Malcolm had the drive and passion to start a new movement but had not been able to maintain a following because of the way he retreated into himself and remained oblivious to the needs of his followers—perhaps Flora would have more success.

Betina slowly came to realize that aspects of Malcolm's nature were not so different from Theodore's personality. Betina and Evangeline both had fathers who imposed their vision upon them. They both tried to escape from their control—Evangeline fled to the streets of the French Quarter, while Betina roamed the African Savannah and later the Canadian forests. Malcolm had been a southern preacher, while Betina's father had been a missionary doctor in Kenya, and like Malcolm, he was so set in his beliefs that he could never consider another perspective. Betina's teenage years were spent in rebellion against her father's rigid belief system that allowed for no appreciation of any of the indigenous gods or traditions in the region where they lived. He never had any regard for their rituals or for their healing practices. Her father, though, had died at a relatively young age, while Malcolm was still going strong. Nevertheless, Theodore was still with her—his voice lingered in her mind.

Evangeline sensed that they were getting closer to Malcolm's shelter, but the trees were thicker than in previous years and things looked unfamiliar. Her sense of direction became confused and she began to fear that it would be impossible for them to find the shelter. They drove around in circles for a while until Evangeline finally noticed several tree trunks that had carvings on them. Evangeline's eyes lit up, "I recognize that...it's a sculpture that's been there forever."

They looked at the wood figures. One was of a woman, with tears streaming like a river from her eyes—her breasts were baby egrets with their mouths open wide gasping for air.

Evangeline pointed to an area that was dense with shrubs. "It's in there. I know it is."

Betina pulled over and got out of the car, pushing aside several branches of thorn bushes. Then they wiped away dirt, dead leaves, and branches that covered a hidden door to the shelter. Though they struggled to open the door, it wouldn't budge. After more scraping and digging they finally got it open and were immediately repelled by the stench of rotten food and feces, blended with the sweet putrescence of sweat, urine, and mold. Betina found an oil lamp near the cellar door and lit the wick. Breathing in a few last gasps of fresh air, they made their way down the cellar stairs. The light from the lamp illuminated the room with a dim glow, casting shadows on the walls. Evangeline called out for her father, but there was no response.

The walls were covered with writing—sentences that took the shapes of clouds, spiraling tornadoes, and thunderbolts. Betina saw a wild stampede of horses that spelled out quotes from the *Book of Revelations*. Holding the lamp close to the eye of the horse, she read the word 'Endtime' inside the iris. She had never seen such tiny writing—it covered every bit of wall space and continued onto the table and chairs. There was a kind of psychotic brilliance in it all that made her shudder.

Malcolm even had an elaborate computational device with calendars and astronomical charts that he used to predict the day of the Final Judgment. Betina was amazed to see the effort he put into coming up with the date. On one chart he had rigorous mathematical calculations that displayed the entire 4.5 billion year history of the earth, delineating the age of the dinosaurs, the discovery of fire, the first civilizations, and the end of civilization or the Endtime (as he called it). The table was stacked with dozens of pamphlets including Benjamin Franklin's *Poor Richard's Almanac* and Robert Bailey Thomas's *Old Farmer's Almanac.* He even came up with his own calendric system, which did not use the names of the pagan gods for months but named the cataclysms that would come to pass at the end of each cycle, until ET—the Endtime.

In the far corner of the cellar, he had a seismograph and astronomical charts tacked to the walls, showing the movements of the stars and planets. He had papers notating calculations derived from lunar calendars, as well as solar calendars, and calculations based on ancient stone alignments. Charts of ancient calendric systems from Mesopotamia, Greece, Rome, China, India, as well as the Julian and Gregorian calendars covered another wall. He even had a Mayan Calendar, which predicted the abrupt end of a number of cycles at the beginning of the 2nd millennium, and there were notes about Hopi prophets who predicted a New World born from a great cleansing fire.

Looking through his paintings depicting the apocalypse, she was surprised to see one that showed a peaceable kingdom in the tradition of Edward Hicks. It reminded her of the gathering of animals at the cave in Ephesus. Holding a light to the ceiling, she saw a painting that must have been one of his early visions of the end of the world. It depicted a sinful world redeemed by Holy Fire. He was a prolific artist, but his only subject, it seemed, besides the one painting of the peaceable kingdom, was the apocalypse. Next to his apocalyptic visions, Betina noticed several paintings, which she realized were drawn by Evangeline, when she was a child. It brought tears to her eyes as she imagined how desperate that period of confinement must have been for her.

Just as they began to believe that Malcolm was not in the cellar, Evangeline lifted several blankets. The stench in the room multiplied as she uncovered her father's crumpled body. Trying to suppress waves of nausea brought on by the odor, Betina breathed through her mouth in short breaths, as she shined a light in his direction. Evangeline knelt beside him, looking down at his pale and emaciated face. When she put her ear on his heart, he moved his head slightly, then put his arm over his eyes to block out the dim light from the lamp. He suddenly let out a terrified cry that pierced the silence, causing several rats to scamper over stacks of papers and dishes, and rush out the doorway.

"It's me," she said. "I've come here to help you."

Squinting at the light, as if he'd been living in total darkness for weeks, he tried to move away from her. Too weak to stand, he fell back down on the floor.

"The cataclysms are over. The storms have quieted. The locust and the scorpions have disappeared. The snakes have retreated. Earth is spinning calmly. You can step outside now. There is nothing to fear. It's time to see the light of the sun, shining down on this new day," she said, suddenly illuminated by a brilliant ray of sunlight coming through the doorway.

Lost in confusion, Malcolm spoke in a weak and timid voice, "Is it an angel that speaks to me?" He moved like a blind man, touching everything around him to get a sense of where he was.

She continued to speak in a reassuring voice and eventually he stood up. He leaned on Evangeline and Betina as they helped him out of the shelter. Shielding his eyes from the light, he peered out at the land through slightly parted fingers. Helping him into the car, Betina took the wheel with Evangeline beside her and Malcolm in the back seat. They passed a group of alligators in the water by the wood sculptures.

Evangeline smiled at Malcolm as she recited a Biblical passage that referred to the alligators. "His eyes are like the eyelids of the morning. Out of his mouth go burning lamps and sparks of fire."

Malcolm continued, "Out of his nostrils goeth smoke. As out of a seething pot or cauldron. His breath kindleth coals, and a flame goeth out of his nostrils. Upon earth, there is not his like, who is made without fear."

Evangeline looked relieved to find that Malcolm was lucid. She recited the next line, "He beholdeth all high things. He is a king over all the Children of Pride."

If Betina had wondered why Evangeline persisted in rescuing this man, it was in this moment that she understood. Beyond all the pain and hurt that Malcolm inflicted on her, there was an occasional moment of resonance when they could share the power of a common history.

The mist turned to a thick layer of fog, creating an eerie mood throughout the land. Believing that he was seeing the aftermath of a holocaust, Malcolm whispered, "The cataclysms must've been unspeakable. How did you survive?"

Neither one answered. Barely able to see two feet ahead, Betina stuck her head out the window to get a clearer view of the edge of the road. Despite her best efforts, the car slid off the road into a muddy pothole. The wheels spun in place, splattering mud on their faces. They tried to push the car out of the pothole, but it wouldn't budge—they were stranded.

CHAPTER SEVENTEEN

LOST BETWEEN WORLDS

They abandoned the car and walked down a muddy path. Uncertain of their direction, Evangeline and Malcolm followed Betina. They noticed a man stepping out of a canoe and tying it to a tree. After reaching into his canoe for a seven-foot longbow and arrow, and several fish tied together by a cord, he walked barefoot, with perfect balance, from one tree trunk—which lay flat in the water—to another, until he reached dry ground. His skin was light brown and his black hair was shoulder length with thick bangs. He wore shorts without a shirt and had well-developed pectoral muscles. Although the trio watched silently and made no noise, the man sensed their presence and looked back in their direction.

"I only had a glimpse of the man that stole your painting, but it seems to me that he had similar facial tattoos...even the same muscular build," Betina noted. "What do you think?"

Evangeline looked him over and nodded in agreement. "Yes. Whiskers and spots…like a wild cat."

"Must be from the same tribe," Betina added.

"Seems familiar to me too," Malcolm said, suppressing alarm. "Let's follow him."

"Yes, let's. But are you really up for it? Are you strong enough?" Evangeline asked.

"My energy's returning…and so are some very…disturbing… memories," Malcolm mumbled.

The Indian walked gracefully and effortlessly over a path covered with broken limbs, low branches, and potholes; Betina, Evangeline and Malcolm followed along with great difficulty. When Malcolm carelessly stepped on some branches that cracked in half, the Indian spun around, though the trio managed to hide behind the trunks of a cluster of eucalyptus trees.

"Where do you think he's from?" Malcolm whispered.

"South America, I imagine. If I could hear him speak, I could get a better idea," Betina answered.

They were surprised that the long and twisting trail took them to a central clearing, which was encircled by a dozen huts, made of woven webs of branches and leaves with green roofs. Emaciated dogs patrolled the courtyard with limp tails between their legs and tongues hanging out of their mouth. Many of the Indians were naked; others were covered in red paint or dust. A couple of old men had labrets in their lips and similar facial designs on their cheeks and around their mouth. Betina watched as one man sat on a hammock and painted patterns on another man's chest with white paint. Next to him was a small boy who looked into a broken mirror. He inserted the spine of a plant into holes pierced in the sides of his nose so that he looked like he had cat whiskers.

Two dark-skinned women came up another path and noticed Betina, Evangeline, and Malcolm hiding behind trees watching the activity in the central courtyard. One woman, with whiskers made of cactus needles, modestly covered her bare breasts with one hand as she looked over the small group. A woven cloth was attached to a string that went around her hips and covered her like a bikini. She held a pet squirrel monkey in her arms and stroked its cheek. The other woman had a nose pierced by a shell and a necklace of beads. She was nude except for a small bikini bottom made of fluffy feathers and fringe. She also covered her breasts, then adjusted the feathers that covered her genitals. Betina noticed the woman's self-consciousness and it made her think of Adam and Eve, after they lost their innocence and sense of oneness with nature when they were expelled from the Garden of Eden.

The two tribal women quietly motioned for Betina, Evangeline and Malcolm to join the group. They were reluctant at first, then followed them into the center of the courtyard, uncertain of what they were getting themselves into.

The Indian woman led the trio to an old woman who sat in front of a hut and mixed a thick white concoction in a number of large gourds. It seemed they were preparing for a group ritual, and hallucinogens were an important part of the celebration. The woman chewed on a root and spit the substance into the gourd, mixing it with the rest of the paste. Betina sensed it was *ayahuasca*, though she didn't know if the dried roots, leaves, and vines needed to make the blend were available outside of the Amazonian region. She had heard that *ayahuasca* blends could be made in so many different ways, causing a range of experiences. Certain mixtures produced strong auditory hallucinations and visions of the future, others produced visions of green snakes, and there were even mixtures that produced visions in red.

The pet squirrel monkey reached in for a taste of the concoction but was overpowered after a few licks. His eyelids fluttered, then glazed over. Betina amused herself with thoughts that perhaps he was seeing himself trapped in a human body, walking though the world without the ability to swing through the treetops. Maybe he imagined himself dressed in a business suit, navigating the human world with severely limited senses. The tribal women exchanged brief comments and laughed at the monkey. They didn't notice when Malcolm picked up one of the gourds and drank from it.

One woman ran her fingers through Evangeline's hair, shook her head, and said a few words to her friend. The other woman's eyes lit up when she noticed a wooden box on the table that contained red pigment. With a little brush, she drew a red line down Evangeline's nose and continued the line down her chin. Across her cheeks she painted black jagged lines of thunder, then placed a necklace of feathers around her neck. Turning to Betina, she drew circles on Betina's cheekbones and put a few feathers behind each ear. After completing the makeover, she stood back, nodding with satisfaction at her handiwork.

A little girl with an intense, unwavering gaze watched them. Around her neck were a dozen strands of beads, with caps from beer bottles as medallions. She held a small green parrot that spoke a few words in their Indian dialect. The little bird pecked at the hairs above her lip, then playfully hid its red-feathered head under her chin, shyly looking up at her once or twice, before burying its head again, in a private game of peek-a-boo. The girl's father had red pigment around his eyes, like a raccoon, and wore a necklace of claws. He watched the three strangers out of the corner of his eye, as he strung together a necklace of blue, yellow, and green feathers.

In the distance, a group of men were adding objects to a large altar, set in the middle of the courtyard. Evangeline was stunned to notice her painting, still partially wrapped in sheets, near the center of the altar. It was alive and radiating a throbbing glow, just as it had in the hospital. Everyone's attention was on the painting when the veil of sheets was removed. A few women placed flowers, leaves, and feathers around the painting. Baskets filled with papayas, mangoes, bananas, apples, oranges, grapes, and guavas were also placed on the altar.

Malcolm took another sip of the white pasty concoction, noticing that the gourd he was drinking from had an unusual shape. Then he studied the painting and muttered, "I've seen that face before. Why is it alive?" The more Malcolm examined the image, the more the colors in the background swirled around. Soon the roses that encircled the woman in the painting lifted off the canvas into the air. Watching the purple, pink, crimson, and gold holographic roses circling the altar, he felt waves of euphoria and began swaying to the hypnotic melody that he heard coming from this living image.

Evangeline whispered, "Why is my painting on their altar?"

"Maybe it's an offering," Betina suggested.

As she spoke, an old shaman, with a headdress made of hummingbird feathers and a dried hummingbird's body behind his ear, emerged with a torch. He was naked except for a string that dangled from his waist and wrapped around the foreskin of his penis, which looked like the knotted tip of a sausage.

Evangeline studied his withered face—his eyes were hidden by a sagging brow and his epicanthic folds were particularly wide. Looking into his eyes was like viewing another universe. Evangeline knew he had seen things that she couldn't even imagine. "Can't you understand, that painting is mine," Evangeline explained. "I made it. It's part of me. I want it back. It doesn't belong here."

He looked at her blankly, while adjusting his headdress. It was clear he didn't speak any English and had no intention of delaying this ritualistic burning.

"Hablan Español?" Evangeline asked. "Parlez-Vous Français? Parlez-Vous Pig Latin?"

"Falan Portuguese?" Betina queried, believing this Indian tribe was from Brazil and probably from the Amazon, since they had the distinctive cat-whisker tattoos of the Matis or Mayoruna.

He responded in a monotone and referred to the woman in the painting as *tita*.

Betina heard the word *tita* several times and sensed that it meant "mother."

Evangeline grabbed hold of the shaman's arm, but he shook himself loose from her grip, setting a torch to the dead leaves and branches at the base of the altar. The cat people began chanting as flames attacked the baskets and painting.

Betina, Malcolm, and Evangeline were swept away in a whirlwind of movement circling the fire. They joined in on a repetitive chant—not knowing the meaning of the words. Betina looked down, noticing that they were walking on burning coals. "Good grief," she muttered to herself. Feeling flashes of pain on her feet as the soles of her shoes melted away, she knew she had to get back into a trance state, to avoid getting burned. She quickly joined the chant of the barefoot firewalkers as they took a few steps to the left and a few to the right, around the pyre. They made more than a few dozen circumnavigations, during this electrically charged celebration, moving toward greater heights of excitement.

As they circled the pyre, Malcolm noticed a familiar face in the crowd. How could he forget the teenager that disgraced him and beat him up, in front of Catacombs? The boy had the same heavy chain around his waist and the same cat whiskers with three lines of scars running down each cheek. He also had a motorcycle tattoo that had the head and tail of a jaguar. The drug-induced euphoria that Malcolm previously felt soon turned to aggression. His face became purple, his eyes popped out of their sockets, the veins on his throat bulged, his hair stood on end, and his body shook with rage. He pointed his crooked and bony finger at the boy, shouting, "Don't think I've forgotten, scumbag!" Taking one last sip of his drink, he realized he was not drinking out of a gourd but out of a human skull. He threw it at the boy with repulsion, screaming, "Cannibal!" He threatened and swore at him, but his words were drowned out by the chant—the Indian never heard a word he said.

Evangeline and Betina took him by the hand, pulling him away from the circle of dancers.

"Let go of me. Don't you understand…he tried to kill me. It's time he gets his comeuppance," Malcolm screamed.

Though he struggled to break free, Evangeline and Betina managed to lead him down the path they had taken when they entered the clearing. Just as they thought his interest in revenge had dissipated, he ripped free of their grasp saying, "I got a certain matter to tend to. You'll have to wait a moment." He was out of sight before the women could stop him.

"I can't imagine how he has any energy at all after all those months underground," Betina said.

"He still has enough to get into some serious trouble," Evangeline sighed. As she sat on a log next to Betina, to wait for him, she listened to the mating call of a cricket and the raspy grunts of a frog which accompanied the distant tribal chant.

Betina thought of the tribe's efforts to retain their traditions, despite living in a world where languages and cultures were dying out more rapidly than animal species. It was devastating that these indigenous people, stewards of the earth's mysteries, had been expelled from their homeland in the rainforest by steel mills and forest industries, and were forced to celebrate ancient traditions in secret, surrounded by cultures that could not respect or acknowledge their wisdom. The greatest tragedy was the children of the Mayoruna who had mixed feelings about their own culture and traditions—they were lost between worlds—and many of the Mayoruna youth roamed the city streets seeking revenge for the silent decimation of their culture.

Betina thought it tragic that they didn't want to study with the shaman to learn the knowledge that had been passed down to him from one generation to the next, for thousands of years. That legacy of unwritten wisdom could die with the shaman since the Mayoruna youth were less interested in becoming apprentices and more interested in shaping themselves into what she referred to as Neo-Primitives. They took what interested them from popular culture, blended it with what they needed from their own Amazonian culture, and let go of the rest. Unfortunately, they were motivated by rage and shame and lived in a state of overwhelming despair.

Betina told Evangeline that she read *National Geographic* reports about the discovery of this elusive tribe that avoided the civilized world. She remembered that several-hundred cat people lived close to the source of the Amazon, considering themselves ancestors of the jaguar. Growing up in Africa, she always felt an affinity with the leopard, and by extension with the jaguar of South America. She said that sharing this totem inspired her interest in this reclusive tribe.

A guest lecturer that spoke during her junior year at Harvard described his life-threatening journey to visit these mysterious semi-nomadic people. More than a decade later, Peter traveled to remote regions of the Amazon, but his descriptions were radically different. He described tourists flocking into Mayoruna territory to see the people who were known for the ability to communicate telepathically. Peter told Betina that for the longest time he ridiculed the tourists every chance he could, as they attempted to bring all the comforts of home with them on their journey into the wild. He said that they might as well have brought their RVs, since they had everything else—hair dryers, curling irons, down pillows, elaborate make-up kits, and enough clothes for a year. Eventually, he recognized that in significant ways, they contributed to keeping the wisdom alive. While most of the world cared little about the traditions and abilities of the Mayoruna, the tourists were eager to learn how to beam and telepathically transmit their thoughts. Betina wondered if the Mayoruna still had this ability, or if years of exposure to other cultures and learning a written language shifted their thinking from right to left brain, diminishing their ability to beam and to experience a consciousness of the cosmos and an understanding of the order of the universe. Beaming was the old language of the cat people, a language without words that existed in the form of picture feelings and images.

Betina also remembered that the cat people had a different sense of time; in their rituals they believed they could return to the beginning. But what was the beginning? Perhaps it was a time before technology, industry, domestication and civilization; when only the natural world existed. A time before there were words like nature or animals, when all were one. She had heard that they enacted rituals of going back to the beginning. Perhaps they were re-enacting it today since time for the cat people was non-linear, and any point in time could be entered through doors or tunnels.

As she thought about these things, Malcolm returned to the clearing and watched the strange behavior of a group of men in trance states. The arms of one man were spread out. With only the whites of his eyes showing he made a clicking sound as his face darted from the left to the right. Perhaps, in that moment, he was a pterodactyl with a ten-foot wingspan, flying over the bayou or over a virgin and pristine Amazon rainforest. Another slithered along the ground like an anaconda. The squirrel monkey stood upright, running between them. The shaman was on all fours, moving like a wild cat.

Malcolm saw the teenager that had beaten him and broken his eyeglasses. Unlike the others in his group who were having expansive visions brought on by *ayahuasca,* he was drinking straight from a whiskey bottle, and was dead to the world. Malcolm didn't know that this young man had once been the shaman's apprentice, nor would he have cared. Now he was the tribe's problem child. Years of alcohol abuse destroyed his potential and with that went the brightest hope for the tribe's survival.

"Bet you thought you'd never see me again," Malcolm said as he grabbed the whiskey bottle out of his hand and smashed it. Then he kicked him over and over till he slumped down in a heap. "I remember it all, the night you kicked me around without pity or remorse…but you have it too easy. I can't hurt you back, cause you're dead already." Malcolm was about to give him a final kick when he heard a voice from the altar.

"Let him be. He will rise again and carry the wisdom and traditions of his people. All is not lost. Malcolm? Malcolm?"

"Who said that?"

"Don't you remember me?" asked the voice.

Malcolm looked around and sensed that the voice was coming

from the painting. He noticed that it had not been completely destroyed, in fact, the original colors and form slowly began to reappear as he looked at it. At moments he could see the face of a woman shining through the charred canvas.

"You never understood who I was. Can you see me now?" she asked.

While a few remaining men chanted and pounded the ground with their dance steps, Malcolm stood directly in front of the altar, looking into the eyes of the re-emerging woman in the painting. Surprised at the power she had over him, he reached into the ashes, pulling out what was left of the living painting.

Malcolm climbed the narrow, serpentine path, holding the painting close to his heart. The brilliant and alluring image that had called out to him moments earlier had faded and was completely black. Evangeline and Betina couldn't understand why he wanted to keep it, since there was nothing left of the original image, but he insisted that the image of the woman would emerge again.

One narrow path led to another, and another, until they finally reached a dirt road. The driver of a creaky old pick-up truck pulled over, offering them a ride to a town on the Mississippi where there was a midnight Christmas celebration. Evangeline and Malcolm rode in the back and Betina sat in the front. The good-natured, forty-something driver, dressed in overalls and thigh-high swamp boots, didn't believe Betina's reports of the cat people. Stroking his beard, he said he was a country hick who knew nothing about the world, but everything about the bayou, since he had lived there all his life.

Betina wondered if there was anyone else who had seen them, or if anyone would believe the truth of her descriptions. She had so many questions. For starters: How had they crossed so many borders to get there? How was it that no one knew they were even there? But more importantly: What was their ritual about? What was their relationship to the painting and to the mother? She needed to know these things and told herself that she would come back at a later date, to learn more.

Thinking of the shaman, who spoke no words of English, she held his face in her mind, and asked for an explanation of their ritual. Suddenly, she experienced a curious sensation—a thought form beamed into her: "In the return is the new beginning." As she thought about that, she saw a giant cat spirit leaping over her. She wasn't sure if it was a jaguar or leopard, but was awed and terrified by its power and wildness.

CHAPTER EIGHTEEN

MIRACLES

Evangeline, Malcolm, and Betina enjoyed the comforting sound of Christmas melodies coming from several of the homes that they passed, along the Mississippi. In front of one house was a crèche in which Mary held the baby Jesus in her arms. Looking closer, Betina thought she saw Mary Magdalene beside the Virgin. Behind them was the shadowy figures of the black Diana, Cybele, Isis with her child, Spider Woman, Tara, White Buffalo Woman, Inanna, Kali, Kuan Yin, Artemis, Aphrodite and many others. It seemed that the Mother in all her forms was tenderly held and comforted in the arms of the most primordial Great Mother of all.

Betina wondered if Malcolm or Evangeline also shared this curious vision, but didn't have a chance to find out. Malcolm was overcome with wonder at the sight of an approaching comet, racing through the evening sky, that had a cloud-like head and a dust tail.

"It's right on schedule. It's a sign. It's time!" he cried.

As they continued walking, they saw piles of wood, stacked on the levees in structures that were more than twenty feet high. In front of one of the tallest structures stood a gray-haired Cajun woman, wearing a red bandana, a long billowy red skirt and a white ruffled blouse. She stirred a pot of soup, over a butane flame. Her grown children sat around a picnic table, while half-a-dozen grandchildren ran around them playing a game of tag. They were all waiting impatiently for the lighting of the bonfires.

She called out to Betina, Malcolm and Evangeline, as they approached. "Come join us for a bowl of gumbo z'herbes. It's got pepper grass, collar' 'n mustard greens, beet tops, sorrel 'n dandelion greens. A lil' chicory, cabbage, onions 'n ham hock. That's just for starters." Before they could refuse, she filled three bowls with soup and handed it to them.

"This surely hits the spot," Malcolm said, as he took a few spoonfuls. The others nodded in agreement.

"Help yourself to cookies and cakes. Don't be shy now. Take a seat. It's almost 7:00 PM. That's when the show begins. My family been working all month stacking wood. We mighty proud. Perfect, ain't it?"

Betina studied the stack made of willow wood that must have been fifty-feet long. "It is beautiful," Betina agreed.

"Why a Viking ship?" Evangeline asked.

"No good reason 'cept'n my grandson here's been studying about 'em." The old woman patted the teenager on the head and he smiled proudly.

When the clock struck seven, they could see more than a hundred bonfires being lit at the same time, on both sides of the Mississippi. Most of them were smaller, shaped like pyramids. Cane reed cracked and popped like fireworks as the fire began to burn. Many of the children lit sparklers and set off firecrackers.

"This is bonfire alley," the old woman exclaimed.

"Wish I could see it from the air," the grandson added.

"Must look like a runway with landing lights," Betina contributed.

"It lights the way for Santa on his sleigh—'n I don't want him skippin' our house this year," said the seven-year-old granddaughter.

As Betina watched the brilliant flames and smoke fill the night sky, she recalled how the Druids built fires, at the time of the winter and summer solstices, to pay homage to the sun. After the birth of Christ, the fire ritual took on religious symbolism. In her visits to Alsace, in France, with her mother and grandmother, she remembered seeing dozens of bonfires. She knew that the Germans also had a similar celebration and had read an article suggesting that it was the early French and German of the Louisiana region, in the 1700's, who brought along the tradition of lighting bonfires. She pondered the possible history of this Christmas Eve celebration until Evangeline poked her in the side, suggesting that they move along.

They thanked the old woman for the soup then made their way along the river, passing dozens of other bonfires. One structure was shaped like a train, another had the shape of a steamship, there was even a shrimp boat with nets, and a sleigh with reindeer. All were made of willow wood.

They joined a crowd of Cajuns and tourists, who were dancing along the banks of the river while a group of musicians stood on a platform playing Cajun music. Betina felt as if she had been swept back in time to a celebration from the Middle Ages. Evangeline began dancing and motioned to Betina to join her. She spotted Julian, Adonis and several belly dancers from Catacombs, and they all danced together.

Not long after that Maw-Maw, Salome, Christian, Raider and Tex wandered through the crowd. Christian was pushing Salome in a wheelchair, while Tex and Raider walked on either side of her. Maw-Maw had insisted that Salome leave the comfort of her bed to join this bonfire celebration, even if it was to be her final adventure in life. Maw-Maw's sense of urgency grew with each step they took, while Salome carried a quiet faith that something important was about to happen.

Malcolm looked at all the groups of people that were coming together and in a confused state yelled, "There's been no cleansing. What is this demonic carnival?" He turned to Evangeline and cried, "You've tried to deceive me, child. The cataclysms are not over...they've barely begun! Our land must be cleansed of these obscene and shameful revelers."

Several Cajuns began shouting when a number of Neo-Primitives drove through the crowd on motorcycles. Their style of dress seemed more outlandish and rebellious than that of their brothers in the bayou.

The cross between leather, spikes and chains, intricate tribal facial tattoos, and red and green feathered necklaces, set them apart from the local townspeople. The Cajuns resented their intrusion into their holiday revelry; soon a fight broke out between the two groups. In no time, the brawl spread through the crowd. One person knocked into another, tempers flared, fists were raised, angry words were exchanged, and the festival became a battlefield of discordant forces.

Dancing Star slowly made her way down the Mississippi, toward the crowd along the riverbank. In spite of the fog mixed with smoke, many of the angry revelers could see the twinkling colored lights that adorned the approaching houseboat. As the boat neared the shore, they heard a pleasing melody that came from a calliope. Calm began to descend on the crowd as greater numbers of people noticed the brightly-lit vessel coming toward them. They looked with wonder at the radiant figure of Eartha Mae dressed in her brilliant red velvet gown. Sitting on a chair covered in white satin, she looked like a queen on a throne.

Eartha Mae had not been the same since her sojourn in the hotel where she sensed that every painful and angry thought was mirrored in turbulent weather conditions. She had begun to understand the power of thought and became more aware of how she handled herself, since she believed that her thoughts could transform the world. She convinced herself that peace was all around her and believed she was approaching a garden of tranquility. With all her senses, she imagined the sweetness of reuniting with her daughter—she could even see the two of them embracing. The light that radiated from Eartha Mae illuminated everything around her and she swayed in the whirling mist.

Evangeline waited in anticipation, with her heart pounding and her hands trembling. Her breathing was so rapid she thought she might faint. Turning to Betina, she whispered, "Do you smell roses? She's coming. She's really coming."

Malcolm asked, "From whence do they come?"

Evangeline looked into the mist. "From the Fountainhead, father."

He nodded, with tears swelling in his eyes. "It's happening." Then with great seriousness and devotion he said, "Not from the hills and the mountains of this lower earth, but from the Heavenly Zion. He showed me a pure river of water of life proceeding out of the throne of God and of the Lamb."

Evangeline continued, "How excellent is thy loving-kindness, O God! Therefore the children of men put their trust under the shadow of thy wings. They shall be abundantly satisfied."

Evangeline and Malcolm looked at each other, with a moment of tenderness and understanding, sharing the wonder and beauty of the miracle.

As the houseboat got closer to the crowd assembling on the shoreline, Virgil blew into his conch shell creating a loud powerful otherworldly tone that signaled their arrival. He tied the houseboat to a post while Oakie helped Eartha Mae step onto a dock. Chloe followed after Eartha Mae carefully arranging the train of her elegant dress. In moments, a crowd of people gathered around her and watched as the luminous Eartha Mae stepped down from the dock and stood before them in the sand. Her presence quickly dispelled violent feelings. A mood of serenity descended on the crowd as the loneliness of separate hearts united in a fellowship of solidarity. Eartha Mae radiated a calming light and milk flowed from her many breasts like a fountain. When she walked through the crowd, she left a trail of flowers behind her that filled every footstep. Virgil again blew into the conch shell, announcing Eartha Mae's presence with each powerful blast.

Malcolm studied her suspiciously and mumbled to himself, "Why that's crazy Eartha Mae. Whore of Bourbon Street." He stood at a distance, watching in disbelief. Without a thought, he switched the charred painting from his right to his left hand, when he felt a blast of heat come out of it. "Why is she dressed like royalty? Just look at her...her face is like a rotten tangerine. How dare she think she's something that she's not." The painting sizzled when he said that and Malcolm put the painting on the ground for a few moments, since it had gotten too hot. It occurred to him that the painting was reacting to his criticism. Then he told himself that he was being ridiculous, imagining such a thing.

Flora, and the seven women that aligned themselves with her teachings, appeared in the crowd. They walked in grace and beauty, dressed in white flowing robes with finely embroidered collars and sleeves, sashes on their waist, and white turbans on their heads. They were radiant. Reaching into their baskets, they took out candles and handed them around. Flora hesitated, then made her way to Malcolm and gave him a candle.

"Why can't you see her for who she truly is?" She asked, looking directly into his eyes.

Malcolm shook with anger then stood back and studied her for a moment. Memories of the months they shared in his underground shelter flashed through his mind.

Flora lit the candle that Malcolm held and said, "You have never seen anything clearly. You have been intoxicated with visions of the Endtime, blinded by your lust for suffering. This is the time for a new beginning, a time for celebration."

Malcolm wanted to talk to her some more and tried to grasp her arm, but she slipped away from him and disappeared into the crowd with an entourage of women that followed behind her. She gave candles to three Cajuns, who had been haggling before Eartha Mae's arrival. Soon every person in the crowd held a candle in the air, with a bright flame, celebrating the arrival of Eartha Mae.

As Eartha Mae walked past Malcolm, he screamed, "Why do you walk with pride...when you're nothing but a whore. Hang your head. Where is your shame? You're nobody."

She glanced at him and turned away—her relationship with Malcolm retained no more importance in her life than that of the family she was born into. She was on her own private journey and her world was vibrant with life—she had no energy to waste on him. Several children chased after her and skipped between the hyacinths, tulips, and poppies that grew in her footsteps, as she continued to make her way through the crowd.

Watching as Eartha Mae walked a few yards in front of her toward the stage, Evangeline whispered to Betina, "I've dreamed of her since the day we separated, when I was six. She's more than I ever imagined." Evangeline followed her to the foot of the platform as Eartha Mae climbed the steps.

Oakie and Chloe carried the train of her dress and Virgil played his drum with a group of musicians that had collected on the stage. The music stopped when Eartha Mae stood before the astonished audience and looked down from the stage—each person felt the compassion and love that she radiated. A profound silence descended upon the crowd as the wind ceased to blow, and the waters of the river became still. Standing in this perfect stillness, they did not know that their life was about to change forever.

Eartha Mae began to hum a song that Evangeline recognized as the one she sang when she was a child. The words no longer mattered—it was the tone that affected her as it vibrated with a rich resonance. Evangeline's ear, like a golden helix, was hungry to capture this divine music and carry it into the deepest recesses of her being. She began feeling ascending and descending currents of curvilinear motion, running up and down her spine, like a caduceus of serpentine energy. Spinning wheels of energy, like whirling vortexes, moved from her forehead, to the base of her spine. She could also feel her heart blast open, like a gigantic sunflower, with spirals spinning in opposite directions.

Evangeline heard a most amazing sound—it was the singing of an angelic choir. Looking around into the faces of those around her, she knew that they were hearing and feeling the same thing. A few stood with outstretched arms, absorbing the fullness of all they heard and saw, several others fell to the ground, intoxicated and overwhelmed by the otherworldly voices. As the singing began to build, Eartha Mae swayed to the melody with a movement that created a gentle wind, which comforted the crowd with its tender, loving caress.

Wheeling Salome through the peaceful gathering, Maw-Maw made her way to the front of the stage where Eartha Mae stood in a meditative state—dreaming of peace, visualizing harmony. Deeply drawn to Eartha Mae, Salome felt the illness leave her body as she stood at the foot of the stage, absorbing the light that radiated across the crowd. Feeling the return of her strength, Salome was able to stand on her feet for the first time in months.

Eartha Mae looked down into the crowd—and then her eyes locked with Evangeline's. As she looked at this child, she saw a slideshow of images of their years together. She recalled the scent of her daughter's hair and the strawberry fragrance of her skin. She could even hear the sweetness of her daughter's laughter. The child had the same magnificent, unforgettable lavender eyes, the same dimple in her cheek, and the same smile that lit up her face. Eartha Mae lost all awareness of the crowd, seeing only her daughter's indomitable dancing spirit that remained transcendent over whatever burdens she had endured. Feeling that luminous thread that connected the two of them, she was filled with gratitude that Evangeline had managed to survive their ten years of separation.

Descending from the stage, Eartha Mae walked toward her daughter. Holding out her arms, Evangeline stepped forward and embraced her. Tears welled in Eartha Mae's eyes and dropped from her cheeks, mixing with Evangeline's tears, creating a puddle of water around them. Out of that grew a ring of bright fragrant flowers. The gratitude that they felt at being united rippled out beyond them like waves of atomic energy. It moved beyond the banks of the Mississippi, past the East and West Coast of North America, and for several unforgettable moments it encompassed the world. Every living creature on planet Earth felt waves of peace and thankfulness until that field of loving energy spread throughout the universe.

Later that night, they walked along the shore of the Mississippi, with the bonfires burning all around them. Evangeline held her mother's hand and whispered, "There is so much I want to tell you and so much I want to know."

Eartha Mae looked closely at her and said, "When you were taken from me, I covered the streets of this town. I couldn't find a clue as to your whereabouts. Finally I began to believe that you weren't here...so I left New Orleans and traveled from city to city, looking for you. I was desperate...zigzagging across the continent...knocking on doors...posting pictures of you on lampposts and post office bulletin boards...passing flyers out in bus stations and railroad stations. If only I had known that you were just north of here."

Evangeline wiped away another stream of tears.

"All these years I dreamed of finding you," Eartha Mae continued. "Then there was a time when I gave up and had no desire to go on. We found a cave by a lake and I slept for days, maybe weeks.

Could'a been years. I was weary to the bone. Maybe on the verge of death. Virgil and Oakie tried to wake me. They shouted and pounded my body—but I was dead to the world. Then finally, in that deep, dark sleep, the North Wind took pity on me and brought your voice to me. It was so clear. So sweet."

Evangeline smiled, "I always called for you."

"I heard you."

"I believed that if I said your name enough...you would hear me one day and come to me."

"So I did."

While Evangeline and Eartha Mae talked through the night and into the next day, catching up on years of living separate lives, Betina sat on the balcony of her hotel room, replaying images of Eartha Mae's meeting with Evangeline. Malcolm sat alone by the smoldering bonfires, struggling to make sense of this mysterious sequence of events. How had it happened that on the muddy banks of the Mississippi, flowers had sprung up in Eartha Mae's footsteps? Why did people honor her? How was it that she calmed them and took away their desire to fight? He thought of the miracle of the five loaves and two fish from which Jesus was able to feed a multitude. He could not deny that there had been miracles. Eartha Mae had given the people exactly what they needed—a miracle of beauty and peace. She had turned a battlefield into a peaceable kingdom.

Distracted by the fragrance of roses that permeated the smoke-filled air, he followed the trail of flowers that went from the platform, where Eartha Mae stood the night before, back to the houseboat. He climbed onto Dancing Star, placed Evangeline's charred painting against the deck's railing, and sat in a chair that had been Eartha Mae's throne on the ride from Lake Itasca to New Orleans. Somehow he understood the importance of the black image in the painting. As he studied it, he saw that it was coming back to life—the colors were re-emerging as the black ash began to dissolve. He hadn't realized that the painting was of Eartha Mae when he first saw it on the altar in the bayou, but now he was certain that it was a vision of her, in all her glory.

The moment he made the connection, he was flooded with memories of how he treated her throughout their years together. He shuddered when he recalled the time he pushed her down the stairs. He recoiled with remorse at the names he used to call her—names that trashed every aspect of her being. He wept profusely when he remembered the way he would punch her and kick her, and thrash her around. He realized that he never knew who she was and had been blind to the potential within her.

Malcolm was overcome by loneliness as he wandered along the banks of the Mississippi. Not knowing where to go since everything of his Old World was collapsing, he found himself making his way back to the home that he once shared with Eartha Mae and Evangeline. He had not been back there in years—now the house was empty with a "For Sale" sign tacked on a post in front of the porch.

After opening the gate, he circled around to the back to see if he could still open a window that had a broken lock. Since it had not been repaired in all those years, he was able to slide through the window, into the house. Finding their old rocking chair in the basement, he brought it up to the empty living room and rocked back and forth in it. The more he rocked, the more he recalled his life with Evangeline and Eartha Mae. Sitting there for hours, replaying mental home movies, he realized with great sadness that he had squandered opportunities of happiness by creating a reign of terror in their home.

In the evening, he mounted the painting on the wall, above the fireplace. Then he built a fire and studied the remarkable image that glowed in the dark, magically filling the room with the fragrant scent of roses. As the original colors of the painting became more vibrant, his mind grew calm, the glare in his eyes softened, and a new rosiness spread over his gray complexion. Wild stallions galloped out of his mind, as he absorbed the healing light from the painting. For the first time in years, he began to feel a sense of peace and well being.

CHAPTER NINETEEN

ODE TO A SINGING FLAME

Betina sat at a table in a small dark coffeehouse, on Bourbon Street, where no two chairs or couches matched. Overwhelmed with thoughts and images, she began a letter to Jane, hoping to reach some understanding of what she had seen in the past few months.

"Dear Jane," she wrote, "I am stunned by the events that have occurred in my life, since leaving Harvard. As you know, it started with the women I met in Malta, the cave in Ephesus, the children at the church ruins in Bosnia. Then there was the antiquities collector who gave me a manuscript, visions in the cave at the lake, Evangeline and her painting, the cat people, meeting Eartha Mae…so much has happened. If I thought these were random events, I wouldn't be so perplexed. My head is spinning as I try to find the bigger picture in all these fragments.

"In my student days I explored Alexandria, that once great Old-World center of learning on the Nile delta, where all thoughts converge. Now I find myself in this southern-most city, not far from a New-World delta, meeting with Evangeline and her mother, the great Eartha Mae. Andrew would say that in the realm of sub-atomic particles, the act (or art) of perception influences what is perceived. Everything that happens in a certain situation affects everything else.

"I find that I am without interpretation for these events. I am weary of analyzing. I seek no answers. Maybe you could say I no longer seek to ask the perfect question—I am questionless. I guess it's all about letting go. It all came to me in the diminishment of my desire and ambition. The great paradox. It is the *not wanting*, but in simply *being*. I sometimes think I sought to understand history as a way to ignore my own personal history, to run from myself. All these years you told me I was strong because I worked so hard and made my way up the academic ladder. I believed you. But now I see it all from a different perspective—I've simply been running and hiding—burying myself alive in piles of papers. Analysis has been a shield for experiencing. What I had once thought was courage now seems to have been weakness.

"I met an interesting woman here, they call her Maw-Maw. She told me that I would see miracles and that they would give me happiness, only if I did not feel the need to convince anyone of their reality. I hear those words over and over in my mind. I have spent so much of my life trying to convince others of my theories that I have been left frustrated. Now I am taking a personal sabbatical to bask in the beauty and radiance of my discoveries. I have surrendered and at this moment it is enough that I know." She paused for a moment, noticing how easily she had embraced Maw-Maw's advice. Then she asked herself—why was it only enough that she knew?

She continued writing, "If I told you all that has passed, I'm afraid you might not believe me—perhaps you'd even think I'd gone mad. I wouldn't blame you at all. I attended a Christmas Eve celebration last night, in a small Cajun town. Bonfires were burning along the Mississippi as they do every year—but this year was like no other. We knew something profound was about to happen. It all started when Eartha Mae appeared on her houseboat. She is no ordinary woman, she has powers..."

She looked up when Oakie and Virgil entered the bar. They ordered drinks and sat at a table near hers.

Oakie tapped her on the arm. "Writin' a book?"

"It was meant to be a letter. But you're right, it's beginning to look like a book," Betina said.

Oakie smiled proudly, "Virgil here's a poet. He wrote an O-de for Eartha Mae. He's gonna read it!"

The tables in the café were quickly filling up with people. Eartha Mae, Maw-Maw, Evangeline, Salome, Christian, Raider, and Tex stood at the entrance to the cafe and sat down at the only remaining table in the back. With her arm around Evangeline, Eartha Mae looked blissfully into her daughter's eyes, forgetting everything around them. Christian looked with devotion at Salome, overjoyed at her recovery.

When Tex asked Salome if she was glad to be up and about again, she didn't hear him. He waved his hand in front of her face, but she barely noticed. He smiled at Evangeline, but she didn't respond either. He looked around the room, then whispered in Raider's ear, "There's that lady. She's sitting alone." Just as he stood up to join her, the owner of the café made an announcement into a microphone.

"The first poet to read in our open poetry night is Virgil Kennedy Sexton."

Sitting on a barstool, in front of the mike, Virgil played his own introduction on a drum. Then he put the drum aside saying, "This is an Ode to Eartha Mae, by her humble servant, Virgil Kennedy Sexton." He cleared his throat as if to speak, then closed his eyes. A calm descended on the group, a moment of complete silence and attentiveness, when all coughing and fidgeting stopped. They waited for Virgil to begin his poem, but he said nothing and the silence became more intense. The silence was his poem...but it was no ordinary silence.

In a moment it started. Betina heard the tinkling of glasses as they knocked into each other—everything became fluid. The wind pulled her into its shaft along with colliding chairs, raincoats, umbrellas and glasses. It was the swirling Holy Wind that leaves whorls on the tips of ones fingers and toes, the wind that brought humans the breath of life. In this galaxy of tables and chairs, checkered napkins and mugs, beer bottles, menus and silverware, Betina began to hear the chant that she had heard so many times before.

She was swept into a vortex that took her back to the desk that was at the top of a high platform. It was a continuation of a vision she had in her hotel room. Positioned above dozens of twirling, free-flowing dancers, like an island in the eye of a storm, she worked on a page in the manuscript that had a central image of a mandala, which was inspired by everything going on around her. In the center of this temple stood a large multi-breasted woman. Groups of dancers whirled around this mysterious being who was now radiating light and whose breasts had become fountains of milk. A concentric ring of singers, holding torches, walked counterclockwise around the ecstatic whirling dancers. Several carried incense burners that filled the air with the scent of sage and cedar.

Betina found herself drawing and then writing at a rapid pace, describing this central figure, with auras of every color, rapidly transforming like an image in a kaleidoscope. The figure became a rainbow of flickering light; a moment later, all that was left was her fiery spirit, which became a Singing Flame.

It seemed that the incantation and recitation of the singers caused the flame to oscillate and change color, shifting from gold to orange, to blue to lavender, to yellow and to red. It produced a harmonic buzzing. The sound amplified, causing echoing voices to be reflected back with greater intensity in this underground temple. The Singing Flame projected pulsing pictures in 3D onto the walls. Betina imagined that the pictures had been encoded in the sound waves. Brilliant rays of light streaked through images of forests and giant flowers. The images soon broke down into thousands of fractal images of cellular structure. The Great Mother reigned in this mysterious cavern, the earth's womb, and the greatest treasure in this echo chamber was the elusive one found in the sound waves.

The spell was broken when Betina felt a hand on her shoulder. Slowly opening her eyes, she found Evangeline staring at her. Tex stood nearby and watched with a curious intensity. Waves of electricity ran up and down Betina's body—she didn't know if Evangeline was shaking her, or if she was shaking of her own accord. She was betwixt and between worlds as she looked around the tilted room with pulsating walls and slowly realized that Virgil had finished his presentation.

"We're leaving now," said Evangeline. "Would you like to join us?"

"I wish I could but I need to pack for my trip home," Betina responded.

"When are you leaving?" Tex asked with a sense of urgency.

"First thing in the morning," Betina replied with surprise at Tex's sudden interest.

"Hmm." Tex became pensive and joined Raider by the door.

As Evangeline left with Eartha Mae and the others in her group, Betina looked around, hardly recognizing where she was, since part of her was still in that underground world. Energies swirled in her mind as she tried to slow down her rapid accordion breath. Sensing that she had been initiated into the mysteries of the divine feminine, she knew she was both participant and record keeper.

In the evening, Evangeline and Eartha Mae walked toward the house where they once lived with Malcolm. The "For Sale" sign had been removed and only the post remained on the front lawn. Evangeline said to her mother, "I've watched the families come and go...always they reminded me of what we could've had."

They didn't notice Malcolm, who stood at a distance from the house, nor Virgil, who followed after them as they walked through the gate and climbed the front porch steps. Evangeline looked through the windowpane in the door and was surprised to see that the living room was fixed up in a fashion similar to the way it had been when they lived there. Finding the door unlocked, Eartha Mae followed Evangeline into the house.

A crackling fire in the fireplace took the chill out of the air and comforted them. Evangeline looked at the rocking chair, the braided rug, and her painting of Eartha Mae, hanging on the wall. She was amazed to see that it was no longer charred. The colors had all returned to their fullness and the image of Eartha Mae was more radiant than ever. Eartha Mae took a soft hairbrush off the mantle above the fireplace and tenderly held it in her hands.

Malcolm watched from the side window and felt a surge of warmth at the prospect of Eartha Mae and Evangeline settling into the home where they had all lived together. It did not take long for him to realize that they did not share his fantasy and did not want to recreate the past. Eartha Mae and Evangeline moved on, while Malcolm eventually moved back into this house, sharing the rest of his life in conversation with the image of his wife that spoke to him through the painting. In time, the little home became a pilgrimage center. An altar was erected around the painting, where people brought gifts of flowers and fruit and received guidance and even healings.

Eartha Mae and Evangeline left behind the home that was never their true home, but just a pale imitation of what home could be. In their hearts, they knew that home was not the picket fence, the little box they called a house, the fireplace or the rocking chair. Home for Eartha Mae and Evangeline was as vast as the universe.

When Eartha Mae sat down on a bench overlooking the river, she opened her arms, and Evangeline climbed into her lap. Taking the soft-bristled brush out of her pocket, Eartha Mae ran it through the long silky strands of her daughter's hair. As Evangeline looked into her mother's eyes she wondered: Who was this woman who held her in her arms, whispering tender words of affection? This woman was always in her dreams, yet she was someone too vast and mysterious to ever really know. Closing her eyes as she rocked back and forth, she drifted into a primordial dance. Her hair grew longer with each stroke of her mother's brush. In it emerged luminous butterflies, sweetly chirping birds, frolicking dolphins, singing whales and sparkling stars. It became the Mississippi, all rivers, the River of Life.

Standing on the banks of the Mississippi, Eartha Mae and Evangeline were joined by Maw-Maw, Salome, Christian, Estrella, even Flora and the women in white that traveled with her. They watched an eclipse and agreed it was a harbinger, heralding an age of gold. The astrological configuration of the Grand Sextile—linking the Sun, Jupiter, Mars, Saturn, Chiron, and the Moon—was their sign.

Hearing the ocean beckoning to them, they turned toward the delta. The Cetacean Nation was calling. Approaching them through the murky waters of the Mississippi was a pod of Atlantic Spotted Dolphins. One dolphin, with her calf by her side, singled herself out and made her way close to the shore. As they looked into the dolphin's eye, they experienced a communion. In offering a telepathic transmission, the dolphin showed holographic images of the group spreading their gifts in foreign lands. They knew that a transformation could occur beyond the personal, to a planetary level. In that moment, they understood that they had much to say and places to go. And so they soon set off in boats, to travel to distant lands, with all manner of gulf whales and dolphins, pinnipeds and sirenians, leatherbacks and loggerheads, leading the way across the wide ocean.

One ancient humpback, which had long ago departed from a northerly migration route, spoke of the coming of this small band of wanderers in a song that was carried along the songlines of the great oceans, by every species of whale; from the sperm to the pygmy, from the blue to the northern right whale. This cetacean music reached the ears of a tribe of aborigines who carried this modern tale along their ancient dream-journey routes, as they made their way across the desert in a walkabout. Soon, news of their coming spread to some of the most remote regions of the earth.

With time, things came full circle as Eartha Mae's group eventually encountered Vesna, who now had a young son, as well as Samir and Zoran, and the rest of the lost and raging tribe of Bosnian teenagers. They shared their life stories and dreams of world peace in the music they played and the songs they sang as they walked down highways that took them through dozens of countries. This nomadic group continued to grow and in their wanderings they passed other nomadic groups, including the old Maltese women, who left their cave dwelling to join 'the walk,' and who came together in tribal councils springing up in places all across the planet. Their dream was taking hold.

CHAPTER TWENTY

ORPHAN VOYAGE

As Betina put her suitcases in the trunk of her rented car she thought of Evangeline, Eartha Mae, and Virgil, traveling to distant lands with Salome, Christian, and Maw-Maw. It was as if their life had been a mythic journey and now they had set off on part two of that journey. Betina, on the other hand, would soon be returning to the harsh realities of a bitterly cold winter in New England. She looked at her map and imagined what it would be like for Oakie, who was returning to Memphis with Chloe and Boots—he announced plans to marry her in the spring. Tex and Raider also had surprising plans of their own. Betina discovered their luggage in the back seat of her car and asked where they were going.

"With you," Tex answered as if it should have been obvious. "You have no kids of your own."

"What does that have to do with anything?" she asked, as she got into the car, ready to start her journey home to Boston. When she realized they were serious she said, "It's out of the question."

"There's no question about it," said Tex as he hopped into the car and motioned for Raider to follow. Immediately closing the back door behind them, they curled up in their seat, securing their position.

"Out," Betina said as she looked at them in the rearview mirror. They didn't budge. She got up and opened the back door, motioning for them to exit the car, but they still didn't move. "This is ridiculous," she cried. "I can hardly manage my life as it is. I don't have space for the two of you."

"Do to," Tex insisted.

"Absolutely not."

"Yes. Absolutely."

"Absolutely not!"

"Absolutely yes!"

And on and on it went as they spoke in increasingly loud voices, until Betina became silent. She tapped her fingers on the steering wheel as she waited and thought about what to do. "Don't you have any family?"

"There's no family," said Tex.

"Maybe an Aunt."

"No Aunt," Tex answered.

"Well, what about you, Raider? You haven't said a word?"

"He don't talk much," Tex said.

"Do you have any living relatives?" Betina asked.

"What d'ya think," Tex replied.

"Let Raider talk for himself," Betina said.

"I had a mother, couldn't get here without one…or could I?" Raider asked.

"Yeah, OD'd, red rum. He found her in a dumpster," Tex inserted.

Betina sighed.

Raider looked with disinterest out the window, while Tex watched Betina closely, realizing that maybe he should have held back the information—she looked scared. It was a delicate walk: getting her pity without alienating her.

After ten minutes of silence, it became clear that they weren't going to get out of the car, so Betina hesitantly started the engine. As she drove down the road she argued with herself about what to do. She could take them to an orphanage or have the police remove them from her vehicle. She could pull over and drag them out of the car, but they'd probably resist. But then, how could she leave them on the side of the road, or with the police, or at an orphanage?

She wondered why they hadn't gone off with Evangeline, or if they had discussed their decision to remain behind with her. After all,

Evangeline had been the one caring for them for the past two years. And to think, Evangeline was only sixteen and had given so much of herself to these boys.

"Evangeline just left you two behind?"

"No...we were with her," said Tex. "Now we're with you."

That cleared up very little for Betina, but they weren't in the mood for any more questions. They shut their eyes, pretending to be in a deep sleep, leaving the rest of Betina's questions unanswered.

She wrestled with a hundred thoughts as she headed northeast, leaving behind the city of New Orleans. Wouldn't they destroy her life? How could she continue with her work? What work was that, anyway? How could she care for them? Weren't there laws about taking them out of state? Of course, there had to be laws. She'd probably be charged with kidnapping minors, she told herself. She'd stop at a police station in the next town. Instead, the only place she stopped was at a dozen diners off the interstate. And each time they left the diner, she caught the boys filling their pockets with candy and cigarettes. She watched them through the rearview mirror as they silently slipped their coveted loot under the car seat, into the ashtray, and into any nook and cranny they could find in the back seat.

At a rest stop along the route home, she nervously reached into her purse for a cigarette while the boys ran to the men's room. When they emerged, Tex reached for the pack of cigarettes from the hood of the car, taking a cigarette for himself and offering one to Raider.

"I like this brand," Tex chirped.

Betina grabbed the cigarettes out of his hand. "None for you."

"Got my own then since you're gonna be that way about it." Tex pulled another pack out of his shirt pocket.

"How long have you two been smoking?" Betina asked.

"Three years. Since I was eight," said Tex.

"And you, Raider?" Betina asked.

"Forever," Tex answered for him.

"I'm asking Raider," Betina responded.

"Earl an' me always smoked," Raider replied in a bored tone.

"Who's Earl? A relative?" Betina asked, hoping that he had a family somewhere.

"Brother," Raider responded.

"A dead relative," Tex added. "Gunshot."

"Good grief," Betina whispered to herself as she put out her cigarette and got back in the car. Tex and Raider jumped in immediately after her, taking no chances of being left behind.

"Where did you get the name Raider?"

"I named him that," Tex replied proudly, "cause he kept raiding my dumpster."

"What was your birth name?" Betina asked, hoping that such an innocent question wouldn't lead to more disturbing revelations.

"My real name was Jesse Lawson Bridges," Raider replied in a barely audible tone.

"Well, that's a beautiful name," Betina noted.

"It's his father's name…he got the chair," Tex added cheerfully.

Betina became silent—that was about all she could digest. She had no intention of asking why he was electrocuted.

Tex slept with his feet resting on the head rest of the empty seat next to hers. She noticed large holes in his shoes, and cuts on the soles of his feet. There would probably be snow on the ground in Cambridge, so she took them both to a shoe store at a mall in Atlanta and watched with amusement as Tex tried on different pairs of sneakers. He settled on a style that had red lights circling the sole so that they glowed in the dark like a couple of UFOs waiting to take off. Tex moonwalked from one mirror to the next.

Raider tried on a similar pair and suddenly he was hopping down the aisle, jumping from chair to chair, rapping in a soft but energetic voice. "Ya gotta reload, ya gotta change the program. Ya gotta let go, of yer old kinda knowin'. " Raider grabbed a pair of red shoes with stiletto heels off a shelf and placed them at Betina's feet, motioning for her to try them on. "Ya gotta put on, a new kinda shoe, as you move through this vir-tu-al re-a-li-ty…"

"Tear it down, brother, keep it real, mother." Tex joined in at the top of his lungs.

"Oh, good grief. They're rappers," Betina whispered to herself as another wave of terror passed through her and perspiration formed on her temple. She wondered what to make of Raider's grin as she slipped her left foot into the red shoe.

"Trippy," Raider nodded.

Just as she lifted her foot into the right shoe, she felt a large blister on the arch of her foot. She recalled that she had been burned when she crossed the hot coals with Evangeline and Malcolm, as they made their cosmic journey around the pyre with the cat people. Not having remembered reading that they were firewalkers, she wondered if firewalking was something they recently incorporated into their sacred ceremonies—just as they spontaneously included Evangeline's painting on their altar. She knew that the !Kung of the Kalahari Desert said that firewalking is possible when a person's energy equals the energy of the fire. She shivered, knowing that something remarkable had happened—they had all taken on the energy of the fire.

Betina thought of Virgil's poetry reading and of the whirling wind that mysteriously swept her off to her underground world. She still didn't know if he had, indeed, read a poem, or if he had somehow inspired her temple vision, of a central fire that was the force behind the fertility powers of the Creatrix. She knew she would hold forever in her mind that image of the Creatrix whirling at such a great speed that she burst into flames, in a kind of Spontaneous Combustion, becoming a Singing Flame. She believed that the fire of the Earth Mother's spirit had been tended to by the fire bearers, since the beginning, so that it could once again ignite and give light to the world.

Fire, brought by Prometheus, was a catalyst for the beginnings of civilization and the arts. In time, however, fire itself became a metaphor for hell, a place where Christians believed that those who were evil would burn. The meaning of fire was debased, like so many other sacred symbols. One image led to another and Betina went off on a series of tangents until Tex interrupted her train of thought.

"Message to earth...Beep Beep Beep...E.T. to earth. Anyone home?" Tex asked through a megaphone made by holding two hands together at his mouth. "Let's see how you look."

Making a note to herself that she'd have to explore the symbolism of fire at a later date, Betina stood up and took a few steps in the high-heeled shoes. Beneath her feet, she still saw the burning red-hot coals.

"You're blazin'," Raider grinned.

"A phoenix from the ash," Betina laughed. She looked down at her legs wondering what kind of fantasy they were offering her by suggesting that she buy the shoes. "Do you know the fairytale by Hans Christian Andersen?" When they looked at her with blank expressions, she continued. "There was a young girl who couldn't stop dancing as soon as she put on a pair of red shoes."

"That's exactly why you need them," Tex insisted. "And it's less than a Benjamin!"

Raider took Betina's hand and twirled her around in her new shoes, trying to convince her to buy them. "Those'll get you outta your matrix," he asserted.

"They're elegant but not very intelligent." She was about to put them back on the shelf, but on an impulse changed her mind.

Stopping in several clothing shops at the mall, Betina bought the boys warm clothes for the cold New England winters. Tex and Raider pirouetted all the way to the car, dancing with shopping bags filled with recent purchases. They said it was the first time they had new shoes, since their attempts at stealing them had always failed. Soon they were bursting with excitement as they imagined their new life in Boston.

"Ever seen snow?" Tex asked Raider.

"Nope," Raider answered.

"What's it feel like, *Maw*?" Tex asked Betina.

Betina froze.

In the evening, they checked into a motel off the interstate. Emptying their pockets, the boys made a little pile consisting of two souvenir ashtrays, a miniature car, several packs of cigarettes, and two cans of spray paint. Grabbing the remote control for the television, Raider blasted through a hundred channels, pausing on a car race and an underwater shark hunt. Tex noticed Betina watching him with a nervous expression.

"She's getting amped," Tex whispered to Raider. "Better cool it."

Raider nodded then set the channel to a Christmas concert performed by the Vienna Boys Choir. He put the remote down, sat up straight and smiled sweetly at Betina as he joined the ninety-five choristers between the ages of ten to fourteen. Tex joined him in a round of *Dona nobis pacem*—their voices were filled with passion and precision, matching the heavy vibrato of the lead singer.

Betina did a double take as they shapeshifted into angels before her very eyes, pulling at her heartstrings. "Little tricksters," she whispered to herself. "They know just how to get to me."

Raider grinned, "Yup…you're in for the ride of your life."

Tex jabbed him in the side and frowned at him.

Betina's heart was rapidly beating.

When Tex took off his shirt, she noticed that he had cigarette burns and knife wounds on his chest and stomach. He jumped into bed, yanking on the blankets that were tightly tucked under the mattress, ripping them completely free of their confinement so that his feet were exposed.

"It'll be cool, you'll see," Tex reassured her.

He seemed to know that her mind was exploding as she considered what she had gotten into by taking them home to Boston. She gulped when she realized she could slip into a permanent parenting role if she wasn't careful. She wondered what she could do for these boys; could she give them the sense of endless possibility that seemed to be the birthright of Jane's son, or would she resent the infringement upon her freedom and the demands for her time? Turning out the light that stood on a stand between their twin beds, she sat down in a chair in an adjoining room, contemplating their future.

Just as she managed to fall asleep, the sounds of cartoons, blaring on the television, woke her up. It was impossible to fall back to sleep so they grabbed a quick breakfast—at 6:30 AM they were back on the road. It pleased her that Raider chose to sit in the front seat. Taking control of the radio, he flipped through all the stations, over and over again, pausing on an occasional commercial that he sang along to in a loud and energetic voice. While pounding the dashboard with his new sneakers, his hand slapped the roof of the car, to the beat of a particularly nasty rap song. Noticing another terrified look on Betina's face, Raider turned to Tex who signaled at him to turn off the radio. Immediately, Tex and Raider straightened their backs, joining in on a soothing round of *Dona nobis pacem*. Eventually, Tex insisted that Betina sing along. During the next thirty miles she was cradled by this song of peace, which brought back memories of summer camp in Quebec.

Yes, Raider was coming out of his shell, but Betina was apprehensive about who he might be, and what hidden qualities might emerge. She watched him quietly, until he fell asleep with his head resting so trustingly on her shoulder. She secretly wiped away tears as she allowed herself to realize the fullness of their tragic situation, and of their courage and fortitude in spite of it.

Soon the boys began fighting over which one of them would get to sit up front, next to her. She was so uncertain about any of this, but it had been a while since anyone had fought over her. This time, Tex raced to get into the front seat. He innocently put a wad of gum under the dashboard, smiled sweetly at her, then turned the radio on ever so softly, folding his hands in his lap. He looked straight ahead till they took off, then raised the volume on the radio in small increments until it was blasting.

Betina's repetitive litany of silent questions continued, as new fears surfaced. What if she started really caring about them? What if she loved them and something happened to them? What if she found that somehow she had an instinct to nurture? And what if after showering them with her love, they took off at seventeen or eighteen only to start lives of their own on the other side of the country, or the other side of the world...never calling, never writing, never remembering her? Or worse than that…what if they ended up in prison…what if Raider followed in his father's footsteps? What if and what if? How could she survive it?

The boys were determined to be as helpful as possible when Betina shopped at a grocery store, just a few miles from her home. Grabbing a shopping cart, they pushed it up and down the aisles. They also insisted on carrying all the grocery bags to the car. Tex struggled with three of them while Raider held another three. Although Tex dropped one of the bags, broke a jar of pasta sauce and cracked a dozen eggs, Betina was moved by their desire to help out. She quietly considered that she might find unexpected joys in sharing her life with them.

CHAPTER TWENTY-ONE

ASHUDDER AND AGLOW

After arriving in Cambridge in the early evening, the boys quickly settled into Betina's guestroom. Tex and Raider jumped on the twin beds then played with the antique toy collection that she had carefully arranged on a shelf. They filled an empty cabinet with new toys and the bureau with clothes. Betina was struck by the way she had decorated it months earlier, before she set out on her trip. Perhaps in the deepest recesses of her mind, she knew she would bring a child into her life.

The piles of mail that waited for her were enormous. There were hundreds of Christmas cards, but the first one she read was from Jane. She was stunned to learn that Jane had separated from her husband and would be filing for a divorce. Shortly after her visit, Jane discovered that Phillip had been having an affair for many years, with a man who belonged to their boat club. Phillip revealed that since their marriage had never been fulfilling, he would be building a new home to share with his boyfriend. Betina wondered why Jane had not seen that he was drifting from her or that he had never been faithful to her. She suspected that she probably knew, but it was something she chose not to discuss.

Betina sat down by the bay window, wondering if Jane might take this opportunity to finish her dissertation, sell her house and move to another town, or go back to work. She remembered Jane's early study of abandoned girls in China. She had written about child abuse in China during her years in graduate school, but left the world of lost children and dropped out of her program after getting pregnant with Petie.

Betina returned for the last time to her office at Harvard to get the things she left there when she moved out with great haste, at the end of the spring semester. The one kindness extended was allowing Betina to keep her cubicle space after her departure. Whirling around her like dervishes as she walked down the hall, Tex and Raider raced ahead into her old office the moment she opened the door.

Looking up from the papers he was sorting through at his desk, Humbert gave her a frown of disapproval. Then he studied the boys with even greater irritation as they fingered everything in their path. Betina grabbed hold of their hands in an effort to subdue their unbridled energy. Humbert tried to speak, but couldn't utter a word, and shook his head in frustration. The left side of his face was frozen, his eyelid drooped, his jowls and mouth sagged, and his arm hung limply at his side.

Staring at Humbert, Tex asked, "What's happened to him? He's half dead."

Betina felt a surge of sympathy for Humbert, when she realized he had had a stroke. Struggling to find comforting words, she thought of thanking him for redirecting the course of her life, and for helping her get the courage to leave academia. She wanted to tell him that she had seen things she never imagined possible, but stopped herself from saying anything, knowing he would not be interested in her good fortune.

She watched as Tex slipped a letter opener into his pocket. Struggling to lean forward, Humbert tried several times to cry out 'thief,' but it required too great an effort. He slumped down in his chair, defeated, without a whimper.

Finally Betina said, "They're constantly coming out with new drugs...there's always the possibility of recovery...I once had an aunt who..." She stopped trying to comfort him when she noticed Tex and Raider imitating Humbert's zombie-like mannerisms. She glared at them until they dropped their antics then looked at Humbert apologetically. His fingers trembled and his left eye welled with a tear that lingered in the corner of his eye, then rolled down his cheek. As he continued sifting through papers with his functioning hand and packing them in a box, it occurred to Betina that he was either taking a leave of absence or had resigned. Just as she made her final departure from academia, she realized that the doors could reopen if a more sympathetic chairperson replaced Humbert. How curious, she thought, that new paths always seem to become available just when the path that you are on turns into a dead end.

Betina finished packing a box of books on archaeology and files of papers for articles that she had been in the process of writing. She also found bottles of wine that she kept on hand for impromptu celebrations. It made her realize that she hadn't had a drink or even thought about drinking since her trip. She left the office juggling several boxes but couldn't prevent the bottom of one of them from opening. She hurriedly fixed the box then filled it back up with books while Raider and Tex paused at the department door. They quickly spray painted it with the words "Break the MaTriX." Betina coughed at the toxic fumes from the spray can. Just as she was about to look back over her shoulder to see what they were doing, Tex joined her and smiled angelically. Taking the boxes from her arms, he hummed *Dona nobis pacem* and hurried her down the stairs.

As Tex and Raider put the boxes in the trunk of her car, Betina mentioned that she planned to visit her mother in the nursing home the following day. She was eager to see her since their only contact had been by phone for the past few months. She hoped the boys would be able to entertain themselves for a few hours, but to her surprise they insisted on joining her.

Betina always braced herself before entering her mother's room at St. Mary's Home for the Aged, since she expected Frances to look at her with dull and lifeless eyes. Her mother's confusion about who she was had made each visit more painful. But something stirred within Frances when she saw Betina with the boys. Frances was suddenly filled with a sense of excitement at spending a Sunday afternoon with new friends.

"I think I'm Frances, Frances Sharp," said Betina's mother with a sparkle in her eye as she extended her hands to the boys. "Not too sharp though anymore. And what's your number?"

Raider and Tex looked at her and laughed, "She's funny," said Tex.

"Yes. I'm a funny bunny." Turning to Betina she said, "Mother, why do you leave me here?"

Betina always found it disconcerting when her mother reversed roles and played the child.

"And where is Father?" Frances asked.

"He died," she said.

"But how could that be?" Frances said, wiping away a flood of tears.

Betina silently reprimanded herself. Even though he had been dead for more than ten years, Frances always reacted as if his death had happened yesterday. "I mean, he's away…working" she said.

"Well tell him to come and fetch me now," said her mother. She brightened-up when Raider took out a package from an oversized jacket-pocket and presented it to Frances. Betina wondered where he had gotten the gift, and assumed he had stolen it from a pharmacy they were in the night before. It was wrapped in gold foil and tied with a bright pink ribbon.

"I love pink," Frances said as she untied the ribbon. "Mother, may I wear this pink thingy? It's such a special special."

Betina nodded and helped her tie the ribbon in her hair.

Frances winked at Raider and said, "Did you know that I have a daughter your age? She would look good in pink. Haven't seen her lately though. What has become of her, Mother?"

The boys burst into laughter when she called Betina "Mother." The laughter was contagious and soon Betina joined in. Frances looked delighted at their amusement as she unwrapped the present: a velvet-covered jewelry box. Turning a key to wind up a pink ballerina, Betina watched as it began to spin to the music of Swan Lake. Then she took out little perfumes, lipstick, and nail polish from the tiny drawers in the jewelry box.

"I could polish your nails," Tex offered.

"Yes, that would be plu plu-perfect." Frances smiled broadly, holding out her hands, while Tex made a serious effort at giving her a perfect manicure. Although he had trouble keeping the nail polish on her fingernails and off her finger, Frances didn't mind in the least. When he was done, she admired both her hands and applauded his effort. She watched with enthusiasm as Tex painted Betina's fingernails as well. Then Frances dabbed perfume on her neck and smeared her lips with the lipstick.

Raider had another surprise for Frances—a pair of elegant slippers. As Frances tried them on, Betina suppressed her concerns about where he had gotten them. This wasn't the time to address his shoplifting habit.

"I had a pair like this when we lived in London," Frances exclaimed. "We were quite a couple. We would dance at all the clubs…we were always the last ones to leave. I thought there was nothing here, but now there's a pleurisy. Oh we were always flashing."

Raider laughed, "You're trippy, Granny."

Frances winked at Raider and took his hand, "You see the blue me. How about a quickening?"

Raider paused for a moment then burst into laughter. "She's coming on to me," he whispered to Betina. "Did you hear what she said?"

Betina was relieved when a young priest poked his head into Frances's room. She motioned for him to come in.

"You must be Frances's daughter," he said.

Betina nodded.

Frances grabbed his hand and said, "This is Father. She said you were dead. See? He's not dead! He likes to lie in the green pastures with me." She coyly lifted the sheet up so that it covered half her face and adjusted the ribbon in her hair.

The priest patted Tex and Raider on the head, while Betina said goodbye to her mother. She took one last look at Frances as the priest sat in a chair by her bed and began to recite the 23rd Psalm.

"Maybe I might want to be a priest—a priest or a rapper," Raider said, as they walked through the halls of the nursing home. "Maybe I could be both."

"Why not?" Betina said with a laugh.

"You just need a collar…with spikes," Tex added, as he spray painted his name on the base of a statue at the entrance, while Betina's back was turned.

Nearly an inch of snow had fallen while they were with Frances. Tex and Raider immediately launched into their first snowball fight. It took a great deal of coaxing for Betina to get them into the car so she could drive home.

As they drove through the streets of Cambridge, Betina asked them several times not to stick their heads out the window to catch snowflakes on their tongue. The snowfall added enchantment to the Cambridge streets—all of them admired the magical landscape. But for Betina, this feeling of wonder was mixed with anxiety as she asked herself if she could survive having Raider and Tex around day and night. Did they have any idea of the life they were choosing?

Tex sensed what she was thinking and said, "It's like this, Maw. When nothin's going your way, and nothin's ever gonna go your way...you gotta go for that sliver of possibility. Maybe it'll only come once in a lifetime. You gotta turn it around."

What a miracle to see the faith that Tex possessed despite all odds. Like Oliver Twist, he had an expectation of justice. He could still ask for more and *twist* things around.

"Ya gotta turn it 'round, ta keep from burnin'." Raider stuck his hand out the car window and tapped out a rhythmic improvisation on the roof of the car.

Betina was stunned into silence.

Soon after arriving home, Andrew called and told her that he had returned from a conference in San Francisco. After inviting him to come over, she wondered if he would tell her that she was out of her mind, bringing home Tex and Raider. She could almost hear him say, "You're an intelligent woman. How could you do something so rash and impulsive? This is so unlike you."

She was completely unprepared for the excitement he displayed upon seeing the boys. Talk about hokey. Showing them some amateur magic tricks, he tried to impress them with his ability to make things disappear and reappear. Betina was careful not to interfere as this new side of Andrew finally had an opportunity to emerge.

In the evening, Betina received a surprise visit from Peter Fagan. Andrew answered the door while she looked out from her study, finishing a paragraph in a chapter she was writing.

"I'm sorry for the intrusion...I should've called," said Peter trying to hide his embarrassment at finding Andrew at the door. Shaking some snowflakes off his hat and muffler he continued, "I'm passing through town on a book tour."

Betina watched from her study as Andrew invited Peter in and gave him a warm handshake. Peter held his new book in his hand, wrapped in elegant holiday paper and tied with a ribbon. Andrew responded enthusiastically to the subject of Peter's book, agreeing that tonal resonance in the pyramids was an intriguing subject. Peter explained that the book started out with a study of the harmonic structure of the pyramids, but expanded to include a focus on the labyrinthine underground systems at places like Tikal in Guatemala and the subterranean complex beneath the Egyptian pyramids. He said that the pyramids were markers on the earth's surface that signaled vast underground cities. Sometimes he could project himself into these tunnels and read the messages on the walls. He explained that the ancient tunnels were all connected and lead to the center.

Listening from her office, Betina felt goose bumps as she imagined the different pathways that led to the center. Maybe these were the same ones she visited in her dreams, through the tunnels and doors that opened in her mind. She always believed that Peter was a discerning scholar who would make significant advances by using a cross-disciplinary approach in his research. Perhaps it was his free-spirited manner, that spring in his step, that natural flow of exuberance that made some people think he was a lightweight in terms of scholarship. She was certain that he gave presentations at academic conferences, not because he wanted the acceptance of the scholarly community—he would most certainly have a much larger audience outside of that circle—but because he believed that shifting their perspective would lead them on a quest for deeper truths. With truth comes wisdom and the possibility of earthly harmony—that was Peter's ultimate pursuit.

Betina listened as Peter asked Andrew about some of his latest projects. She was pleased at the curious resonance and respect they had for each other, despite their tangled history. She heard Andrew excuse himself when a lamp crashed to the floor in the boy's room—moments later Peter tapped on the door of her study.

"I see that Andrew is really in touch with his past," Peter remarked.

"What do you mean?" she asked.

"Everything he's working on now...the new energy systems...it's all related to the technical devices that he once used...things he designed in other lifetimes."

Betina looked puzzled.

"Why do you think it all comes to him so effortlessly?" He picked up her kaleidoscope and looked through it, then said, "Andrew was over-educated and lost the memories of those lifetimes. Maybe he doesn't want to remember, but the technology stayed with him." Peter paused and with a twinkle in his eye he asked, "You're not really back together, are you?"

She answered, with a sense of disbelief for everything that had transpired in the past month, "Things have realigned in ways I never would have imagined."

His cheerfulness momentarily disappeared as his jaw tensed and his smile dissolved. Peter tilted his head, took in a deep breath, and soon his eyes brightened again as he handed the kaleidoscope to her. "Well, the only thing that's permanent is impermanence." Then he quickly changed the subject. "Tell me about the manuscript that Wolfgang gave you."

"It's blank," she said. "You know how much I love cryptography...but there's nothing to go on. No language to crack...no coded words. Just wingless book-lice...roaming the pages of the manuscript, like Tuaregs crossing the Sahara."

Peter did not seem surprised by her comments. "There's nothing for you to crack, it's easier than that...after all you wrote it."

She looked at him blankly.

Peter added, "Wolfgang told me that the writing and images would appear when the moment was right."

"And what makes the time right?" she asked, as Andrew joined them and listened in on their conversation.

"It has to do with the earth's cycle around the sun and the

movement of Earth toward the center of the galaxy. The configuration of the Grand Sextile signals the way. In this new stage of the earth's cycle, feminine energy in all things will take the lead. The true history of humanity will be revealed when an eclipse covers the sun causing a shadow to fall between the paws of the lion constellation in the sky and on the lion-sphinx in Egypt. As above, so below. The lion guards the entrance to knowledge of the earth's history and the manuscript is a piece of that forgotten history."

Betina couldn't tell if he was being literal or speaking metaphorically but decided to hold her tongue, remembering how it often took months before the meaning of Peter's thoughts fell into place, though sometimes they never did.

Andrew considered Peter's perspective and said, "Earth does have a heartbeat and you could say it's speeding up. Its pulse is also rising and its magnetic field is diminishing."

"It's a galactic New Year," Peter exclaimed. "A shift in ages from the Piscean to the Aquarian Age. We're at the end of the Kali Yuga and the Maha Yuga...The ending of one Yuga is just the breathing in of the Godhead and the creation of a new Yuga is the breathing out. It's all divine breath. Then there's a 4.4 billion-year cycle, called the Kalpa, which is coming to an end. The cycles are all converging and electromagnetic wave patterns are shifting."

"Where're you getting this information?" Betina asked.

"It's in all the sacred texts, from the Vedas to the writings of the ancient Greeks. It's in the spiraling mathematics of the Mayan calendars. This ancestral knowledge has even been passed down from one generation to the next among indigenous people. You could even say it's encoded in our DNA."

"Do you have archaeological evidence, beyond veiled ancient texts?" Betina asked.

"Evidence of previous Yugas is turning up everywhere...it's in the newly discovered underwater ruins off Taiwan, in India...and south of Cuba. Ruins of highly complex civilizations, like Atlantis…much more advanced than we ever were. It's also evident in new discoveries in astronomy of a hundred solar planetary systems and in new findings about the galactic core. There's also evidence of a binary system in which our sun rotates around a twin star."

Betina couldn't quite understand what the galactic core or a twin sun could have to do with the subject at hand.

Peter recognized her unspoken confusion and continued, "Every living thing has a cycle, men have cycles, women have cycles—menstrual cycles, menopause. It's easy to see the cycles in our own body and in animals…when a caterpillar turns into a butterfly, or a tadpole becomes a frog…but it's harder to see the slow cycles in the planet and in the universe—but they're happening. How could they not be happening—change is the only constant. The universe is living—it's not dead. It has cycles within cycles, within cycles, within cycles." He took a pen from his shirt pocket and carefully drew several diagrams depicting the ending of these cycles. He also drew sketches of the alignment of Earth with the sun and its position in the galaxy. "I don't know how this will all manifest…I have my theories…they're all in my book. Here, this is for you." He held out his book for her.

She slowly unwrapped the starry wrapping paper then ran her fingers over the elegant cover. "I'll read it and get back to you." Betina realized that for Peter, logic and spirituality were balanced and braided in their wholeness and unity like a double helix. She was intrigued by the way he described the shift toward the feminine coming about because of earth changes rather than the result of a social movement that began, at least, with the great democratic revolutions of the eighteenth century. It was a perspective that would not have been embraced by any of her former colleagues. Although he managed to alienate practically everyone in academic circles, he was building a following of his own outside of that world. There were often points where their thinking found a curious convergence, as if they were getting to the same place although they traveled along different paths.

"The time has come...your mysterious manuscript will reveal itself," Peter said, returning to his original point.

Betina knew in her heart that the book would speak. In a way, it had been speaking to her all along. When she had it in her presence, it affected her so completely, it altered her moods, it inspired visions, it transformed her even though it remained indecipherable, uninterpretable, and an incomprehensible mystery. It helped to lead her out of the shadowland by reminding her of the truth of who she was. She hadn't looked at the book for months and was eager to sit down with it again. Perhaps this time it *would* reveal itself.

She introduced Peter to Tex and Raider before he left.

"Got any tricks," Raider asked immediately.

Betina wasn't surprised that Peter also had a bag of tricks. When he demonstrated some wrestling moves, they were more than impressed.

"He's hokey," Tex shouted to Betina and Andrew.

Betina was stunned and shrugged her shoulders. Where did he get that word from? Andrew looked at her for an explanation and Betina whispered, "They recycle words from decades ago, and they love to reverse the meaning."

It was true, Peter looked anything but hokey as he skillfully maneuvered both boys at once into headlocks.

"Well then...that's what I meant that time when I said that your proposal was a little hokey. I meant it in reverse," Andrew whispered back.

"But you said you never said that," Betina replied.

"Well...I'm saying...that if I did *indeed* say that...how can I remember everything I say...You were the one who said I said that...though I'm certain it was never something that I said…oh never mind."

Despite Peter's expertise, Tex and Raider managed to pin him down and shouted out cries of victory. But their victory was short lived. Peter flipped them over and made his escape. "That's it, tigers, I'm off." Andrew handed Peter his coat and hat and he put them on.

Betina wrapped the muffler around his neck. "It's cold out there."

He whispered in her ear, "I'm glad to see you've brought these raw and untamed jungle creatures into your home. These little cubs compliment your leopard spirit."

Betina was moved by the comment and kissed him on the cheek.

I'll be in touch," he said, as he hugged her then bounced down the stairs and was off.

She put Peter's book and the kaleidoscope on a shelf above her desk and thought about how life is like the wheel of the kaleidoscope—just when you think your life is one way—it becomes something else when all the pieces fall into a new formation. As she sat at her desk and opened the mute book, she realized that the dial of life had shifted for all of them. Staring at the empty pages, she knew that the book had something to communicate, but she still did not know how to penetrate the silent language.

Betina didn't notice Andrew standing over her until he rested his hand on her shoulder and whispered, "Maybe it was written with invisible ink."

If only it was that simple. If only in a split-second the words and images would appear to her after all these months of silence.

"Hey Pop," she heard Tex say, "Just one more trick!"

Pop? She couldn't believe he called Andrew 'Pop.' She watched as Andrew returned to the bedroom and pulled a coin out of Tex's ear. The boys feigned amazement and Andrew left the room feeling a buzz of satisfaction at his ability to amuse them.

"Night, Maw," shouted Tex from the bedroom.

Tex and Raider were weaving them into a kind of storybook family. Betina wondered where they had gotten the concept? They had come from broken homes and lived on the streets most of their young life. The more she thought about it, the more she realized that a family might be their ultimate dream—and these two young dreamers were manifesting their desires with every step they took, because their vision was fully formed and foremost in their mind. When they called her *Maw*, she felt fear, fascination, and pleasure. She wanted to be that all nurturing, all loving Great Mother, but feared that she would be unable to fulfill their endless need for attention and devotion. But then, Peter had said these boys were from the jungle. They knew how to take what they believed was theirs. She was somewhat relieved by his comment—in a sense these boys would not let her fail. Although she was intrigued at the thought of excavating the internal strata of her mind regarding motherhood, this expedition would have to wait—Andrew had other plans.

She held the mute book in her hand as he led her into the bedroom. Then he turned off all the lights, except for a black light that she kept in an antique lamp as a memento of their college days. When he put on a cut from a newly released Doors Anthology, memories of their early years together filled her mind. She remembered how he played *Break on Through*, after their first night together, and how her black light illuminated everything that was fluorescent in the dorm room: the fish in the tank, the butterflies that hung from the ceiling, the peace sign on her door, even his T-shirt with its fluorescent mushrooms. It was also her first experience at recognizing the possibility of moving through new doors of perception, and soaring into unexplored worlds with another human being.

Here they were again. She left behind this earthly realm and became an astronaut, blasting off with Andrew, on their private cruise ship. Holding her close, he breathed in the scent of her skin. Circling her breasts with his tongue, he ran his hand up her inner thigh. How was it that they had come back to each other and made their way home, after years of going separate ways? It was Twelfth Night and they had a night of epiphanies. They were more than two people holding each other, they were the fullness of the universe itself. In that moment they were a miracle of perfect love. They were the magi bearing the gifts of their love to one another. She had wandered far from her homeland, crossed mountains and deserts, guided by an inner star, only to find her way home to Andrew, wanting only to offer gifts of adoration. The word had new meaning for her. Adoration—she knew there was no greater wisdom or beauty than that of adoring another.

They entered low earth orbit and floated in each other's arms at zero gravity. Through the window of her luxury cabin she saw Earth as an anagram for heart, and watched it spinning beneath her. She felt overwhelming love for this precious blue-green world as they soared toward the moon. She could see the astronauts taking their first steps on that lunar landscape; soon they drifted past the other planets, into distant solar systems. They were celestial voyagers, quivering, rippling, rhapsodizing, tingling, trembling, tenderly holding each other with their hearts wildly throbbing on a breath-taking journey.

Inhaling. Exhaling. Aching. Arching. Widening. Pulsating. Together they became the perfect rhythm of the primordial oceans. Ebbing. Flowing. Rocking. Rolling. Receiving. Relieving.

They entered into a cosmic heart that was rapidly beating. They were hearts within greater hearts and she could see the ribcage that protected them, expanding and contracting. She realized that the lines of the ribcage were created by words or thoughts. They moved so rapidly that they blurred together and gave the illusion of being stationary lines. It reminded her of the way the words that Malcolm incorporated into his paintings had become outlines of horses and people.

They were out-of-body lovers and one image merged with another. In this altered state, the ribcage morphed into Marletta's text, in holographic form. As they rose up the spine of this body of thought, from one level to the next, she found that they were moving through a scale of tones. Each tone corresponded to a spectrum of colors and expressed a truth that she could feel, but could not translate into words. These tones created a harmonic chord that was so magnificent, that every cell in her body resonated with it. But mixed with the ecstasy that she felt at hearing this most exquisite music, was a sadness that this harmony had been lost through a lack of interest in remembering and through mundane pursuits.

Betina was certain that Andrew was seeing all this with her, as orgasmic waves washed over them. They were centripetal and centrifugal forces in an undulating cycle of vibration around a still point. Soon, strands of DNA lovingly merged with each other and gave birth to additional strands that blasted apart their bodies. Their veins and arteries shot out into the cosmos like a vast network of dark blue rivers. Their bones pulled apart at the joints and drifted through space while their spinning cells exploded into a galaxy of shining stars. They were neutrons and electrons dancing and singing. They returned to the beginning of creation, as their cells merged with each other becoming atoms of the Creator.

Inhaling. Exhaling. Inhaling. Exhaling. Inhaling. Exhaling. Inhaling. Exhaling. Inhaling. Exhaling. Inhaling. Exhaling. Inhaling. Exhaling. Inhaling. Landing.

They rolled over onto their backs, catching their breath with hearts still wildly pounding. Betina heard the shaman's words: "In the return is the beginning." She knew she had returned and savored the experience of oneness with all creation. It was a perfect and pure moment—an epiphany for both of them. After countless breaths, Betina focused her thoughts on the love that existed between them. Soon, she stood outside herself, watching as renewed fears surfaced—she recognized how much she needed Andrew in her life.

Andrew sensed her fears and smiled lovingly, "I've missed you terribly. I've missed everything about you."

He never chose sarcasm over sincerity or cleverness over kindness, and this was what made her powerless around him. He could only speak the truth. He lay with his head on her breasts and she stroked his forehead. But she soon became restless; she wanted to tell him about all her visions, but she was hesitant. After struggling with the pros and cons of revealing her deepest thoughts, she said, "I've seen so much in these past few months, but if I spoke about it to anyone, I'm sure they'd think I was crazy."

Andrew said, "It doesn't matter what people think. You are a lightspark returning to the light."

She shuddered as she remembered how Fogarth had called Marletta 'lightspark.' Where had Andrew gotten this word? He had never used this word before and she wondered how it had become part of his vocabulary. She thought of how she no longer met Marletta as a separate person, rather she seemed to have merged with her. In these visions, Betina found herself wearing Marletta's habit as well as a velvet cloak that was exactly like the one she bought in Amsterdam. Andrew reminded her of Fogarth. The world had become a much more mysterious place than she ever imagined, and she was filled with awe at the *mysterium tremendum.*

Betina marveled at the way she had felt so completely connected to Andrew just moments earlier, but now he seemed to be as unfathomable a mystery as the universe. But then, so was she. With all the years she had spent sifting through the layers of her conscious and unconscious mind, she still had made only a small dent in terms of self-discovery, and if she remained a mystery to herself, how could she expect to comprehend the limitless universe of Andrew?

Still naked, she got up to get a glass of water from the kitchen, forgetting that Tex and Raider were staying with her. When she heard them giggling, she grabbed her bathrobe and threw it on.

Tex was sitting up in bed smiling at her when she looked in on him. "Satisfied?" he said, grinning from cheek to cheek. "Sounds like you got yours."

"Good grief," she muttered.

"How's a person s'posed to get any sleep?" Raider snickered.

"So sorry. It won't happen again." Betina shuffled off down the hallway and sighed as she listened to the boys imitate the sound of their lovemaking.

"More...more, Andy. Oh darling, deeper, deeper. Faster, faster, oh *Dona* oh *nobis* oh *pacem*," Tex moaned in a feminine voice.

Betina returned to the bedroom and looked at Andrew as the boys continued to carry on in the next room. "I never said any of that, well except for the *Dona nobis pacem* part."

"Oh good grief," Tex whined.

Andrew looked too surprised to comment.

"I've only had them for a week and already I've done just about everything wrong. I completely forgot they were here."

When Tex and Raider did a perfect imitation of their moaning, they looked at each other with excruciating embarrassment until they could no longer bare the weight of it and simultaneously burst into fits of laughter. Tex and Raider became more imaginative in their outrageous imitation of Betina and Andrew, throwing in the sounds of grunting and snorting pigs and the cries of wild cats in heat.

Andrew was beet red. "Can they be returned?"

"Maybe your mother could take them on." Betina suggested in a dry tone. "You always said she was the perfect mother."

Andrew agreed in an unconvincing and enigmatic manner.

Soon the boys launched into a dead-on imitation of Frances, scolding Betina for her reckless behavior in front of two minors. Raider had a perfect ear for capturing the sound of Frances's voice and this had Betina bent over with laughter so that she couldn't catch her breath.

"Wait'll I tell Father," Raider screeched. "Just you wait till Father comes home, Ms…Not So Sharp Anymore. Parading yourself…in front of minors."

"Sounds just like my mother!" Betina laughed.

This inspired Andrew to join in with a tirade delivered in his mother's nagging and hysterical voice—it was a voice Betina had never heard before.

"My perfect son. I knew when I first saw your face…when the nurse put you in my arms…I knew you were the son I longed for. Not like James and Thomas. Such terrible disappointments to me. Heartbreaks, really. Chasing anything in a skirt. Disgracing the family name. Spitting image of their father. But you…Andy…You were so pure. Singing in the church choir on Sundays. Like an angel. There was none of your father in you."

"Is that really how she sounded?" Betina interrupted in a disturbed tone.

"You're too smart to give your heart away, only to be ridiculed. And trust me, Andy, trust me on this. All you can count on in this world, is a mother's love. It's the only thing that won't be taken away."

Everything Andrew said about his mother amused Betina at first, since it was juxtaposed against the boy's imitation of Frances. But soon her mood changed as she became disturbed by the portrait Andrew was creating.

Andrew continued, slurring his words, in an intoxicated tone. His playful manner turned serious, as he realized that even though he had pushed his mother out of his life, her voice still spoke within him and had determined so much of his behavior. The boys became absolutely quiet and still, they were most likely trying to make sense of Andrew's outburst.

Andrew's mouth snarled, the furrows in his brow deepened, his eyes glazed over in a stupor of fury till he was transformed into some dark Goddess. He ranted and raged like the Black Dakini, Throma, as he began to recall the stories that controlled him. "Others will promise their loyalty, devotion, and faithfulness. They will deceive you, manipulate you."

"Good grief…she sounds as mad as Malcolm, raging against the coming of false prophets," Betina whispered.

"Once they gain your trust, they'll turn against you. That's exactly what your father did to me. Left me for the fool. If it weren't for you, Andy…I don't know how I would've survived."

"She was an alcoholic?" Betina interrupted.

Andrew nodded.

"I always thought you were crazy about her."

"Hated her…"

"How come you never told me that before?"

Andrew had more to say and ignored her interruption, "Don't you see, we're all we have. Each other. And there's nothing that should take the place of that. Nothing could be better than the two of us, the love we share. My beautiful boy. Trust me on this. Never let another into your heart. I'm the only one that will always love you. Remember. Always remember."

Betina shook her head in dismay, wondering about this intense, passionate love or control this mother had for her son.

Andrew had stored these memories in a wall that he built between them—a wall he insisted didn't exist. The Berlin Wall had fallen soon after they first met, and now the time had come for the fall of this great wall, the wall in the head that divided east from west. Andrew wanted to cross to the west; he wanted his freedom and a permanent end to their personal cold war. So he circled the truth, and walked the outer edges of a spiraling labyrinth coming as close as he could to the central fire, without sustaining third degree burns.

Betina was used to working with cryptic messages. She could build stories about lost civilizations based on pieces of pottery, fragments of paintings, and partially deciphered text. They were fluid stories…always ready to shift directions based on new information. As she sorted through pieces of Andrew's childhood, a not-so-perfect mother began to take form. She was a woman who had crossed boundaries on so many occasions by demanding that Andrew be her loyal emotional consort.

The boys created the opportunity for this shadow voice of this dark feminine to emerge, and miraculously, this unexpected role-playing brought about the release of the confused tension between Andrew and Betina. This dark mother's controlling voice and emotional manipulations held Andrew back at every turn. This dark mother, who devours her young, gives life and takes it back. The dark feminine erupted out of Andrew like the volcanic Pele, with Medusa's fury. And in this release of Andrew's repressed rage and fury, he began the process of liberating himself from her control and from the dark dream that possessed him.

He lay motionless in bed contemplating all that had transpired. For once, Andrew felt no embarrassment but a strange and unexpected sensation of relief. He was the calm after a storm and finally he was free from a burden he hardly knew he carried.

Just as Betina got up to turn out the black light, she noticed that it illuminated images and words on a page of the mute book, which she had left on a side table in the corner of the room. She called out to Andrew, and as he studied it they agreed to take it to his lab to examine it more closely. Betina reached for her raincoat in the hall closet but accidentally grabbed her antique velvet cloak that she had found in the thrift shop in Amsterdam. She put it on and was about to run out of the house with Andrew, but paused for a moment to tell the boys. Finding them both sound asleep, she adjusted the covers so that they wouldn't be cold, then rushed to the car with Andrew.

Though they were both anxious to get to the lab, the slippery roads, covered in ice and snow, forced them to go at a snail's pace. Betina was on the verge of tears from excitement. Her leopard mind raced from one idea to another. She thought of the way Peter spoke of earth changes. He said they were building with a momentum that was increasing like a trickling stream that merges into a fast-moving river, that becomes a rapid, that flows over a waterfall and into a vast ocean and touches everyone and everything. He said that in these changing tides, a new way of thinking would emerge, where intuition stands above evidence; where a higher heart-felt knowing resonates with truth throughout the body, standing above a dull and feeble mental certainty that lacks the full radiance of truth. She was beginning to understand what he meant when he said that the body would become like a tuning fork and that this shift would herald the beginning of a new-world destiny, where knowledge of the unseen rises above that which is visible. She knew she was ready for what the book had to say and could tune into its frequency and receive its signal.

After reaching Andrew's laboratory, they studied an emerging image under ultra-violet light. The central figure was similar to the Great Mother image of Eartha Mae that Evangeline painted in the hospital. She was round and heavy-set with large breasts; her facial features were small, but pleasant. Even the dresses were similar—both were red with yellow trim. This central image was set against a map of the heavens, reminiscent in style to the hand-colored map engravings displayed at the Rijksmuseum. In the lower left-hand corner of the painting was an image of Marletta, in the very same velvet cloak that Betina was now wearing. She was leaning over the very desk that Betina sat at in her vision, with Fogarth standing behind her. Surrounding them were women drummers and dancers.

Another page depicted an underground temple at the center of the earth. It had a dozen levels, connected by staircases and tunnels.

Frescoes of temple rituals, like the kind Betina had seen in her visions, lined the walls. Stained-glass windows were illuminated by the light of the sacred fire burning in the center of the complex. Betina imagined that the song of the flame was shooting out through underground passages in places all over the world. She had found the temple within, and understood that once that temple is accessed, it is constructed in external form, since truth is a fractal that repeats itself and multiplies—like the leaf on a fern tree that so perfectly mirrors the fern tree itself.

"*Et inhoresco et inardesco,*" she whispered.

She was 'ashudder and aglow.' She had heard so many voices, calling out from the forgotten ruins of the past, courting her from underground passages, reaching out to her at every turn and crossroad until she could no longer ignore them or convince herself that these voices were figments of her imagination. Now she entered into the sanctum of her heart and asked that the meaning of the text be revealed. She let go of the clamor of obstructive thoughts, focusing on the breaks between thoughts, until there were no more thoughts. Descending deep into that still place within, she expected to hear an ancient voice from the past, carrying the wisdom of the ages. Instead, she heard a most unexpected voice.

Coming to her from the slowly emerging images and text covering the pages of this precious manuscript was a child's voice, filled with magic and possibility. Betina realized that this child in her mind's eye was what Peter would've called the new Yuga, born in the flames of the inner temple. She could see her spreading her greening power as she danced across fields of grass, slipping into the dark recesses of a cave. She could hear her laughter and her song as she swung from one treetop to another, flying from flower to flower, celebrating the beauty of all creation. The voice of the new Yuga spoke with such sweetness and exuberance, saying:

"I come to you as the voice of infinite possibility. I offer you a renaissance of remembrance, renewal, and rebirth. You have become what you pursued. You are the mute book that now speaks. You are the living book of change, you are the singer and the song. You are the keeper of the dream."

At breakfast, Betina thought about all that she had seen over the past year. There were so many lives to choose from—she could settle into a quiet life at home or go out into the world with all that she had witnessed. They listened to a news report on television and watched scenes of warfare and destruction, flaring in the numerous hot spots that had metastasized around the world like a cancer. These images blended with images of the ancient prophecies that Malcolm and others were resurrecting in their millennial madness. Silencing her mind, Betina made an effort to distance herself from these images. Turning off the television, she replaced pictures of famine, plagues, and nuclear disaster with images of the miracles that Eartha Mae created in the lives of everyone she touched. Looking deep into herself, she drew from the source of that same power. With unwavering intention, she saw only peace.

Out of nowhere, Andrew said, "The future is undetermined. It's in our hands. There are six billion people on this planet, but it only takes a critical mass to create peace. Peter suggested it would be one-tenth of one percent of the world population." He paused for a moment to make some calculations in his head, then added, "That's less than the population of Boston."

She studied his face, certain that he was beaming into her an image of how focused intent can change the world. She realized they shared a new language—they had discovered the lost art of beaming.

In the afternoon, Betina took the boys to a local indoor swimming pool that was open year round. She sat watching the boys splash around, while snow fell outside the windows that surrounded the pool. Tired from hours of floating, diving and dog paddling, they lay down on lounge chairs on either side of Betina and napped. She couldn't help but notice how the water made the scars on Tex's body a dark purple. She knew that his scars would eventually fade, but would never go away completely. Raider's scars were all internal. In taking these wounded children into her home, everything was shifting: abstract theories were becoming concrete and had turned into action. Andrew was going to rent out his house and would start moving in with her later that day.

Betina was settling in, looking forward to designing a life apart from academia, with Peter as an inspiration. She recalled a Zen koan he recited when he decided to set off in his own direction and leave behind plans to teach. He told her about a Japanese master who received a visitor, a university professor who wanted to learn about Zen. As the master served the visitor tea, he kept pouring tea into the cup, even after it was full. Finally, the professor said, 'It's overflowing, no more will go in.' The master replied, 'Like this cup, you are full of your own opinions and speculations. How can I show you Zen unless you first empty your cup?'

Later in the evening, while sifting through cabinets of papers, trashing file after file, Betina saw the opportunities that lay before her in letting go of some of the information crammed in her head. She was soon distracted when she heard Tex and Raider serenading her with angelic rounds of *Dona nobis pacem*. They didn't see her peeking through a curtain from a window in her study. When she didn't respond, they quickly became engrossed in intercutting and fusing the formal postures of the Vienna Choirboys with hip hop, rap, and even capoeira movements. She watched as they moved, catlike, then shifted into amazing gymnastic feats—spinning on their heads and somersaulting through the air. Tex sang rounds of *Dona nobis pacem* in a falsetto voice with heavy vibrato, while Raider added a bass line of "Break the MaTriX...Break the MaTriX." It was a stunning performance and Betina secretly applauded the genius of their dance steps, as well as their brilliant psychological maneuvers that had landed them a permanent place in her home. Before she had a chance to wave to them, the phone rang—her life was about to shift again.

A brilliant scholar from India replaced Humbert as Chairperson of the Classics Department. She had read several of Betina's books over the years and was intrigued by her unique perspectives. She contacted her about redesigning and teaching a full load of classes that would clearly bring forth the eternal truths found in the forgotten treasures of the past.

"There's no time for irrelevance! Set the students on fire! Turn them around! Give them a dream! Now's the time. Turn it around!"

Betina was stunned by the intensity of her concern and commitment. She accepted the offer, hiding her hesitation and trepidation. Soon she felt a surge of energy to take on the challenges of this new assignment. Having thrown out old lecture notes, she had nothing to teach. She was forced to start from scratch, offering 3Rs for a new kind of education and a new cycle of life: Remembrance. Renewal. Rebirth. What she had to say was so far removed from the theories she had previously expounded, and perhaps parroted, the previous year. No wonder their impact had been minimal. Now she could begin to speak of truths that resonated throughout every cell of her body.

She watched as the cynicism, which she clung to as a kind of protective addiction against disappointment, began to slip away. She had thought that cynicism offered a wiser and more realistic point of view and a firm grasp of reality for a world that had so little love or light. But where would it get her, and where would it get the world? It occurred to her that she had been nothing more than a sleepwalker, too afraid to embrace the possibility of change with every ounce of her being. Now she wanted, more than ever, to participate in redirecting the course of events so that the wisdom of the ancient cultures, whose artifacts she had studied so carefully over the years, could be applied to reshaping society. She had never before understood so clearly or so fully that nothing had to be as it had been. Old patterns would be torn asunder and replaced by new ones. There could be a New World, a world without hungry and wounded children roaming the streets of New Orleans and Calcutta, hiding in bombed-out churches in Bosnia or the ruins in Kabul or Baghdad. A new society without young and old women and men dying of desperation and heartbreak. With one more twist of the kaleidoscope, all this could be turned around. She had gone from theory into action.

She prepared for her upcoming class, returning to images of figurines from Willendorf and Laussel, which held a vision of life without violence encoded in the stone. Then she set aside these precious artifacts and cleared her mind of all thought.

Betina no longer felt burdened by the voices that spoke to her from all directions. Her head no longer whirled from the revelations coming from the earth, from ancient manuscripts and paintings, from forgotten voices whispering songs of change. She recognized there was no complexity. There was just one simple message that great numbers of people were hearing, speaking, feeling, knowing, and beaming. It was not that all the pieces of the puzzle suddenly fell effortlessly into place, telling her about the time they had been waiting for—it was simply that the pieces of the puzzle no longer mattered. She would never find enough pieces to create a picture of this great Mystery. She knew that more important than laboriously collecting potsherds from ancient civilizations or cryptic fragments of future civilization was the simplicity of effortlessly entering into the flow, the Cosmic Dance where all great wisdom resides. She let go and let the knowing lead her into right action.

In letting go, Betina stepped into the River of Life and joined the Creatrix, Eartha Mae, Evangeline, and all the other self-proclaimed Creatrixes who hold and protect the future of this bright planet as they travel with her in spirit, across oceans and through foreign lands, spreading a golden dream of possibility.

They were turning it around.

GRATITUDES

Although *Keepers of the Dream* was a private labor of love from beginning to end, early thoughts about this project began to stir in me during my college years when I studied ancient near-eastern languages and was blessed to share my passion for ancient culture with William Ernest Herbrechtsmeier. Anthony Szulc enriched my life in countless ways and brought magic into our years together—memories of our time together always fill me with joy. Ryck Bird Lent opened his soul to me and gave me the gift of unconditional support for my life's work.

A big thank you to Julie Sitney, who took time from composing music for the frame drum, to review an early draft of this novel. I am deeply grateful for the many generous ways that she contributed to help bring this project to completion. At the start of this project, my remarkable friend and soul sister, Yuki Yamamoto, entertained me with unforgettable tales of her extraordinary life. Her stories always touch me because of her profound gift of honesty. Donna Strong offered the priceless gift of faith and generously gave of her time to comment on an early draft. I was blessed to share regular conversations with John Dering, who always amused me with his stories and stunned me with his brilliance. I deeply appreciate the generosity of Gingi Caswell and Mary Duprey who offered valuable editing suggestions. Kriag M. Hill was kind enough to set aside precious hours from his new novel to offer editorial comments on my manuscript. The lovely otherworldly Creatrix, Raven Z, offered joyful and enthusiastic comments in the final stages of writing, which sent chills down my body.

Huge hugs and kisses to Lois Ross, who enriched my life in countless ways, throughout all the years of my life. Thank you to Sky Sitney and Blake Sitney, for being so cool and terrific—and for being family. Much gratitude and lifelong love and affection to Billy White, for the letters we exchanged in our childhood, and for having the generosity in his heart to care for me even after all these years. Through the consistency of their friendship Jeanie Vandam, Eva Au, Thea Soroyan, and Sheila Laffey contributed to my mental and emotional health that enabled me to do my work. Christina Williams's spellbinding dancing made my spirits soar. I greatly appreciate her careful reading of my manuscript. I was blessed to have the joyful energy of Rachel Meyer around me during the tail end of my journey in finishing this book. Much gratitude to Choctaw Shaman Many Knives, for showering me with the golden wisdom that flows through him, and for opening a gate to the Lightning Dance pathway.

A big thank you to Alex Djolakian for so generously contributing his outstanding graphic talents. Many thanks to Gus Dawson for typesetting. Christina Hamlett and Karen Deborah Farris took the time to give me helpful publishing advice—many thanks to them for sharing their expertise. Graphic and website designer, Jean Marie Mayer, at Whirled Wyde Web, was a pleasure to work with as she brought to life my vision for the cover image. Thanks also to Cary Ellis who posed as a model for the cover shot.

I was influenced by the pioneering work of archaeologist Marija Gimbutas and am also grateful for the visionary writings of Riane Eisler and for her comments, which inspired me to redirect the ending of my story. She read an early draft where Betina accepted that inner knowing was the ultimate goal of her journey. Riane encouraged action in the world over inner knowing, and in moving one of the lead characters into action, I also made a profound shift in my own life.

I first saw footage of the Mayoruna while working as a Sound Editor on a six-part series on the Amazon, directed by Jacques Cousteau, but it was in reading Petru Popescu's gripping tale, *Amazon Beaming,* that I learned about their ability for projecting messages. I am also grateful for the wisdom imparted to me by many of the people I interviewed for various metaphysical magazines—their ideas on earth changes and cycles influenced the direction of my own thoughts. Many thanks to my beloved friends who made the pilgrimage to the Casa de Dom Inacio in Brazil, to access higher levels of wisdom and to overcome health challenges. To Sargon, my beloved spirit friend and to Allegra, my spirit daughter, who is always in my heart, and always dancing with me.

I appreciate the support of Celestial Pictures, which held an option on an early version of this story, when it was in screenplay format under the title *Daughters of Babylon*. Thanks also to the Djerassi Artists Residency, in Woodside, California, which provided me with a studio, wonderful meals and excellent company, and was the starting point in my journey of writing this novel.

ABOUT THE AUTHOR

Celeste Allegrea Adams traveled around the world, exploring ancient and modern mythic traditions and ritual. She is the recipient of screenwriting awards, writes documentary narration, is a prolific writer on metaphysical subjects, and leads workshops and retreats. She started *Keepers of the Dream* in New Orleans, wrote parts of it at the Djerassi Artist's Residency, and completed it in Southern California.

WORKSHOPS

For workshop dates,
information on consulting services,
to comment on *Keepers of the Dream*,
to order additional copies of this book or to reach the author:
write to,

Creatrix Studio
PO Box 3775
Santa Monica, CA 90408-3775 USA
Tel: (310) 829-6407

To be placed on our e-mail list,
send an email with the word subscribe in the header to:
CreatrixStudio@aol.com

Visit our Website: www.CreatrixStudio.com

CREATRIX STUDIO

for a little heaven and earth magic

Creatrix Studio's Reading Insert for

KEEPERS OF THE DREAM:

A Myth for a New Age

Celeste Allegrea Adams

Creatrix Studio's Reading Insert

Q & A with Celeste Allegrea Adams, author of Keepers of the Dream

1. Why did you write *Keepers of the Dream*?

One purpose of *Keepers of the Dream* was to create a feminine metaphor for the sacred life energies that live in all things. All religions have their own set of metaphors, but as Joseph Campbell points out, trouble arises when people get stuck in the metaphors and interpret them as fact. Imbalances have occurred in Western civilization for thousands of years because the dominant metaphor has been the trinity of Father, Son, and Holy Ghost.

In the feminine trinity depicted in *Keepers of the Dream*, Eartha Mae is the self-proclaimed incarnation of the Great Mother, and Evangeline is the divine daughter. Their story is book-ended, in the beginning, by Betina's references to the ancient Great Mother spirit (whose archaeological remains are the focus of her studies), and at the end in her daughter, the young earth spirit, (who emerges as the voice of the mystery text announcing the possibility of a New World of pristine beauty).

2. How can we transform into a Creatrix, like your character Eartha Mae?

We become a Creatrix when we lose interest in living as a victim of circumstance and decide to live in a world of our own creation. As a Creatrix, we recognize that we can choose how we respond to any situation. By creatively finding opportunities in all situations, events do not shape our life—we shape the event. Our life is more than a reaction—it is an act of creation. Those who choose to see themselves as creators of their world, move into a place of enormous personal power. A Creatrix enjoys taking responsibility for everything in their life and feels compelled to shift the things that aren't working in the world.

Eartha Mae's journey down the Mississippi is about her transformation into a Creatrix. When we first meet her, she is in a depression and sleeps for days on end, waking only to eat. The wind carries Evangeline's voice to Eartha Mae, bringing with it an idealized image of her mother. This dream helps Eartha Mae transform from a victim of her husband's brutality, to a Creatrix of all things. Like most people, there are times when she believes in her highest self and her greatest potential and other times when she doubts that she is capable of anything extraordinary. She is stunned when she realizes how seriously her misery impacts the world and slowly recognizes the power of her intention.

We all have this same power to affect the world. The idea that the flapping of the wings of a butterfly could alter local wind patterns, so that they would affect the formation of tornadoes, came from Lorenz's work on chaos theory. This concept is a reminder that our influence and power is far greater than anything we imagine.

3. The two minor characters, Malcolm and Peter, have very different perspectives on the earth changes. Why are these shifts happening and what is your perspective on the idea of earth cycles?

Both Malcolm and Peter are knowledgeable about calendric systems, though they respond very differently to the shifts taking place. Malcolm hides out in an underground shelter to survive the apocalyptic cataclysms. Peter, on the other hand, sees it as a galactic New Year and is excited about the changes that will occur.

The shift in cycles is popularly described as an end of the Piscean Age and the beginning of the Aquarian Age. The Piscean Age began at the time of Christ and is symbolized by two fish swimming in opposite directions, a time when polarities of perception dominate. Now we are at the beginning of a new 2,000-year period, the Aquarian Age—it is described by some as a time when there will be a balance between male and female energies and by others as a time when feminine energy will reign. According to the Hindu tradition, quite a number of cycles are coming to an end. The 438,000-year cycle known as the Kali Yuga, the 1.8 million-year Satya Yuga, the 4.4 million-year cycle the Maha Yuga, and the 4.4 billion-year cycle called the Kalpa are all ending at once.

Change is the only constant in the universe, since the pulse of life moves through everything in cycles. Women have body cycles (menstrual, menopause), caterpillars become butterflies, tadpoles becomes frogs, the moon cycles around the earth giving us day and night, the earth cycles around the sun giving us the seasons, our solar system cycles within our galaxy. We can choose how we want to respond to the changes that naturally occur in our bodies, on the planet, and in the universe as we experience these cycles of life. By choosing faith and trust over fear, in response to earth changes—and even to the current threat of terrorism, and the potential of war—we move into a position of our greatest personal power.

4. You describe *Keepers of the Dream* as a myth for a New Age. What old myths do we need to release?

Demythologizing old millennium concepts that are no longer constructive to individuals and society is essential for maintaining personal and environmental health. These are just a few of the myths we need to release:

• We need to move beyond the Genesis myth that man was given dominion over all things, since humans are not the pinnacle, or crown of creation, but are one of the jewels in the crown. We also have to let go of the myth that the earth provides an infinite wealth of resources. We cannot afford to continue to lose more than a hundred species of life every twenty-four hours, or hundreds of thousands of acres of rainforest everyday.

• We have moved beyond the misogynist time of the early church fathers, when it was believed that women did not have souls, but we still need to release all traces of the myth of original sin. The myth that it was a woman who tempted man to eat from the tree of knowledge, causing the wrath of the creator and the oppression of women continues to have a devastating effect in many societies.

• We need to move beyond myths of cultural and racial superiority, since all cultures and races have a significant piece of the puzzle in terms of understanding the meaning of human existence and our purpose in the universe. Our planet, and all the people on it, will evolve into a higher state as technologically advanced cultures open to the wisdom held by its indigenous people.

• As the wisdom of physics and spirituality converge, we are also moving away from the limiting myth of space and time. String theorists have discovered that there are traversable wormholes that connect dimensions and link physical and temporal time. Shamans from all different cultures have known this and have been moving effortlessly through these portals or stargates for millennia. Perhaps these breakthroughs in physics will inspire release from enslavement to the Gregorian calendric system. By moving beyond the artificial categorizations of time that keeps us disconnected and out of balance with natural earth cycles, people in technological cultures can begin to reconnect to the earth. The health of this planet will be restored through gratitude and respect for all that the earth provides.

5. What new kinds of myths do we need for the new millennium?

We need more myths and stories about healing and nurturing and less stories about aggression, destruction, and warrior power that dominates our national mythology and Hollywood films. By creating new myths for the earth, and reviving and reinterpreting old earth-centered myths, we can take a stand for nature and our environment. The role of the artist is crucial in helping people to become more aware of the transcendent beauty of the earth and of all creatures on it. This new mythology needs to be created in all forms, including television, novels, short stories, poetry, and paintings and in the feature films that Hollywood sends to countries all over the world.

6. Where did your ideas and images for this mystical tale come from?

One source of inspiration for this book came from reading the works of the classical archaeologist Marija Gimbutas who demonstrated that cultures that worshipped the Great Mother lived in peace.

Images in the story came from travelling around the world, exploring archaeological sites and ancient and modern mythic traditions and ritual—the archaeologist, Betina Sharp, visits many of the sites I explored. The idea for the character, Eartha Mae, came from spending time in sites devoted to the Great Mother. The region of Cappadocia, north of Ankara in Turkey, also made a deep impression on me. There were homes carved out of conical structures made of stone, and underground cities carved out of limestone, that were once inhabited by Christian refugees. Visiting these underground tunnels inspired images of the tunnels that led to the central fire in the earth, (the earth's womb), where Betina joins Marletta in a ritual, during her dreamtime explorations.

At one point in my life, I moved to New Orleans to write about Voodoo, but my interest shifted to a group of teenage street musicians in the French Quarter. A girl who wore lavender and sang on the street corner caught my attention—she became the character Evangeline.

7. You talk about worship of the great mother in prehistoric times and also allude to Marletta and Fogarth's heretical worship of the feminine in Medieval times. What is the connection between the two and what effect will the emergence of the divine feminine have on society in the new millennium?

Western Civilization once had an earth-based spirituality where society was built on partnership rather than domination. These egalitarian societies worshipped the Great Mother in the Mediterranean region before patriarchal systems took over. The pervasive power of the feminine did not completely end when Christianity and the trinity of Father, Son and Holy Spirit were embraced. The feminine aspect of divinity still continued to be worshipped in the form of the Virgin Mary, though the myth of Immaculate Conception made her into a chaste vessel and stripped her of her former power as Creatrix and fertility goddess.

Recent scholarship suggests that heretical groups like the Freemasons, the Cathars, the Knights Templar and the Priory of Sion secretly embraced the feminine, in the form of Mary Magdalene. The black Madonna was worshipped along with Mary Magdalene, in places that might once have been pagan centers. Scholars such as Lynn Picknett and Clive Prince, in *The Templar Revelation*, suggest that the black Madonna may have been Mary Magdalene. Worship of the power of the feminine and of sexuality as a pathway to God went underground during the 2,000 years of Christianity.

Now we have entered a new millennium and can no longer allow religion and its dogma to be the root cause of violence in so many regions around the world. A contributing cause of the war in Bosnia-Herzegovina, (mentioned in the first chapter), was the conflict among three religious groups: Muslim, Roman Catholics, and Serbian Orthodox. Americans experienced the aggression of Al Quada on 9/11, in its efforts to promote a worldwide war between Muslims and non-Muslims. Religious differences have caused conflict in places like India, Indonesia, Middle East, Northern Ireland, Pakistan, South Africa, Tibet, and many other countries around the world. The re-emergence of the feminine aspect of divinity in this new millennium should shift cultural values away from war and aggression, to peace tolerance, and sharing.

8. Will feminine energies dominate in the new millennium or will we move into a balance between the masculine and feminine?

I think there is a continual evolution between cycles of masculine domination, periods of balance, and cycles of feminine domination, since change is the nature of being alive. At the present time, we are experiencing feminine emergence which will lead to a period where there will be a dominance of feminine energy. I've enjoyed hearing my friend, Choctaw Shaman Many Knives, speak of these shifting energies as a beautiful dance, between the sky father and the earth mother, with each one allowing the other to take the lead at different times, and each one caring for the needs of the other. I like the term 'dance' since it implies that there is no judgement placed on the cycle we have left and the new one we are entering. (Note: In American Indian culture, the feminine was always honored. I was intrigued by several scholarly studies on the impact American Indians had in shifting the European settler's attitude towards women in the Americas. The Iroquois culture, for instance, even influenced early feminists in upstate NY.)

The current language used to describe feminine emergence is sometimes confusing because our perception of it is shifting and evolving as we struggle to understand the nature and possibilities of the true archetypal feminine. This is unexplored territory, since it is something we did not experience in its fullness during the millennia of patriarchal dominance.

The dichotomy between feminine and masculine energies has commonly been reduced to pairs of yin/yang opposites like: intuition vs. logic; heart vs. mind; and partnering vs. dominating. This is a 'Piscean Age language,' which sees things in opposite. As we develop an 'Aquarian language,' our way of categorization may change so that it may seem overly simplistic, too black and white, to classify partnership and heart as feminine qualities, and logic and domination as masculine. A new language may emerge as man and woman become whole and balanced within themselves, holding both masculine and feminine qualities.

9. How did you find the voice of the ancient mystery text?

Discovering the voice of the ancient text was one of the most electric, emotional, and mystical experiences of my life. Chills ran up and down my body like a current, while tears streamed down my face. I was blinded by the radiance of this young earth spirit and realized that it had to be the voice of the ancient mystery text as well as one of the final voices in my novel. I started typing and there was magic all around me—sparkling light and singing. I believe that above all else, this will be the voice of the future—the voice that brings the renewal of wonder, mystery and celebration of life. I look forward to the luxury and blessing of accessing and sharing the exquisite fullness of this voice in my next book. *Et inhoresco et inardesco.*

10. Do you feel a particular resonance to any of the characters?

I've enjoyed being all of the characters and exploring aspects of myself that exist but are not necessarily developed or dominant in my personality or nature. I learn from all of them. I loved going through the process of solving the pain of abandonment that haunt the tribe of lost children in the ruins of Bosnia and the street kids in New Orleans, by creating families of friends and discovering true life directions. I feel infinite tenderness for Zoran, Vesna, Samir, Salome, Tex, Raider, Christian and Evangeline in their struggles to create a life for themselves, in a world that has forgotten them. It was interesting to explore Malcolm's frustration and rage as he madly grasps for answers and insists on spreading his fear by preaching the little he knows. He often lives underground, in a kind of oversized box or coffin (without tunnels to the central fire), out of his inability to trust in the *Mysterium Tremendum*. Peter, on the other hand, has no attachment to knowing, and in his lightness of being effortlessly connects to greater truths. Andrew's journey to self-discovery takes a unique path, since he is at an impasse and needs to be cracked open and liberated from a self-imposed box that prevents him from connecting to his potential in love, and perhaps in his pursuit of knowledge—the children bring this gift of truth, on Twelfth Night. I loved living in Betina's whirling mind, like a kaleidoscope, that always shifts directions and is ready to run off on tangents of association. She's a bridge between the academic world that is grounded in proof, and new-age thought that embraces inner knowing above external verification. I enjoyed the experience of watching her move from theory to practice. Virgil and Oakie reminded me of the blessings and mishaps of serving, since Eartha Mae is a powerful leader, yet unpredictable and often moody. Eartha Mae, as she moves from victimhood to Creatrix, awakens in me an understanding of what it could mean to own everything in my world, as an act of my creation. She teaches me a powerful pathway of possibility.

11. What is your spiritual background and orientation?

As a child I attended Unitarian services where we honored the wisdom found in all religions and appreciated the many different pathways to the Great Mystery that is in all things. As a teenager, my focus and passion was on tuning myself to the celestial Music of the Spheres—my artwork and short animated film was a daily meditation on this theme. During my teenage years, I read everything from Gurdjieff, to Carlos Casteneda, to writings on Pythagoras, and then began exploring ritual and spirituality in cultures all around the world. I camped out with the Bedouins, Berbers and Tuaregs, explored ancient ruins around the world, and participated in shaman gatherings and modern day rituals like Burning Man. My faith is deeply personal and has no name. I feel an electric connection that alerts me to profound truths—these moments tell me everything I need to know and guide me on my path. You could say that sometimes I'm an ecstatic, often I'm a Creatrix—when I write and create my world—but always I'm a Celebrant in that I live the dance and song that celebrates the *Mysterium Tremendum*.

This insert is available for download at:

www.CreatrixStudio.com/dreamguide.html

ORDER FORM FOR ADDITIONAL COPIES

Name		
Address		
City	State	ZIP
Tel (_______)	email	
Ship to: Name		
Address		
City	State	ZIP

TITLE	Price for one	Add. Books
Keepers of the Dream–SOFTCOVER BOOK (Tax included)	$21.60	
Shipping and Handling in United States	$ 1.40	
(England – add $8.70 for postage Australia – add $9.70 for postage)		
Add $1.00 for each additional book		
Total Amount	$23.00	

Make Check or Money Order payable to: CREATRIX STUDIO

Mail to:

Creatrix Studio
PO Box 3775
Santa Monica, CA 90408-3775

Tel: (310) 829-6407
Email: CreatrixStudio@aol.com
Visit our Website: www.CreatrixStudio.com

DREAM NOTES

We can all be Keepers of the Dream by holding a vision of possibility in our hearts.

What dreams do you want to keep for yourself?

DREAM NOTES

We can all be Keepers of the Dream by holding a vision of possibility in our hearts.

What dreams do you want to keep for your community?

DREAM NOTES

We can all be Keepers of the Dream by holding a vision of possibility in our hearts.

What dreams do you want to keep for the planet?